FREELANCE BUSINESS WRITING BUSINESS

How to make a living
as a full-time freelance

by William R. Palmer

Heathcote Publishers

P. O. Box 135, Monmouth Junction, New Jersey 08852

Printed by Adams Press
30 W. Washington St.
Chicago, Illinois 60602

Contents

Introduction

"Ernest Russell, a frequent contributor to magazines, *earns his entire living* from free-lance writing." This thumbnail sketch introduced a new writer to readers of one of our more prestigious journals. The name is changed; the italics are ours.

The remarkable fact about Mr. Russell seems to be that he can actually make a living at freelance writing! And right there the editor made a Freudian-slip! For he that marvels is he who buys Russell's creative output! Many editors do not expect their contributors to "make a living" at writing.

The fact is, many editors *expect* to be subsidized by writers. They are accustomed to it, because for many of them it's "always been that way." Myriads of writers derive their basic income from steady jobs. Or they have a working spouse or parent, Social Security or pension, or some other independent means to support the privilege of "selling" their literary creations at less than cost of production.

In a business where for many just seeing one's byline in print is highest heaven, our statement is not so cynical as it may seem.

And to be quite fair, many editors and most freelance-writers haven't the foggiest idea how much writers do subsidize many publications. Nor are many of these writers even aware they actually do *not* "make a living at freelance writing!"

This book, then, tells how to make a living at freelance writing—especially business writing. It can be done. It is being done. You can do it.

The percentage of writers who keep body and soul together solely by freelance effort probably matches the percentage of successful freelance plumbers, TV-repair men, cooks, stock market advisers or management consultants.

In this book we concentrate on business writing for five reasons:

(1) That's where *our* experience lies;

(2) It's a journalism cliche that one can start "at the bottom" writing for "trade journals," and work one's way up. Hence, *if* you make a living at business writing (goes that philosophy) you can survive at any kind of journalism.

(3) In business journalism a writer does get exposed to business practices which, when applied to one's own writing, do raise the potential for "making a living."

(4) Business writing exposes a journalist to the full spectrum of society, opening areas one might miss completely in other disciplines. This will become more apparent later.

(5) Finally, as the black sheep of journalism, business writing is grossly under-evaluated. Something is badly warped in a society that heaps riches on mindless recitations of sex exploits, while stingily rewarding the creator of an intelligible insurance policy!

The author does hope that writers who freelance in other disciplines may re-examine their own writing efforts in business terms. For most business principles, in final analysis, do apply to all types of freelance writing.

Paradoxically, when a writer does treat literary production as a business, his or her mind is freed from economic harassment. Then it really is possible to concentrate much more effectively on the creative part of writing.

In this book we presume the reader is articulate, and is reasonably well-grounded in basics of grammar, composition and manuscript preparation, and is self-motivated to be a writer. Comments on style and presentation, therefore, assume these basic conditions.

Prologue

No "how-to" book, however carefully written, is free of author's bias. For any writer, it is at least awkward to present as truth that which he himself does not believe. Unless, of course, the writer is deliberately mis-informing his readers.

Personal experience, education, family background, ethics and mores, all mold an author. So even a writer's selection of outside references in support of his or her "facts" as presented tend to reflect a scribe's own personal values.

Hence a little biography may explain attitudes expressed in the following chapters.

In the summer of 1953, at the mutual age of 43, Hazel and Bill Palmer severed all organizational ties in order to freelance in business journalism.

Working from a Westchester County apartment, we found ourselves on the road more often than home. Hence when our lease expired, we sold the furniture and bought a 28-foot travel trailer. This became our permanent and only home for the next 5½ years.

In the trailer we roved this country's whole southeast quadrant, probing after material for business magazines desirous of greater and better Southern coverage.

Does it sound exciting, glamourous? It was a very rugged internship! Illness and operations brought real testing as we learned the hard facts about freelance business writing.

Prior to the break, Hazel devoted half her working time to freelance writing, in fiction and in general features. Before our marriage in 1950, she supported herself with part-time jobs as reporter and researcher for various publishers in Washington, D.C. This included a stint "on the Hill" reporting legislative action in Congress for *Law Week*. Hazel's earliest training was as a legal secretary.

I came up through ten years on the editorial side. I now have been editing or writing in varying degrees for 45 years, mostly in the business field. Before free-lancing, I was seven years editor of *The National Cleaner & Dyer* (now defunct).

Trailering ceased when the same editorship was resumed "temporarily" as my successor died in a plane crash. Three years later the magazine merged with three others, and we returned to freelancing.

The latest 15-year span of freelancing has been in the Boston-Washington megalopolis. Our central New Jersey home was chosen as being mid-point of the megalopolis, accessible to major highways, and relatively free of metropolitan smog (at this writing).

My magazine writing is now mixed with extensive research and feasibility studies, consulting, PR writing, and a stint of preparing and conducting small business management workshops. While all this "side" work *is* done freelance, business magazine writing is still the core function. The side-work is usually "spin-off" from this magazine writing.

Link To Associated Business Writers of America

When we returned to New York in 1960, Hazel backed into being executive secretary of Associated Business Writers of America. As its handful of members multiplied, ABWA became a full-time occupation, squeezing her freelance writing to a shadow.

Yet ABWA gave Hazel close contact with many top-notch freelance business writers—the real pros. She learned much at first hand about *their* problems, their techniques, their triumphs and setbacks. This knowledge supports our own very strong convictions about freelance business journalism.

Hazel was also in almost daily contact with business magazine editors and other users of freelances. They would be seeking a writer in a specific geographic area, or one with knowledge of a particular field, or both. A typical query might be, "Hazel, do you have someone in Oregon who knows electronics?" Moreover Hazel was often called on to arbitrate or clarify editor/writer misunderstandings, by phone and by letter.

So Hazel Palmer was uniquely a vital line of communication between the business writer and the business editor or writing client. When she died of cancer in 1975, the author succeeded her as executive director of Associated Business Writers of America.

All of which led to this book. Much mis-understanding and friction between editors and writers is due to ignorance on the part of each about how the other half lives and works.

Moreover, much of the "blue-sky, anybody-can-do-it" froth written about freelance business writing must share blame for the confusion. For assumptions on both sides, that have no basis in fact, often have their source in such forthy writing.

Therefore this author aims to "tell it like it is" (which cliche-phrase will probably be one with Moses by time this appears in print).

Chapter 1

Do You REALLY Want to Freelance?

Are you ulcerously fed up with the boss? Do your associates give you the hives? Is your job a dull sea of detail? Is there active distaste for the kind of work you do? Does the organization discipline gall you? Is your sense of good ethics or morals bruised daily?

To put it bluntly—do you *really* want to be a freelance writer? Or do you merely see freelancing as the handiest escape hatch from current job conflicts.

Let's take a hard look at what freelance writing entails, especially in the business writing field. To get the cold shower over with quickest, we'll start with some negatives.

As a freelance, you have several or many bosses to get mad at. Their requests or demands conflict. Nor can you any longer testily ask a single boss, "Look, do you want "A" first, or does "B" get priority, or must "C" come ahead of the others?"

Nope—*you* work out all the priorities yourself, as best you can. These many bosses may humor you and make some adjustments to help you, but not often nor very much.

You'll get a bellyfull of boresome work, too. The term "potboiler" comes from freelance writing. A pot-boiler is a deadlyboring job that you do, or an article you write, simply because it pays cash and "puts meat on the table." It's a very lucky, or very sharp, freelance who garners engrossing "creative" assignments more than half the time.

You'll do many distasteful jobs, simply to keep fully employed. We don't mean violating your ethics, either. But you'll do phone surveys, even if the thought repels you. You'll stand on aching feet in exhibit halls. You'll smile encouragingly at some bloated egocentric, while trying to winnow a credible fact or two from his verbal eruptions. You'll get home at three a.m., because a meeting didn't start on time, only to arise at six to prepare and phone in a report against your deadline.

Why? Because the same editors who have those nice creative assignments expect you to also take the bad with the good. Otherwise they'll line up a writer who *can* handle the whole job.

1

Therefore, the *self*-discipline a freelance must exercise, merely to survive, can often be a far tighter straight-jacket than disciplines imposed by an organization job.

Chapter 2

Advantages and Drawbacks of Freelancing

If you *want* to be a fulltime freelance writer, to make a living at it, there are many advantages or benefits. If you're *truly motivated,* these outweigh the drawbacks. For careful analysis shows all negatives can be controlled, when you recognize them for what they are.

1. You *are* your own boss. Credit and blame, profit or loss, inspiration and perspiration, joy and regret—they're *all* yours. Some folks are never happy on a payroll. That's why we have solitary mechanics, management consultants and music coaches, reasonably content at what they're doing, even while they probably could earn twice as much on somebody else's payroll.

2. The writer usually has only one person, the editor or client to please per story. State of the industry, advertiser pressures, personal status, all are relatively unimportant to the writer. Just get the facts. Communicate them. Let the editor or client worry about the rest. A freelance writer is simply a transmission belt for facts.

3. You can be "depression-proof." Your income may drop way down. But it need never completely vanish, if you spread risks carefully, and are creative and alert to trends. That is, you need never be 100% out of work.

4. Cost of living is, or can be, substantially lower than for the organization employee. You do not commute daily (unless you insist on the status of a personal downtown office). It's unnecessary to live in or on top of big cities or industries. You can reside out where living costs are less.

5. You spend, as a freelance writer, 40% to 60% of your time at home, or wherever you park the typewriter. You need eat only a third as many restaurant meals as the office-bound writer. You often wear casual clothes, blue jeans or even shorts.

6. You can split off some of your costs (car, rent, utility and phone) as deductible business expenses. But don't overdo it—IRS knows the angles better than you. This does mean possibly owning a car or home you couldn't otherwise afford.

You can sometimes partly subsidize family travel. However it's

3

never really a vacation for the breadwinner to be tied down on interviews while the family sees the sights.

7. You escape office politics. You avoid office parties and collections. (And you're utterly crazy if you waste your valuable time on a client's internal politics. It rarely puts any bucks in your jeans).

8. You can spend more time with the family. This is especially important when your presence is badly needed at home. It's vital for writers with physical limitations.

9. Around whatever firm commitments are made on a day-to-day basis, the writer's time is flexible. But flexibility may not be abused. Every goof-off hour requires an hour's solid work some other time, even if you arise at 3 a.m. to do it!

10. Over the years, the freelance can get involved in a wide range of industries and subjects. If variety is your meat, you can have all you want of variety. Of course, repeating the same basic story for twelve kinds of business could have its own kind of monotony. Yet even there a considerable variety exists in the repetition.

11. Except where constrained by client deadlines, the freelance works at his own pace. He has his own preferred tools, in his own personally arranged office or nook (at least until the second baby or grandma comes to live).

12. Freelance writing is "retirement-proof." Nobody will automatically shelve you at age 65, or even 72. A few freelance business writers continue at slowly diminishing productivity well into their eighties, with both pleasure and profit. Fremont Kutnewsky was still writing fitfully, when he died just short of his ninetieth birthday.

13. Freelancing, finally, is a supreme test of whether one can "make it" on one's own! Which may bring us right back to advantage number one.

Well, those are some advantages to freelance business writing. Few are untinged with precautions.

Drawbacks to Freelancing. Here's another fifteen caution-signs, if you're itching to cut loose and freelance. You thought I was through with the first go-round?

1. "Anomie" is the number one drawback for would-be freelances. Anomie is that feeling that, if I died tonight, no one would ever miss me. The freelance writer is virtually unknown, unimportant and entirely expendable to most of the people he or she works for.

Writers first venturing from payroll careers into freelance suffer anomie as severe "retirement shock." Yesterday you had relationships, good or bad, with many people. There was a routine schedule of duties you were responsible for. There was a physical place and things designated as yours.

Today there are no ties with anybody or anything, other than personal. It's a very real feeling of rootlessness and facelessness. It's a traumatic experience! Many freelance business writers never wholly recover from anomie.

2. There's no security in freelancing. No one but the writer supplies his or her own fringe benefits. There's Social Security, yes. But even there a freelance doesn't share costs with an employer. There are no company-paid vacations, sick leave, pensions, hospitalization, clothing allowances, etc.

3. There is no company expense account, either. The writer must maintain working capital, entirely over and above the family checking account. This working capital fund needs to average from $500 to $5,000 depending on the type of writing and amount of travel. If writing freelance full-time, a minimum $1,500 working capital is essential.

4. An initial $5,000 reserve, in savings or other liquid assets, is advisable when one launches fulltime into freelancing because:

First, no matter how optimistic the outlook, getting started at freelancing is all out-go. You cannot expect to live off the proceeds. There is unavoidable time-lag between effort and income. Sometimes this lag stretches appallingly. Mistakes, false moves, indecision, lack of marketing experience and technical knowhow, all chew up cash reserves at a frightening rate. It's not unusual to take three years or more to build up to an acceptable living income.

Second, sickness, accidents, emergencies, can all set you back, with added expenses and reduced or non-existent income. If you don't have a stake left when the emergency is over, you've had it. Because you then face once again that time-lag in getting re-started.

Of course, if others in the family have dependable incomes, this reserve is less crucial. But it's still very much advisable.

5. Be prepared for credit to be harder to get. Cherish your credit most carefully.

6. You will have *less* total productive time than on a payroll job. This is because you'll now be responsible for all your own correspondence, filing, typing, phoning, bookkeeping, tax returns, purchasing, etc., that employer companies pay others to do for you. Or if you hire this done, it will eat into your working capital.

7. Marketing will consume a quarter to one-third of your working hours. Bargaining (haggling, hassling) with editors over fees and expenses, both before and after getting a story, can discourage

writers who expect naively to simply get out there and get stories. Finding markets for good articles, as well as articles for good markets, is an art born only of vigilant persistent practice.

8. The freelance must read widely and constantly, to keep current in many areas of business. Personal reading for recreation tends to be squeezed to a minimum. A business writer, however, usually does enjoy much of this necessary business reading.

9. The successful freelance must be, or learn to be, well-organized, virtually a compulsive planner. To earn a reasonable income, it's rarely possible to work one job at a time. You usually have several jobs or assignments in different stages of completion. All must be nudged along as rapidly as possible. It takes carefully-tended schedules, simple charts and tickler files to keep on top of everything.

10. The writer can work at his own pace, yes. Except most work not involved with deadlines is speculative. It's subject to approval and acceptance, with longer payment timelags. And even the best writers fail to sell some speculative work!

On the other hand, much of one's output can be "wanted yesterday." Freelances are often called on only when editors or clients are in a bind. Their staff people are sick or assigned elsewhere, and the convention to be covered starts tomorrow 100 miles away.

Other editors believe the only way to deal with a freelance is to "keep the heat on." Unfortunately, moreover, there's often real justification for this "heat."

11. It is nice to be with the family more. But then everybody's going to have to give a little, if you are to get work done. Rules have to be agreed on and kept. Frequent interruptions can be easy to start, but can cause hurt feelings when discouraged.

Or *were you* distracted just as easily at the office, too? Maybe *you* must learn to concentrate better.

12. Business always lives with you at home, 24 hours a day. Your typewriter leers at you during every idle hour. Sometimes family members get in the habit of second-guessing your activities. You may have to be defensive with folks who don't understand your business.

13. Not only the writer, but his family also must be able to weather dry spells with some equanimity. Otherwise the recurrent tensions cut deeply into the writer's own poise and efficiency.

When "desperate for dough" your own business values get warped. Instinctively you try to create stories where there aren't any. You press the sale of second-rate manuscripts. *Then* you lose your hard-won credibility with editors and clients.

14. Nobody outside believes you actually *work* at home. Neighbors, associates, townspeople, all are sure you have secret independent means, and are just filling your idle hours. Unless sternly controlled, they have no scruples about phoning or visiting during business hours. Too often these are the exact characters who have all the time in the world to kill.

Most difficult to deal with are those who take it on themselves to volunteer a writer's services for civic and charitable duties. "Say, Bill Palmer doesn't go to work. He's usually home. I'm sure he'll be glad to do it."

15. Fact is, if you make a respectable living at it, freelance business writing is a nose-to-grindstone occupation. Every hour from 8-to-5 has a dollar sign on it! And many, many nighttime hours also have dollar signs.

16. You can't turn a freelance career on and off. It takes time to get rolling. Each time you switch to fulltime jobs, you start at the bottom again if you return to freelancing. Be prepared to stay with it, or else it's better not to start freelancing in the first place.

Shift Part-time to Full-time With Eyes Open. All the above, specifically applies to the writer looking to freelancing as a full-time career, from which a decent living is hoped for.

The least-wary individual to launch out into the deep often is that writer who feels he or she had done very well on a parttime basis. For this writer may not realize his or her previous writing may not have been so profitable as imagined. It could even have been subsidized by steady income from other sources.

Survey of Associated Business Writers of America showed one-half of a freelance writers' income, on the average, goes to *business* expenses. The writer's whole living, including domestic household expenses, must come out of the other half of income.

This means the income from a freelance business writing career must produce total income equal to at least twice what you and your family need to live on.

If all the above sounds too grim, remember *every* line of business has just as many benefits and drawbacks. These are listed for freelance business writing right up front, so we can more promptly get down to the business of learning how to make a living at freelance business writing.

Chapter 3

The Business Buff Who Writes

A "buff", says Webster, is a devotee. There are jazz buffs, pinochle buffs, fire engine buffs, poetry buffs—and business buffs.

Some business buffs are writers. Moreover, *writers who are not business buffs* rarely succeed at business writing. Put *that* down as an axiom!

The good business writer has a "feel" for the dynamics of business. This empathy is as sensitive and knowledgeable as a baseball buff's absorption in even the tense, slow-moving pitcher-batter dual that so readily bores and baffles the uninitiated.

A buff's empathy for business rivals that of a music lover savoring the subtle contrast in renditions of the same aria by different opera stars. It resembles the compassionate thrill of a teacher as a backward child suddenly breaks through to new levels of achievement.

Business writers *like* business people. They *esteem* business creativity, innovation, experimentation, enthusiasm. They admire the lonely entrepreneur with the guts to stake all he has, both current assets and future credit, on a wispy new enterprise with *no* guarantee of success and *no* "security."

Business buffs *believe* in the profit motive. They see profit as a guage of success or failure, a reward for constructive effort, an antidote to waste, and a warranty of economic stability.

Drama Of People In Action. In essence, the business writer tells how executives motivate workers to produce goods and services for customers. But customers, workers and executives are all human. Each, as an individual, is largely self-serving at core. None is entirely above exercising leverage on the others for personal benefit.

Therefore every step in production of goods and services, including their ultimate disposal, is fraught with drama.

Every element of life crops up in business—conflict, teamplay, inspired creativity, bureaucratic sloth, complex programs, the startling solo effort, deliberate skilled planning, intuitive inspiration, greed, generosity, loyalty, defiance, craveness, heroism, hope, doubt, stupidity, wisdom, good, evil, death, life...

And always, every day, everywhere, business men and women confront new challenges they just cannot ignore.

Want spice in your life? Business is *all* drama, *if* you know what's going on. And, as a business writer, you have a front seat in this theatre, without the cost or risk of investing your own assets in the ventures you observe.

Scarcity of Business Buffs. Business editors agonize perpetually over the very real scarcity of writers, reporters and editorial staff who are true business buffs.

One cause for this scarcity is this so-common inference that "trade journals" are the bottom rung of journalism. Actually, telling a novice to "start at the bottom in trade journals and work up" is like advising an ice skating tyro to start by learning to swim.

The several writing disciplines are parallel ladders, not a totem pole! Good business writing is an art as distinct in itself as good drama or good poetry. Junk in any of these disciplines is just as truly junk!

In fact this bottom-of-the-ladder advice is a vicious disservice.

It tamps into the roots of business writing swarms of raw scribes who only strive to escape again as quickly as possible. Never having understood the business environment, they leave permanently scarred with acute antipathy for business and business people.

For non-buffs are just as bored with business dynamics, as non-buffs would be with opera, gymnastics, stamp-collecting or gardening. For them the business climate is thoroughly alien. Better such a writing novice live by clerking, collecting tolls, or serving as watchmen. Then start immediately writing catch-as-catch-can in the field he or she enjoys best! Creative frustrations will be eliminated, and all creative energies can be focused on the true love.

Who's More Moral Than Business People? Such discontent is abetted by another fallacy, cherished by literary pundits and infused in their students. This is the credo that business people are somehow anti-social, less moral, more heartless, than other human beings.

Yet nothing can be more vicious or unmoral than a frustrated novelist's slashing attack on the work and person of a more successful rival! Vilification of a notable scholar by university peers is a well-practiced art! Artists and musicians laud each other's work with double-edged knives! Even the religious are not above fraternal alley-cat feuding!

Once again, we're *all* human. With our human failings we *all* try to manipulate political affairs, social structure, creative arts, sports, hobbies, education—and business. When we ask "What's his angle?" we most certainly don't always allude to a business person.

When we cry out at "capitalist rip-offs," we don't consider that commodity prices include very substantial pilferage by employees and customers, to mention just one facet of non-business morality.

Wide Scope of Business Writing. What *is* business writing? It's roots spread through much more of society than you may realize.

Most visible to the public are prestigious publications like *Fortune, The Wall Street Journal, Harvard Business Review, Business Week, Forbes, Nation's Business, Dun's Review,* and others. These obviously deal with facts and events pertaining to business.

But, take religion, for instance. Could anything be more remote from business and business interests?

Read how *Christian Life,* describes itself in part: "...editorial areas include building plans, financing programs, kitchen equipment, floor coverings, projectors, screens, pews, chancel furniture, auxiliary seating, sanitary equipment and supplies, organs, pianos, choir vestments, books, Bibles, recordings..."

Part of *Your Church's* self-analysis reads: "...help the Pastor/Architect team to build, equip, improve and administer today's churches..."

Church Management expresses concern with: "...ethics, methods, materials, new buildings, architecture, finance, maintenance, publicity, insurance, (plus a) section edited by National Association of Church Business Administrators..."

Religion, the arts, education, charity, government, science, conservation, etc., are rightfully the gems of human society. Yet every such gem is dependent on a broad, firm setting of business procedure.

Science put astronauts on the moon, but business assembled the vehicles, fuel, gear, training units, etc.

The Philharmonic stirs a thousand souls tonight, even while business prepared the hall, supplied instruments and music, marshalled the audience.

Under aegis of many charities, planeloads of supplies jet into the latest disaster areas. Who but business musters planes, provides crews and logistics? The military, you say. Ah, yes, but military logistics are simply good business practice in a special environment.

Business Journalism Describes "Logistics." In fact, the term "logistics" largely describes the scope of business journalism. Its dictionary definition is "The branch of military science having to do with moving, supplying and quartering troops."

Every human activity has both its creative function and its logistics—its moving, supplying and quartering. Creative purists disdain logistical processes as too material and mundane for their sensitive psyches. Yet, without logistics, any creative function is simply a shambles.

A vivid example was the famous Woodstock Music and Art Fair. An estimated 300,000 young people swarmed toward mountain-hemmed Woodstock, N.Y., in August of 1969. Little or no preparation had been made to handle one-tenth that many.

Massive traffic jams tied up highways for 20 miles around. There was rain with no shelter, scant food, sparse drinking water, no restrooms, no medical facilities. Those striving to flee couldn't crowd past those still pushing in. Even the area residents were completely immobilized.

Woodstock was a logistical shambles!

But the business buff knows that, had the logistics of Woodstock Music and Art Fair been in the hands of well-organized management, it could have been a very different story.

Moreover, had the Woodstock event been conducted smoothly, participants would have been barely aware of its logistics. And in that unawareness, those logistics would also have been a "work of art." But only the business buff would recognize them as such.

The "fine arts" are meant to be displayed and shared. Logistic arts should attract no attention, except from business buffs. A logistical genius is as truly an artist in his or her way as is the conductor of the Philharmonic. The God who gave us poetry, music and color, also gave us order and natural law.

Everything Has Its Business Side. It's not only specialty publications, the business papers or "trade journals," however, that are involved with business. Many articles in general magazines are, or could be, authored by business journalists. Here are titles gleaned from just three successive issues of *The Reader's Digest:*

"20 Ways to Save Money at the Supermarket"
"Danger; Hazardous Materials in Transit"
"How to Buy A Diamond"
"Hullabaloo Over Hemlines"
"Our Food-Stamp Fiasco"
"Farming's Fantastic New Look"
"America's Citizen Crime Fighters"
"Mafia War on the A & P"
"Rx for the Family-Doctor Shortage"
"America the Inefficient"
"The Next Industrial Revolution"

11

In some degree these articles all concern logistics, the supply of goods and services. Their facts, of course, are written for consumer viewpoints. Yet, with different emphases and detail, the identical facts can be re-assembled as useful information for business people. In fact, a business version is often written first. Then a consumer version is developed from the same interview material. Versatile business writers usually extract several articles from the same material.

Chapter 4

Many Kinds Of Business Writers

Business journalism is not confined to magazine articles. There are many different functions for writers across the whole spectrum of business journalism.

Each function, moreover, can usually be performed as a full-time or part-time staff person, or else small-scale or large-scale as an independent contractor—a freelance, in other words.

Many functions are not clean-cut, but blend or cross-over. Even titles or terms have varied definitions or descriptions.

A "field editor" for one magazine might simply be a fact-finding legman, researcher, or virtually a detective. Yet another publication would require from its field editors only polished copy measured and marked ready for the printer. For some papers, "field editors" are invariably "staff," (i.e., on the payroll, with all fringe benefits). Yet other publications freely confer that title on regional or local freelances.

Or a specialty editor for one paper could be termed a columnist by another. Yet they'd prepare similar copy. That is, one could be called the "insurance editor" or the "insurance columnist."

Editors Shape Material. So we need to clarify terms as used in *this* book. To *me,* an "editor" is one who utilizes previously prepared material in assembling a magazine or a newspaper. A "writer" or "reporter" researches and writes the original material that is supplied to the editor.

In business journalism, editors frequently are also writers or reporters, especially on small publications. But these, to me, are wearing two different hats. Because good editors are *not* necessarily good reporters or writers. And vice versa. And that's another axiom, my friend!

"Editing" is shaping the copy to conform to the needs and style of the magazine. To edit a writing does not necessarily improve the writing. It simply makes it more usable for a specific publication.

This is exemplified by the trade news release. An identical report about a new product will be sent to several publications. Each editor then "edits" or re-writes this copy to suit his publication's own particular style and format.

13

Hence that writer who deliberately slants his copy toward the style of a specific magazine is actually doing a bit of editing.

Three Kinds of Writers. Most business people are acquainted with writers who gather information for their business magazines. They are less aware there are three general kinds of such information-gatherers.

A *"legman"* (can't bring myself to say "legperson") is a human tape recorder, with a nose for news and fair detective ability. He or she simply digs out facts, whether news, data or case histories.

The legman often reports material piecemeal to editors, as quickly as obtained, without regard for cohesion. Sometimes the information is phoned-in from the interview site, or near it. There is little or no effort at organized writing.

A typical example would be an articulate mechanic, strong on his special knowledge, but weak on composition and grammar.

The *"reporter"* in the business field goes the added step of writing organized copy that needs little editing. Facts are grouped in logical order, with clearly-arranged data and good identification of sources. These usually are news articles or case histories of business practice.

Copy from the reporter is still subject to polishing by the editor, as well as cutting and fitting to a publication's space requirements. The editor often may supplement the reporter's copy with material from other sources. The "reporter" most closely fits the commonly-accepted concept of a "freelance business writer."

An *"author"* produces finely-written material. It is virtually ready-to-print. It is sensitive to trends and forces in the industry, sophisticated in that field's technology. Principles of good management are clearly depicted and evaluated.

In fact, a good author reflects an industry so accurately that he or she often is asked, "What did you do in this business before you became a writer?"

Legman, reporter and author are not degrees of excellence. They are quite different functions. Work by any of these three can be done carefully and efficiently, or sloppily and inaccurately.

However, it is not unusual for the same individual, when versatile enough, to work in all three functions at the same time, for different editors and clients or under different circumstances.

Many an editor/writer hassle could be fore-stalled if they'd open negotiations by establishing in the first place the reporting function desired or most practical.

For there are some editors who are under demonic compulsion to change the smoothest bit of copy, just for "editing's" sake. I once saw an editor almost cry! Tears literally welled up, as with a catch in his voice, he admitted an article was so tightly written he didn't dare touch it.

For such an editor it's sheer waste of time for a writer to do final polishing.

But other editors turn purple, if they must even pick up a blue pencil. They aren't lazy or crazy—just overworked. The latter often pay premium rates for printer-ready copy.

Unfortunately the writer generally must learn who is which by trial-and-error.

Demand For Part-Time Editors Growing. Business writers are often part-time editors. Because of our country's population growth and steady industrial expansion, part-time editors are in ever-growing demand.

As each industry enlarges, its sub-divisions become industries in themselves. Then each sub-division breeds its own special business publications.

A dramatic example is the automotive field. Note the thin slices of automotive industry suggested by the following magazine titles:

Autobody; Reconditioned Car; Auto & Flatglass Journal; Auto Laundry News; Automotive Aftermarket News; Automotive Cooling Journal; Automotive Engineering; Automotive Fleet; Automotive Rebuilder; Automotive Service & Body News; Brake & Front End Service; Car & Driver; Commercial Car Journal; Fleetowner; Gasoline News; Home & Auto; Hot Rod Industry News; Modern Bulk Transporter; Modern Tire Dealer; Motor; Motor Service; Service Station Management; Taxicab Management; Trailer/Body Builders; Warehouse Distribution.

This list is not all-inclusive. Each of these papers has one or more competitors. In addition, in the automotive field alone, there are even more numerous sectional, state and local publications.

Each of these started as the gleam in someone's eye, requiring part-time editorship for some busy person. Often a freelance writer has been tapped for at least some of the work.

Most pro business writers get requests, sooner or later, to edit or produce small publications. These may be tasks requiring only a few hours per week or month. Some writers do such editing on planes, in hotel and motel rooms, or even in restaurants and bars while "on the road."

The pay proffered for such work isn't always realistic! It must be negotiated with fair regard for net return to the writer. Or else the writer must acknowledge to himself that he's being charitable. But more of that later.

Other Kinds of Business Editing. Akin to business magazines are "house organs," which utilize many freelances for both reporting and editing.

A house organ is a magazine or newsletter published in the interests of a single business firm. Or the sponsor might be an association, a union, a professional society, a foundation or other organization.

The "internal" house organ is written for a company's employees, or the members of an association, etc.

The "external" house organ is addressed to customers, prospective customers or the general public.

Sometimes a single house organ is directed at both audiences. More often big organizations have several publications aimed at different audiences.

Another source of part-time editing and reporting is the shopping center "newspaper." These are steadily increasing in numbers as competition intensifies between shopping centers. Some are published by the shopping center managements. Others are private enterprises launched by individuals and supported by merchant advertising.

They vary in format, from external house organ types that blatantly promote the merchants, to weekly newspapers that truly are general-reader publications. Only the former are real variants of business journalism.

So much for editing. Many a freelance stabilizes his or her income with one or two part-time editorships.

Quite often these are handled out of the writer's home. The writer contracts at a fixed fee, with maybe an expense account for specified items. He or she is not on the payroll, but is treated as an "independent contractor."

Specialty Business Writing. Business magazines use a lot of specialty writing, much of it for technical applications in a magazine's field. But there also are treatments of law, insurance, accounting, advertising, marketing, personnel relations, etc., always as applied to the magazine's particular business audience.

These specialty writers are frequently called "editors" (i.e., "legal editor," "engineering editor," "service tips editor," etc.) Yet, despite the title, their usual function is merely to provide copy suitable to the special column or department. Such copy normally is

16

still subject to actual editing for style and composition in assembling the publication.

Best known of the specialty writers is the "Washington Editor," who transmits from our Capital all news on legislation, department or bureau action that affects a given industry. Some business writers make a full career "on the Hill" of being Washington Editor for several magazines.

Sectional and state business magazines often have similar correspondents at their respective state capitols.

Other special "editors" or correspondents frequently are posted in industry core areas, such as Detroit for automotive books, New York's Wall Street for financial papers, Atlanta or Charlotte for textiles, Houston for petroleum, etc.

Business Writing In General Publications. Specialists described so far all write for business publications. But there also are specialists on business matters whose works appear in general or consumer publications.

A newspaper of any stature usually has a bylined editor or columnist commenting on the local business scene. And this particular contributor very often is freelance.

Such a page, department or column may appear only once a week, usually in the Sunday edition. If there is none, it may run Saturday or Monday. Occasionally a business section appears three times a week, and very occasionally even daily.

Market reports are a common example of such business reportage. So are reports of new products, personnel changes, plant remodelings, special services, even business problems that affect the community.

The personal contacts such a "business editor" makes are invaluable if he or she is also a freelance business writer. They provide story leads adaptable to other markets, as well as frequent entreé to local business establishments.

General magazines often have regular business sections. And while *Time* and *Newsweek* maintain permanent staffs for business reporting, others depend on a lone specialist, or even a few freelance correspondents.

A variant on the business section is the column that gives business advice to consumers, on insurance, legal problems, finance, investing, building, purchasing, etc. Sylvia Porter is probably the best known of such freelances.

These columns usually tend toward explaining do-it-yourself

procedures. But always they are re-organization of business facts in a way the average reader can comprehend.

Syndication Is The Shotgun Method. Some columns or articles are "syndicated." That is, the writer prepares copy for a single column, on a topic general enough to apply to many industries or to various groups of people.

Then a syndicate, which is an agency specializing in multiple sales, will sell and distribute this same column to a number of non-competing papers or magazines. Syndicate and author split the proceeds according to prior contractual agreement. Or the author may "self-syndicate" his column, handling sales and distribution himself and retaining all the revenue.

Though similar, syndicated specialty columns are not to be confused with "boiler plate." A piece of boiler plate involves a single idea or group of related thoughts, written up in a very general way, that could apply to almost any human situation. It might be thoughts on human relations, housekeeping, maintenance, self-improvement, etc., etc.

Boiler plate is distributed to wide varieties of publications, with not too much concern for overlap of readers. It is sometimes referred to as "thinkpieces" or "shotgun copy." Very often it is self-syndicated.

Pay for boiler plate is usually bottom-of-the-scale, because of this extreme lack of exclusiveness. The material serves most frequently as "filler," whenever an editor runs short of regular copy, or has a small space to fill on some page. Therefore another distinction is that syndicated work is published regularly, while boiler plate is sporadic.

Ghosting And Collaborating. Least visible to the public is the "ghost writer." This is the fellow or gal whose creative effort appears under someone else's byline. Any writing chore can be ghost-written.

Ghosted speeches are most notorious in politics and government. But they prevail in business circles, also. Few busy executives take time on their own to prepare those more or less florid addresses to their peers at conventions, testimonial dinners and public affairs.

Very often also a businessman's testimony before hearings is ghost written. So are many reports to scientific or special interest meetings.

A variant of the ghost is a "collaborator." He or she does all the writing, usually for a specialist who supplies the facts but hasn't the ability or time to write them up. But, unlike the ghost, a collaborator does share the byline with the specialist. Many "how-to" texts are collaborated.

Such a collaborator is not to be confused with pairs or teams of journalists who mutually share both research and writing chores.

Sometimes ghosting or collaboration is part of an overall public relations program. In the latter, a writer prepares all manner of articles and information on behalf of a business client. These are then circulated in a wide variety of ways.

It's a short step from such PR work to writing trade press releases describing new products and services. These are distributed to publications as news. The PR writer also makes up descriptive literature to be passed out or mailed to prospective customers.

Final step in this direction is the freelance preparation of advertising copy, usually on behalf of small businessmen.

Report Writing Of Many Kinds. A special form of collaboration is report writing. This could be a comprehensive report of a meeting or of a series of conferences. Or the job may be to organize some chaotic taped proceedings into a readable analysis or a consensus.

Committees of all kinds turn to journalists for their final reports to constituents. In a business community, the business journalist is obviously best-fitted for this function.

The annual stockholder report of a company is often put in final form by a business writer, especially if containing descriptive matter about the firm. Also researching and writing the history of a company, association, industry or union is a frequent assignment.

Business journalists are uniquely qualified to perform many kinds of research. For instance, a marketing manager who wishes to investigate a possible new market, may retain a journalist to prepare a survey of that field, its history, trends, influences, "power centers," pitfalls and apparent potential.

Research of this type involves "literature search" in industry publications or association proceedings. Interviews with authorities, inspection tours, field trips and exhibit or convention attendance may also be required.

The final report for such a project is often more elaborate and detailed than any article submitted to a magazine, even though only a single client pays for and benefits by it.

Business writers are also in demand for writing or collaborating on training or instruction manuals. These range from one-page instructions on how to assemble or maintain, up to multiple volumes on training procedures or basic theory.

Such, in bare outline, is the gamut of business journalism. More on the subject appears in Chapter 29 on "Retainers, Sustainers and Sidelines."

Since business, as supplier of goods and services, reaches into every facet of human society, communication of business information must do likewise.

Too often business communication breaks down because busy executives rush through, or even neglect entirely, the writing of adequate reports, analyses, instructions, etc.

A "scribe" can be as important and useful to the dynamic executive as were ancient scribes to St. Paul and Jeremiah the Prophet.

Chapter 5

Who Should be a Business Writer?

Research shows 80% of business errors are either totally the fault of management or management shares the fault with employees. That is, employees by-and-large are *solely* responsible for errors only one time out of five.

But this doesn't mean management is that much more careless. There simply are four times as many things at which management can err, compared to labor.

A "non-business buff" when confronted with business error reacts like others of the uninformed public. Like as not, scathing denouncement of management stupidity or callousness is followed by turning to something more interesting.

But a true business buff is aware of this error-exposure ratio.

He doesn't condone errors any more than non-buffs. But he does mull over the circumstances. What went wrong really? What were meant to be the quality controls? Why didn't they work? What would be logical solutions?

Psychologists tell us a man or woman is what the mind reverts to and dwells on in idle moments. Musicians dwell on melodies and harmonies; boaters daydream of slapping waves and billowing sails; business writers puzzle over business problems.

Reading in the business field must be an avocation. Business magazines and books will take up at least half the journalist's reading time outside a "forty-hour" work week.

Empathy For Employer And Employee. Good business writers identify with their readers. Alert to reader needs, they can assess their readers' ability to comprehend and digest specific kinds of information. They shape copy accordingly, rather than to their own personal tastes.

By contrast, the scribe who lacks business orientation is likely to present business news subjectively, as it impresses him or her personally. Therefore its real import for the readers may be missed entirely.

A typical example of the latter is the often enthusiastic description of something new—a novel incentive wage system, let's say. On paper it looks foolproof!

So all "benefits" are set forth in positive glowing terms. Obviously, this writer may feel any sensible business man would be eager to set up a program just like it, right now.

But a business buff knows the business executive must think in terms of Joe, Mabel, Scotty and Juanita. Can he or she "sell" such a program, however promising, to these faithful and honest but short-sighted, self-serving workers?

Hence a business writer needs empathy not only for business management, but also for Joe, Mabel, Scotty and Juanita.

Curiosity Verging On Nosiness. Avid curiosity is requisite for all business writers. New situations demand to be explored and understood. Familiar situations are probed for the variants? Do they prove a principle? Do they seem exceptions to the rule? Why? Are there seeds of management breakthrough present for an advancement in technique? Or, in case of a project failure, is a new principle or axiom to be learned?

Be a "Beneficent Detective." Two traits ought to be either native to the writer or carefully developed. One is a combination of observation and deduction. This is the ability to see things, to really see them, in the sense of noting their existence, *and* figuring out their possible uses or significance. It's being an habitual detective, always "snooping" for the new, the novel, the improvement.

An almost a routine experience is to stroll through a business facility with its owner and to encounter a dozen things worthy of speculation that he fails to call to your attention. Not because he doesn't want to! He simply has become so accustomed to them, *he* doesn't see them any more. Very often what's "old hat" to him is your best story material.

The other most useful trait, akin to the first, is "visual imagery." This is ability to look at operational details and visualize how they work.

You stare at three meshed gears and visualize that if the first turns clockwise, the next must go counter-clockwise, and the last turns clock-wise again.

Or you see the aisle behind a counter is too narrow for a cart to pass a person, except at the cross-aisle. Or three poorly-parked cars can actually tie up six or eight parking spaces.

No Place For "Wise Guys." Tact is another essential! The popular movie/TV image of brash newspaper reporters heckling government leaders in nagging righteousness rarely belongs in business writing.

Each industry tends to be a community in itself. It has a very lively grapevine. So doors close abruptly and firmly on wise-guy reporters!

This doesn't mean that ethics and integrity are out. Some really hardnosed reporting by a number of business papers, for instance, is said to have aided in fracturing the Mafia. All true industry housecleanings have involved vigorous probing and reportage by the business publications in those industries!

However the "norm" of business reporting is dignity, courtesy, frankness. For even the totally unattached freelance must remember he "represents" some publication every time he conducts an interview!

The ultimate buyer of the manuscript may even not be determined at time of interview. Yet, when the article finally appears in print, writer and publication are instantly married, in the mind of the person interviewed.

A big question-mark in the average editor's mind always is, what image of his paper does a writer project to persons interviewed.

We must remember also that most business publications have the same people as subject matter *and* as readers.

Actually projecting a good image is one major reason publications maintain their own expensive field staffs. Often it would be less costly to use freelances part-time. But many editors or publishers cannot remain comfortable about their image in the field, when using freelances unknown to them.

A Measure of Persistence. Along with tact, however, dogged pursuit of the facts is necessary. The business writer needs a sharp eye for contradictions. Figures, dates, incidents often don't match up. They must be "justified" or brought into agreement.

Contradictions are not usually due to deliberate misleading by business men. Rather it's a too-casual tossing out of information in varying contexts.

A very typical example is in quoting production rates per employee. Supervisors and/or inspectors are lumped into the labor force for one statement but excluded in another quotation.

Hold Your Head Up. Reasonable self-confidence is also important to the business writer. He very often deals with leading men and women in an industry or field. But to be over-awed by them is to dull the writer's mental processes.

Remember, a freelance business writer is truly an odd-fish to business men, or almost anyone else for that matter. People can't pin you into a category. They can't "type" you. Therefore they are most likely to treat you according to your own apparent estimate of yourself.

My own confidence quotient was permanently raised at an early stage when, after a long, complex interview, the president of a multi-million dollar firm asked, "Do you make a career of this sort of thing? You make a living at it? I sure do envy you!"

Self-sufficiency is a very important qualification for freelance business journalism. Most people do not realize how "married" they are to their jobs, ordered home lives, their specific hobbies and civic responsibilities. These give stability and continuity to their lives. They are causes for being, for inspiration. At times they are even goads.

But fleeting importance must be way-of-life for freelance business writers. For an hour or two, a day or so, even for two or three months, the writer can be deeply, intimately involved with some business person, group or organization. The relationship often reaches a close first-name basis. Then, suddenly, it's over! The job's done! They don't need you any more! It was nice knowing you!

To stay solvent, the freelance must be psychologically prepared to "let go" promptly when an assignment *is* done. Occasional contacts to probe for new assignments, or be remembered, are practical, yes. But don't haunt an editor or client simply because of a temporary close relationship. Bluntly—there's no money in it.

Be All Ears. Every good journalist is an attentive listener. In fact, a good journalist becomes so used to keeping himself and his own views out of an interview, that a personal question from the one interviewed is likely to find the journalist briefly at a loss for words.

It *is* a legitimate ruse to briefly cite a relevant personal experience, to get the informant's word-flow started. But for a writer to go on about his own vacation, his car, his flu shots—never! The best thing a journalist can learn to do is to shut up and listen! That's not hard, really, because the other guy usually is happy to talk about *himself*.

Chapter 6

Marketing Comes First!

If you "make a living at writing," you are a business. You produce something that some part of society *needs* and therefore will pay for.

What this society-segment is willing to pay provides your living. Willingness-to-pay applies not only to business journalism, but to *all* forms of writing—poetry, drama, TV scripts, short stories, science fiction, juveniles, cookbooks, research reports, etc., etc.

Filling a need is "marketing." Sound marketing—filling a specific literary or communications need—is *the* key to writing success. Many writers stumble into good marketing procedure by luck or good providence. But if they don't understand the marketing concept, they just as readily stumble out again—and never know what went wrong.

The "total marketing concept" is a term familiar to most people who read business literature. But few ever *fully* understand it—including a majority of business people. Yet, to enjoy a prosperous career of freelance writing, one has to comprehend, accept and apply the marketing concept.

A neophyte journalist assumes eager editors will grab for his manuscript, simply because some creative urge inspired him or her to "do their own thing." Even some old-timers never fully shed this illusion.

In this assumption, novice and shellback alike are 180 degrees opposed to the marketing concept. They are being "product-oriented," instead of being "customer-oriented" or "market-oriented."

Briefly, *"marketing" is finding, then supplying, a consumer need, at profit to oneself.*

The popular conception of marketing as simply advertising-plus-selling is quite inadequate. Marketing is actually the whole backbone of a business, whether recognized as such or not.

So, let's review the elements of marketing—in terms of freelance business journalism.

First, research is done to find and define specific consumer needs. The notorious low-price structure for freelance business writing stems from its prevailing product-orientation. That is, most writers offer for sale whatever they can most readily obtain in the way of material, rather than ascertaining and digging out what editors urgently need most. The former is sometimes termed "stumble-over" material (i.e., what a writer stumbles-over without methodically probing for material). Since any writer can stumble over it, editors are swamped with stumble-over manuscripts.

Such manuscripts at best fill only an editor's need for low-cost "filler." This is a legitimate need, but usually for only a few random editorial pages or columns.

Filler is used to sustain a suitable "ad/ed ratio" in the magazine. (Editors strive to maintain story material at a prescribed percentage of the advertising, such as an ad/ed ratio of 40% story material to 60% advertising). Thus filler need expands in boom times, shrinks during recessions. Therefore, in providing such low-cost filler, the writer competes with cheap "boiler-plate" and free publicity releases in the most roller-coasterish area of freelancing.

Topical and relevant features usually come from the editorial staff, or from specialists—or from the professional freelance who detects a genuine need and fills it specifically.

How To Find "Needs." There are several ways to ferret out these more vital, and more rewarding, editorial needs.

We can ask an editor out-right what he needs. This is rarely fruitful, at least until after an editor has been able to guage our capabilities through use of some of our work.

Also editors tend to be hazy about their own weak areas. We cherish memory of an editor of one major business magazine. He personally detested paperwork and control systems of any kind. He seldom ran articles on them, so we dug them up for him. He always threatened to drastically cut our manuscripts on the subject. Standard phrase was "nothing we can use." Yet he invariably wound up using them verbatim, at his prime rate!

So *this* editor never *asked* for articles about controls or paperwork. But when he received one that was simple and clear enough for his readers (and himself) to understand, he recognized how well it filled a gaping hole in his topical spectrum.

But, note well, this need *did* exist for *that* paper. It wasn't an illusion. This experience must not be confused with the product of creative urges referred to earlier. Your author himself is not too fond of paperwork and controls systems. But he did recognize that particular editor's urgent need, and forced himself to provide for it profitably.

Guides For Writers. Many editors who use freelance regularly will send, on request, a statement of their needs. It's usually labeled "Correspondents' guidelines" or "Tips for writers," or some such. It can be well-organized and well-written, or a hasty rambling letter. These range from outlines so general in nature as to be almost meaningless, to some very complete, specific and helpful guides.

Such guide sheets are often more helpful in their listing of "don'ts," than their "do's," in that the don'ts spare writers from wasting time and expense on matters of positively no interest to specific editors.

Chief problem with guide sheets is that they are designed for use over extended periods. Therefore the editors, lest they miss something "good," tend to include everything, without priorities or qualifications. This often leaves the writer, after reading the sheet, still back at the starting gate.

A very few editors issue information letters periodically to their regular correspondents. These are extremely helpful in steering writers to the theme of the moment. But with these, precaution is necessary not to suddenly flood the editor with manuscripts on one subject. Before proceeding, this is an especially important occasion to query an editor, just to protect oneself.

Talk To Readers And Suppliers. A better way to dig out editorial needs is to question typical readers of a magazine about what information they want from it. Be prepared for each reader to ride his own hobby-horse. But, taken all together, reader comments can expose whole areas of need that are editorially neglected.

Ask readers what their chief problems are. Then ask what the business papers have done to help with these problems. Inquire where else help has come from, if any. This last may even provide the writer a source of material for an article.

A similar approach is to query allied tradesmen or suppliers to the industry in question. Often they are acutely aware of its weaknesses, and even know logical solutions. But here we have to beware of their own product biases!

Study The Publication And Its Competitors. Another method of determining editorial needs is to study a business magazine itself for editorial balance.

One publication may not include enough sales material. Or it may lack maintenance data. Or it's weak in administrative techniques, hiring and training, purchasing, stock control, etc. Most magazines are weak in one or more areas, simply because their editors are less knowledgeable in those areas.

But we must not be misled by numbers. A magazine weak in sales material could have two meaty production stories and five superficial sales pieces. Hence it's still weak in it's sales emphasis, despite the numbers. That's where the freelance can move in.

Such a study, however, must keep the magazine's audience in mind. A sales-oriented book needs only enough technical material to give salesmen adequate product knowledge. A production-slanted book might involve sales only in terms of handling defect complaints or warranty service. A "nuts-and-bolts" paper may have little concern for either administration or sales.

But in the case just cited we *do* know the editor needs sales material. This is because he is making obvious gestures in that direction with those five sad-sack stories. Apparently this editor is unsuccessful in obtaining good material, or is personally incapable of judging what he's getting.

Freelances may not have any better luck! But the odds are good. At least, here's a place to start, a theme to stress. They now know research and digging are a good gamble.

Second element *of marketing is that a product must be designed to supply each need as completely as possible, at a reasonable profit to the producer (writer).*

Designing a product logically follows on finding that a real need for it exists. If we have trouble with product design (shaping our story), we have *not* described the need for it clearly enough in the first place.

Most often a businessman's need is for some sort of help with making specific decisions. After reading a writer's article, he should face four choices: (1) change his present method; or (2) do *more* of what he has been doing; or (3) do *less* of it; or (4) make no change at all.

But if the latter, the business reader should acquire from the article positive reasons for holding status quo, rather than just stalling and procrastinating for lack of knowing what to do.

It is a mistake in business journalism for a writer to feel he or she must push the reader into doing whatever is written about. Just present the facts as objectively as possible. *Let the reader make his own decisions*, in light of his own circumstances.

Exception to this, of course, is the publication's editorial page and certain policy-declaring columns or pages. But such exhortations are usually the editor's or publisher's personal responsibility and private soapbox. Freelance writers rarely get paid well, if at all, for "editorializing." It's enough to marshal the facts so the reader can come to his or her own conclusions.

Third, facilities are built or adapted to provide a product of the right specifications. Facilities for a writer include the obvious physical tools: typewriter, desk, phone, reference books, sample journals, car, camera, credit cards, etc. But for a writer, facilities also include competence in interviewing and writing, plus familiarity with business terms, principles and practices. Being readily available (within reason) and being flexible as to time (nights, weekends, multiple days).

Fourth, production is controlled to result as close as possible to specification with minimum waste of time and expense. Production control is a direct function of specifications for filing the need. The more sharply we have defined the editor's need, the more efficient our effort to fill the need is likely to be.

This means gearing oneself to get and write what's needed, and *only* what's needed, with the least effort, shortest time, lowest cost—and minimum distraction. Involved in the process are planning and organizing on both a short-term and a long-range basis.

Fifth, quality control is exercised to assure the product does fill those specifications declared necessary to supply the specific need. Quality control does not mean producing superb literature as such. It does mean that whatever specs we determine *are* necessary to fill a need, our production must adhere to those specs. Otherwise we waste time and money on products actually designed for some other need!

If the editor specifies 1,000-wds-3-pix, we *might* sell him 2,000-wds-10-pix, but only *if* the subject matter is irresistible—and *if* he can juggle space to fit it in. If the editor requests picture/caption stories, and we submit all-type material, it has to be *very* good to sell at all!

Sixth,—and now we finally come to the step so often misconstrued as the first step in "marketing"—*advertise and promote the product to those particular customers who have this specific need.*

Advertising and promotion are basically the process of creating two images. One image is of the product, the other of its producer.

A neat manuscript with full margins, properly identified, is something an editor can work with readily. If facts follow logically and are supported or documented, he has confidence in the manuscript's content. If the relevance of the subject is made clear quickly, the editor smiles all through the reading. And if the story is *complete,* he's charmed. If a significant part of the story is missing, the editor may suffer a stroke. As to the producer (the writer), a separate set of image communications is involved. A writer who feuds with an editor at the drop of the hat suggests a reporter whose fuse will be short with interviewees also. A wordy correspondent implies a reporter who talks too much during interviews, instead of listening. A sloppy letter or manuscript infers a careless, unkempt person. Frequent delays and excuses imply a disorganized scatterbrain.

These details create the image of a person who presumes to project the image of the editor's magazine to that editor's own readers. An editor may personally be broadminded enough to put up with a writer's idiosyncrasies. But he'll think twice about stamping those foibles on the image of his magazine!

Seventh, make the product easily available, presenting it to those who need it. Making the product available is what freelances do best. They're already on-location. They can usually do the job quicker and less expensively than staff writers.

Presenting the product to those who need it is an automatic sequence of originally determining the need. So much of an editor's "slush pile" involves manuscripts totally irrelevant or only partially relevant to his or her needs. It's little wonder an editor repeatedly pushes the slush pile to the back of the desk, and reaches for fresher manuscripts from writers known to be dependable producers!

Eighth, deliver the product to those who need it, in the condition and at the time specified. This step in marketing should need no comment. Editors have deadlines. Writers' promises are business contracts, whether verbal or written. We must be careful in making promises, but once made, we must "knock ourselves out" to keep our promises at any reasonable cost.

If an assignment or promise of copy just simply *can not* be fulfilled, let the editor know as promptly as possible. The sooner he knows, the more easily he can alter *his* plans. Sometimes, by personal contacts and pressures, the editor can salvage the assignment or provide alternatives. But by all means, communicate promptly!

Ninth, provide suitable warranty service, and support good post-warranty service. Does this sound too far-out for writing, more like selling appliances or automobiles?

For writers, warranty service is taking every reasonable precaution to get facts accurately and to not distort quotes. It means presenting facts so they can not be misconstrued by either the editor or the reader.

It also means ending an interview on such good terms that a writer feels free to call back and amplify a point or clear up a question. This last also lays amicable groundwork for a follow-up story at some later date.

Tenth, monitor consumer feedback carefully. "Consumer" here means both editors and their readers. This final step is to check product suitability, and to probe for changing or diversifying needs. It could even be "Step One" in probing for *new* needs in a *new* marketing cycle!

You can ask an editor what response there was to a given article, but allow three months after publication before you do so. Editors rarely volunteer reports on reader feedback—usually too busy, or possibly afraid you'll want more money.

Better yet, ask a few readers of the magazine, though they're likely to fish it from a pile and glance through for the first time while you wait.

And that's the story of marketing for writers. Many details in this chapter when judged by themselves may seem unimportant or simply too obvious. But when viewed as parts of a single well-knit structure, they all are most vital. A chain *is* no stronger than its weakest link, etc.

Perhaps, then, "the marketing concept" can help more freelances to a truly prosperous future as real "professisonals."

Chapter 7

Story Leads and Assignments

Some freelance writers insist they can work only "on assignment."

By contrast, this author freelanced in business writing for seven years with no more than two dozen specific assignments. At least 90% of my published writing was done "on speculation" during that period.

What is an "assignment?" It is a verbal or written agreement. The writer is to obtain specified information and/or illustrations, for which the editor agrees to make specified payments.

Actually it's an informal but valid contract. Writers have successfully sued magazines for payment on completed assignments. At least one publisher has successfully sued writers for noncompletion of accepted assignments.

Not until the writer has acknowledged and accepted the editor's offer is there an actual assignment.

Therefore the word "agreement" is crucial! *Since the assignment is a contract, there must be agreement on terms.* Lack of clear mutual understanding is the root cause of most hassles between editors and their correspondents.

When an editor or client gives a writer only the name, location and person to contact for a possible story, this is merely a suggestion or a "lead." The editor is in no way committed to use or pay for the resulting copy, until it is accepted. Nor is the writer committed to produce a manuscript.

Should the editor, when giving the lead, also state terms of payment for material resulting from this lead, then he has made a proposal or an "offer." The payment offered should include terms for copy, for pictures and for major or unusual expenses.

Often included is provision for partial payment if, after the writer spends time and expenses, the material proves unobtainable or unusable through no fault of the writer. This is generally referred to as a "kill fee."

An offer should also include a "deadline." This is the date before which the material should be received by the editor.

Thin Line of Distinction. A freelance would save a lot of hassle with editors if he or she asked two questions. "Is this an assignment, or only a lead?" and "Do I get a kill-fee, if there proves to be no story?"

Editors *can* be your best source of leads, once you've established good rapport and they know they can trust you as a sound professional writer. For instance, one might say or write, "Smith & Co. appear to be doing a good PR job. You *might* look in on them. Roscoe Smith is the one to talk to."

But that's *not* an assignment. It's a lead for a possible story. The editor isn't sure there's a story there. Not sure enough to make a commitment. And therefore the writer is not committed either. But in the absence of assignments from anybody, the Smith lead is a good place to look for your next story, with reasonable assurance that particular editor would be interested in it.

However, most editors are unlikely to waste leads on a freelance until that confidence is established. Nor will they make much effort to supply leads to a writer who rarely follows up on them.

On the other hand, if after calling on Roscoe Smith, the writer is uncertain whether there's an acceptable story, the matter may be dropped, or the editor may be contacted for guidance and a possible official assignment.

If an editor does supply leads, it's good to report briefly on those one does follow-up, even when no story evolves. For one thing it helps the editor evaluate the quality of leads he or she is handing out. An editor gets tips and leads from all kinds of sources. Some are trustworthy sources, others are simply PR plugs by persons with no understanding what constitutes a good business story. Allied trades salesmen are often in the latter category.

Assignments Not Taken Lightly. Often, after a writer and editor have worked together, assignments become less formal because the terms are routinely understood. Yet it's worthwhile to run over terms occasionally, if only as a checklist.

This makes both editor and writer think an assignment through. It precludes offers such as the one, by a California client to a North Jersey writer, of "a couple of small jobs at page rates in your backyard—Newark and Atlantic City." Respective round trips for the writer were 20 and 190 miles. (He promptly asked for, and received, mileage and travel time on the latter story, in addition to the page rate).

The obvious advantage of an assignment is reasonable assurance of pay for the writer's work. Also the editor often makes the initial contact with the interviewee. This smooths the way, reducing the time consumed in scheduling and explanations.

But assignments have disadvantages, too. They tend to "lock-in" a writer. There's constraint to get *a* story, even though no story is really there. You can really spin your wheels trying to make substance out of air.

And because the interviewee expects *a* specific kind of story, it's more difficult to switch him or her over to more promising data for a different kind of story.

Assignments reduce a writer's flexibility in planning and actions. The deadline must be met, at whatever cost, short of outright catastrophe. Or, at least, more time and possibly expense, is consumed in getting deadline extensions and re-scheduling.

Should the article ensuing from an assignment have potential for a higher-pay market, the writer is still under moral and legal constraint to submit a full manuscript to the assignor.

Speculation Has Less Constraint, More Risk. Any manuscript *not* the result of a firm agreement (an editor's or client's offer accepted by the writer) is submitted "on speculation." The editor or client is under no obligation whatsoever to accept or use it. So the "on spec" article always stands on its own merits, subject to the editor's or client's needs.

If the interview for a "spec" story doesn't jell, the writer can withdraw at any stage without prejudice or penalty. If an alternative big story looms up, he can promptly ditch the little one, if expedient, to save the big one. Should another market usually pay better for the type of article that develops, a spec story may first be offered to the more promising market.

When it originates with the writer, a spec story usually moves faster through production than the assignment. This is because the writer doesn't wait for a "go-ahead" from the editor in answer to his query.

A Query Must Be Careful Communication. A "query" is the frequent mid-wife between a writer's lead and an assignment. The writer senses a possible story, sends a brief outline or abstract to the editor, gets a go-ahead or a rejection.

If the latter, no time is wasted on futile interviews, pictures and writing.

Reasons for query rejection can be many. The editor may be temporarily over-stocked and not buying anything at all. Or he's loaded with that particular type of story, or has recently just run a similar one. The subject may not suit his readership, or be alien to the publication's policies and format.

None of this necessarily reflects on the quality of the story, but only on the particular editor's need for it at the time. It's not unusual for an editor to write, "If you don't place it right away, try us again in six months."

A query should not be hastily dashed off, however brief. It must be careful communication of enough facts so the editor or client can make a sound decision. If the writer sends in a fuzzy query, he or she is sure to receive back a carefully-hedged response at best.

Are Queries Stolen? It is natural for freelances to worry lest the editor "steal" a story idea and assign it to a staff man or another freelance. That, bluntly, is a risk you have to take. But, in 25 years of intensive freelancing, plus 15 years of moonlighting, I have been thus "tricked" only three times—and only once by a major publication on a major story.

If this should happen, you *are* forewarned at least that you're dealing with a stinker, before you waste too much time and expense on a manuscript. And you still have information convertible to a manuscript for some other publication.

So, my personal advice is, don't worry about it. Include enough information in your query so the client can make an intelligent and positive decision. It saves time for you both.

Sometimes an editor or client may justifiably feel the writer is not technically or otherwise qualified to handle a story, and may credibly find it expedient to re-assign it. It is then proper and common practice for the editor or client to pay the freelance a "finder's fee." This is usually commensurate with the time and expense involved in presenting a query or even an inadequate manuscript.

Manuscript Is Best Query. On the other hand, many writers feel "the best query is a good manuscript!" Then there's no question in the editor's mind about being over-sold, or misunderstanding the facts. If it is a first contact, a manuscript reveals the quality of the freelance's writing and pictures.

As a practical matter, by the time you sense a story, you often are on the verge of an interview you'd hate to shut off. Setting up another interview, after query, entails not only more time and travel but possibly a change in the interviewee's mood.

Also, in the time necessary to prepare a comprehensive query, the first 200 words of the story itself can be written. In fact, one very successful freelance often submits the first page of his manuscript draft as his "query," along with a brief covering note. The key elements of the story, of course, are set out in that first page.

Many editors, it's true, in explaining their buying policies to writers, urgently request queries before articles are submitted. Some editors are real sticklers on this, too. They'll adamantly refuse to consider a manuscript for which prior query was not okayed!

However, most editors will give non-query manuscripts fair consideration. The writer simply must realize the gamble in time and expense is greater, when the query step is by-passed. It's a calculated risk.

When To By-Pass Queries. When is it feasible to by-pass the query? This author moved around by travel trailer continuously for 5½ years in search of article material. Often, by the time responses to queries came back, he could be 500 or 1,000 miles from the place queried about.

So I dispensed with queries altogether. After the first year of by-passing queries, I scrapped about 25% of my output in dog-eared manuscripts proven to be unsalable. By the fifth year, the speculative manuscript submissions were consistently selling better than 95%.

What made the difference? *The secret is knowing, intimately and currently, the industries written about, knowing the magazines buying the material, and knowing the preferences or aversions of individual editors.* This all goes right back to the basic elements of marketing, as described earlier.

Detecting Leads Requires Sensitive Antennae. So—when not receiving assignments from editors, where does a writer find story leads? A "lead," incidentally, is merely the hint where a story *might* be found. A lead is a possibility, not a certainty.

We talk in terms of leads because stories rarely jump out at you full-blown. You have to be a detective!

Start with the newspaper's business section (but don't overlook the rest of the paper). One item reads, in part, "Mrs. Goldie Smith was honored yesterday for going 12-months without customer complaint about her assembly of Gulliver toy earthmovers."

This suggests Gulliver Toy Company just might have: (1) an employee motivation program; (2) good quality control systems; (3) good customer or dealer feedback; (4) excellent training methods; and, (5) an enlightened management that ought to be good for other as-yet-unsuspected stories.

At least half the adults you meet socially or casually work at some job. Keep your ear tuned for any remark that sounds like something unusual at their places of work. Don't hesitate to dig a little. Europeans are amazed at how Americans like to talk about their work. Take advantage of it.

Talking about work has two advantages. One, many leads come this way. Second, it's a major method of learning about industries or processes unfamiliar to you.

When interviewing, be alert for any mention by the person interviewed of a competitor, or of a similar operation in a nearby city or another industry. By all means, don't break the speaker's train of thought, but note down the reference. When the interview is buttoned up, then inquire further about that reference, *if* it can be done tactfully.

Every Enterprise Has Potential. Generating leads is a chain-reaction process that multiples geometrically, if you are truly alert at all times for tips or hints.

When barnstorming, it was my frequent experience to enter a new town or city with no prior leads whatsoever. I'd work it for a week to several months, depending on the town's size and on our schedule. And I'd inevitably leave with a file-folder still full of good leads, many of them useful the next time through town a year or two later.

Every notable advertisement of any kind is not only a possible sales promotion story in itself, but also a hint to some progressive action by the firm doing the advertising.

Any new facility in a community (less than two years old) holds promise of something worth investigating. It should have the most modern equipment and layout. Much of it will be stereotyped, of course, but combing the new buildings in town will yield a profitable percentage of good innovative leads.

Remember, too, that *everything* has its business side. We have written about a church's parking lot and a church's job descriptions. We've discussed the safety provisions of an amusement park, the cafeteria at city hall, water temperature control at the zoo, therapeutic pools for horses, housekeeping in the hospital, special diet in an orphanage, coach-and-four rides at a tourist spot, etc., etc.

Long and Short of It. Articles of any length are grist for the mill, from picture-and-caption on up. But you'd better know your editors and magazines quite well before spending time on long articles (over 2,000 words)!

As a rule of thumb, articles gradually decrease in marketability according to their length. Not only do reject rates tend to increase with length, but longer articles are slower to get into print, as a general rule.

One reason is mechanical. Editors find it more difficult to make room for the long article. Another reason is tactical; editors believe their audiences won't read long articles.

Moreover many publications have a "smorgasbord" policy—the greatest variety of titles possible for readers to browse through and choose from. Which means preference for short articles.

Single pictures with captions up to 50 to 75 words sell the most readily—if they tell a good clear story. The "pic-caps" sell even when the market has closed down on everything else! So they should never be overlooked.

The "product-application" pic-cap especially finds wide acceptance among the 4,000 or more house organs. This is a picture of a company's product being used. That is, its function or "application" is being demonstrated in the photograph. Such pic-caps or shorticles sell to editors of house organs published by manufacturers of the products.

The editor will often buy such a picture even though there are similar ones already in the file, simply because yours is from a new or different locale.

Pic-Caps And Shorticles. We cannot overstress the importance to a freelance writer of both pic-caps and "shorticles" (short articles up to 300 or 400 words). They fill in the chinks and often make the difference between profitable and non-profitable operation!

Freelancing is full of delays, dud interviews, callback trips, and all other forms of wasting time and energy. So the alert freelance is always watching for pic-caps and shorticles to salvage the trip, to "pay the nut," or sometimes simply to increase the total revenue from a given field trip.

For instance, you have a date with a progressive merchant. He's located in a small shopping center in a nearby town. After a 30-mile drive, you learn he just went to the hospital with a heart attack. So, no story today!

But you don't turn right around and go home, writing off the cost of travel and your time! You look around for at least some pic-caps or shorticles to pay for the trip.

It's kind of a sorry little shopping center, but the drug store, the lunchroom, and the rock-and-roll music shop each have one small window display that shows some initiative. You take a picture of each, and ask the proprietor why he chose that particular display and how effective it has been.

Usually you get some response like he or she just thought it was a cute idea and has no idea if it's effective. But occasionally it develops the business man has in mind a definite group of customers to appeal to. Then you're off on a true marketing story of why the focus on this group of customer, what follow-ups or other promotions were pursued, and so on.

Net results is at least $50 or $70 for two of the three pic-caps, to salvage your half-day expenses. And occasionally one leads to a story equal to or better than the one you originally came to get.

We have found that pic-caps and shorticles are a bit like bears! Start fooling around with the cub, and the big mamma-bear story comes running up in a hurry. The pic-cap is always a good probe for something greater. It's a plausible reason for approaching the business proprietor or manager.

Round-ups with pic-caps also help to market some that are not too exciting in themselves. A "round-up" is a collection of short items and/or pic-caps grouped around a single theme. They may show the display panels of several delivery vans, or several methods of displaying guitars, ways of preparing fruit salads, or samples of specific types of advertisements.

Seasonal displays especially lend themselves to round-up treatment. The pay-off tends to be postponed six months or so, but eventually helps the writer cover some otherwise wasted time and expense.

Editor Wants What's Unknown. One final comment on leads and assignments. As an editor I frequently received letters reading, in effect, "I, John Jones, am a professional freelance writer, working an area fifty miles around Blank City. What can I do for you?" The letter may even be accompanied by a well organized resume' with listing of articles and books published.

Our usual response would be, "Thanks for your letter. We'll put your name on file in case something of interest turns up in Blank City."

We had a folder full of such names, but little faith in it. For if Jones simply waited for assignments based on his letter, he will have gone back to an organization job by the time we might have an assignment for him.

Moreover, what an editor wants from freelances is story material that he or she doesn't even know about, until a query or manuscript is received. Editors are much less omniscient than is supposed. Publications are only skimming cream most of the time. They don't really know all that's going on in Blank City, and only a little of what's happening in big metropolitan areas.

39

If an editor learns of something breaking in Blank City, he has three choices. Get on the telephone WATTS line and dig out information for himself, or send a staff member pronto, or check the folder for Jones' name. The editor tends to turn to familiar sources first, meaning the WATTS line or staff member, chiefly because they can be depended on for comprehension of the situation.

If the freelance, however, is first in with the news, and reveals comprehension of its significance, he or she is likely to get the assignment. The area a freelance works is a gold mine that must be worked by the writer!

Chapter 8

Interviewing MAKES the Business Story

Were *you* ever interviewed about something in which you yourself were greatly involved? Not for publication maybe. But hasn't someone sometime just seemed truly interested, and asked intelligent questions, and really listened to your replies?

Were *you* reluctant to talk? Didn't you want that person to understand *exactly* how it happened the way it did, and why, and how you felt about it?

Before women's lib, it was axiomatic that one "caught" a man by listening wide-eyed while he talks about himself. And many a dull Romeo succeeds by giving attentive ear to the woman he pursues.

Most people *want* to talk about themselves, if only *someone* will pay attention. So business people are rarely reluctant to discuss their own business!

Even Mr. Big is usually quite willing to grant you time enough, once you can cross his receptionist moat and scale the private secretary battlement.

There are, of course, always a few Mafia types. Sometimes a flat-faced wariness alerts the writer he's stumbled onto a numbers joint or bawdy house front, such as that elegant "gift shoppe" we once called on, wherein the "salesmen" obviously knew less than nothing about their modest display of giftwares!

No Time for Platitudes. Business journalists share with salesmen that gut-wrenching timidity in confronting a new "prospect!" They are overly concerned with choosing approaches that will produce cordial receptions and fast "warm-ups."

We'll discuss some of these next. But let's understand that in the long run nothing succeeds like wading right into the business at hand. A business writer deals mostly with successful business men and women. These no-nonsense worthies habitually take things one at a time. They give full attention to each matter in turn, then promptly turn to the next matter at hand.

Therefore the person interviewed moves by instinct to the heart of your visit as rapidly as possible. He or she warms up quickest when told what you're after as soon as possible.

It's our experience that to open an interview with a digression about the business man's golf trophies, family portraits or art treasures is likely to prolong this wariness.

We prefer to open with the most complimentary statement we can make sincerely about the facet of his business which we came to discuss.

We say that we've been impressed with his unique advertising. Or we experienced considerate treatment by his sales people, which seems to reflect superb training. Or the firm's on-time contract completions are a community by-word!

The person interviewed is likely to demur modestly. So next you say why you're impressed, listing details that caught your attention. Immediately thereon you and the business person are into discussion of merit of details, and the ice is broken.

Can The Interviewed Person Trust You? While the average business person is more than willing to talk, he or she also does not fully trust you. Will you, the writer, be objective? Are you likely to make the business person sound stupid, or vain-glorious or even villainous?

For business people are more sensitive to the regard of their industry peers than they are to the public opinion in general. The public can't accurately guage a business person's competence, His peers can and do!

Business people are reassured by writers who look to be one of their own kind. Flamboyant dress, manner or speech have their place, perhaps, around businesses serving the arts. Otherwise they arouse suspicion of anti-business bias.

Certainly TV or movie stereotypes of a newspaper reporter with drooped hat and cigarette, or tennis shoes and scraggly hair are to be eschewed by all means.

Please don't mis-interpret here. If the writer *insists* on "standing on his principles" of freedom in dress, manner or speech, that's okay! He or she *can* get the job done. But we're talking about accomplishing interviews as expeditiously as possible.

So, clothing should be conservative, though not severely plain. It can be more casual than business people customarily wear, because writers are expected to be casual. Conservative sports wear is often suitable. But extremes are distracting.

Discretion applies, naturally. For instance, blue jeans or kahkis and storm jackets are certainly more appropriate around construction sites. But they still should be neater and cleaner than average.

Gals dress smartly, but in outfits that don't impede their efficiency. For instance, no floppy hats that must be grabbed in the midst of note taking. No scarves that flutter out to catch in machinery. No long necklaces to entangle when leaning over. Soft-pedal the whistle-bait, too. Most bosses don't care to trail through the plant with a gal who stops production dead as long as she's in sight.

Comfortable shoes are vital to good interviewing, for men and women both. A common misconception is that interviewing is simply dialogue across the desk in a luxurious office. But most interviews don't really start until the executive says, "Here, let me show you."

Actually you stand much of the time, often on concrete floors or pavement, in corridors or store aisles, power plants or on freshly bulldozed dirt.

In fact, the "stand-up interview" is generally the rule rather than the exception. Sometimes this is deliberate, to inspire you to do your work quickly, so the business man can move on to other things. But very often the interviewee is so engrossed in his own recital as to be oblivious to casual comforts, his own as well as yours.

Always Level With Your Subject. Glibness in a business reporter is a red flag to business men! Executives deal every day with people, with employees, salesmen, customers, who try to cover up deficiencies and/or errors, or distort the facts. So executives know *all* the signs, including glibness.

Hence a writer should not try to conceal ignorance of a subject. In fact, it is better to "low-key" what you *do* know, and so draw the interviewee out more. You then fit his or her claims firmly on the base of your existing knowledge, rather than having to always reach tip-toe to the other's level of expertise.

Remember, you've got to listen. You have to quickly grasp new (to you) concepts. And you must make notes as you go. All the person interviewed has to do, usually, is to recall familiar concepts or data, and talk. He or she may, or may not, check once in a while to make sure you're getting it right.

But, to the one interviewed you're a reporter, not an industry expert. You may even be a unique experience. He or she really doesn't know what to expect of you. Therefore you are not likely to be judged by comparison to someone or something else.

So *you* set the pace by your questions. And it is totally unnecessary to pitch questions at tip-toe level just to make an impression.

Striving For Accuracy Impresses. In fact, we find interviewees to be more impressed with careful effort to assure accuracy. Often we will re-phrase a question, even when we're sure we got the answer the first time. But this not only checks on the accuracy; it often causes the affirmation to be amplified with more details, which we would not have known enough to ask about!

It must be stressed that clarity is much to be preferred over danger of appearing stupid! It's the finished article that shows whether an author grasped the subject or not. And, in the final analysis, it's only by his finished articles that a writer may be fairly judged by the editor that pays him, by the person interviewed, or by the industry that reads the writer's work.

It is a communications axiom that all listeners are each influenced by their own experiences, background and preconceived ideas.

In an interview, therefore, it is solely the writer's responsibility to ensure clarity! It's the writer who's supposed to be the expert on communications, not the businessman. Hence it's the writer's fault, if the full true facts have not been gleaned by him, This isn't to gainsay, of course, that the informant *is* at fault if deliberately uncooperative or misleading.

Careful interviewing, moreover, inspires careful replies. The person interviewed gives more responsible answers, brags less, talks more objectively, when he or she realizes you are being careful.

Fighting For Time. Sometimes you have to fight for time to get all the information you need. Maybe the interviewee can spare you only a few minutes. Constant interruption chews up the interview miserably, distracts the executive, with alloted time fast running out.

"Stake out" *a* story as quickly as possible in the interview—some valid story that covers your cost. Make sure you have the cub, before you go after mama bear. Then, if your informant is called away suddenly, you will be paid in part at least for your trip.

A plan or pattern for interviewing helps ensure getting a complete story. Otherwise writer and business person can dwell too long on one phase of it and never get to the rest!

Business stories have three parts. They describe a problem, its solution, and the results, though not necessarily in that order. This, too, is an axiom.

Too often what a writer thinks is a "story" is only a solution. Sometimes editors will buy solution-only articles, if their merits are so self-evident as to be able to stand alone. But better pay-rates are reserved for complete stories.

So the writer is well advised to probe quickly for the problem, solution and results on this bear cub story, this "insurance" part of the interview.

Probe In Three Stages. Not only are there three parts to the story. There are three stages to probing. First stage is to try to establish all the basics in the story, the outline of its fundamentals, so to speak. That is, get the basic elements of the problem. Next, pin down the core points of the solution. Then determine the key results.

Now you are "home free" with a story that can sell. No matter what happens next, you can pay for your trip. All the rest is enrichment.

Now you go through the three parts again to fill out mechanical details—the "how to."

Then, finally, you go over the three parts (problem, solution, results) once more in terms of the informant's management philosophy. This last stage is important for picking out real "quotable quotes." It usually produces the most "color" or "human interest" for an article.

An interview pattern shouldn't be rigid, of course! When the interviewee volunteers details out of the pattern order, just note them down. Don't distract him or her. These details clue you into the later phases of the interview, so no time is wasted.

But interviews, like any conversation, have low points at which it's obvious you're both ready to move on. At each of these turning points the writer controls the discussion by bringing in the next stage of his pattern.

At one time, I even used a clip board with "problem, solution, results" typed and pasted in the upper left corner. "Basics, details, philosophy" were pasted in the upper right corner.

Break Away, If He's Edgey. Sometimes your executive, after granting an interview, proves cryptic and edgey. He riffles mail on his desk, jots notes to himself, jabs his letter opener into the blotter. Obviously he's pre-occupied with something urgent.

As quickly as possible, ask if you may look around a bit, and get back to him later with final questions. Your subject is likely to brighten, tell you to go right ahead, or even summon someone to guide you around.

Then prowl in leisurely fashion. Make note of anything that pertains even remotely to your story. Ask knowledgeable-looking employees how things work (but don't comment about whether they're good or bad).

Don't rush back to the boss, either, unless he set a time for you. Chances are he'll soon get curious about you and come looking for you.

By then he will have read his important mail, made his phone calls, straightened out some employee, done whatever else was urgent.

Now he's *ready* to talk! And you now are ready with a fistful of questions. Some of my best stories have come from such two-stage interviews in which the first stage was somewhat touch-and-go.

The two-stage interview will also often open up a proprietor or manager who has been laconic or non-committal. They aren't edgey or restless—they just won't give out anything useful!

This usually happens in a case where the writer is not sure what the story is, or where to break it open. Yet the business man is the type who lets others take the initiative. By getting out into the store, shop or plant, the writer gets more pertinent insight and can start with effective questions.

Usually when this happens the laconic one suddenly becomes a fountain of information that's sometimes even hard to shut off! We several times have had the experience of fruitless interview for as much as an hour, then got the whole story while standing in the doorway as we were making our exit.

We have only one possible explanation for such phenomena— which happen too often to be accidental. These laconics-turned-fountains must have a sub-conscious fear of reporters or of being written about! Unaware of this fear themselves, they react to interviews by clamming up.

Then, once the formal interview-ordeal is over, they're so relieved their natural enthusiasm wells up and overflows.

Uncle Looks Over Your Shoulder. The most sensitive area in business reporting has to do with figures—sales volumes, costs, wages or salaries, production rates for both men and machines.

Today's business man knows that any statistics published about him are likely to be noted by a half-dozen tax agencies, from IRS down to the local tax board. He suspects one or more unions will scrutinize any claims involving labor. Some creditors may be overly curious. Or he may even not want his wife to learn his real income— especially if divorced; or re-married!

Many proprietors and managers develop pat half-truths with which to fob off casual questions about their businesses. And deliberately, or without thinking, they'll feed these same half-truths to a reporter.

If the latter is sharp, he soon senses discrepancies in the data. And since his article must be credible, for his own reputation as well as the reader's understanding, the writer *must* probe for the truth.

This has to be done as persistently but discreetly as possible, until he gets data that *does* fit together, or at least does not grossly conflict.

There are two ways to go at this. Most face-saving for the informant is to tell him that the data presented must have different bases, that they seem to compare "apples and oranges," to quote the business cliché.

This gives him the chance to say, "Gosh, yes, this figure was at cost, but that one at market," or "Last year's production rate was for workers only, but this year's includes inspectors and supervisors!"

If the reluctance to divulge actual figures is too great, switch to discussion of percentages, fractions and multiples. Find if this solution gave a 13% improvement, or that department's crew was reduced by 1/5th, or the doubled floor area produces 3½ times as much work.

Your reader doesn't *really* have to know the exact figures in a story. What's significant usually is the scale of the change (improvement) resulting from the solution to the problem.

For almost any business, a writer can depict the results of a solution in one or more of the following ways:

Reduced man-hours of production;

Reduction of overtime;

Higher production rate;

Speed of service to customers;

Lower percentage of cost to firm and/or customers;

Degree of skill required (i.e., substitution of unskilled for skilled labor);

Savings in supervisory time;

Improvement in employee morale, customer relations or public relations;

Increase in sales;

Lower sales costs;

Shift to more preferable type of sales (i.e., larger orders, more store traffic, better off-season or slow-day business, etc.);

Reduction in accidents, claims or complaints;

Reduced overhead or paperwork.

All of the above can be satisfactorily measured in percentages or fractions, without revealing a firm's actual before-and-after figures.

Your Readers Can Figure. This is an important facet of business journalism. A writer can tune out his readers quicker with data that doesn't jibe, than in any other way.

Business men, as readers of "trade journals," check the data first. Data establish the credibility of every other factor in an article.

During interview, it is not unusual for an executive to sharply challenge a writer about data in some other article that the scribe has never even seen, let alone written. It's easy to plead ignorance in such a case, but it's proof businessmen do check and re-act to the data!

Chapter 9

"Support the Interview"

So it's better to have no figures than bad ones. And it's best to have sufficient good data to fully support the major points of your article.

Good Stories Illustrate Good Business Principles. Good business operations are not necessarily spectacular. Actually absence of bustle and turmoil is often the most clear signal of an unusually good business. Its story lies in how this order and efficiency is achieved.

Principles of good business are generally common knowledge among the leaders of any industry. But they tend to be "folklore" among the general run of business. That is, perhaps half of an industry's executives will give lip service to various business principles, even while they don't really accept or even fully understand them.

The hard-nosed shop foreman, for instance, is likely to miss completely the value of psychological motivation in employee supervision, even after much supervisory training.

Therefore any story is likely to be marketable, *if* it demonstrates a business principle by a clearcut example at the practical everyday experience level. It will, that is, if the *reader* can be convinced the information is "for real," not just "theory."

This is because the average business man is apt to say, "Yeah, I know all about that theory. But how do you make it work under the conditions in *my* business!" Many a business man is sure *his* business has unique problems that nullify accepted business principles. Hence the function of the story is to convince him that principles *do* apply to him as well.

Eight "Ms" A Check List. One other check list used to be on my clipboard. This is the "Eight Ms," so familiar to many management students. The list's purpose is to help explore each topic thoroughly. The eight are "Men, Money, Market, Machines, Methods, Materials, Management and Maintenance."

By mentally reviewing this M-list before closing an interview, the writer can be assured of a fairly complete report.

49

For every project from smallest to largest is involved with every one of these eight factors. Whether or not the executive has seriously taken every factor into consideration, each "M" does or will have its influence on any project.

Take something as simple as putting a potted plant in the corner of a store, and apply the eight Ms:

"Men" means who got the idea, who performed the installation, and who maintains the plant now;

"Money" includes cost of installation, cost of maintenance and replacement, and net profit or loss if determinable;

"Machines" involve the pot, table, stand or bench, watering pot or hose, trimming shears, possibly a bug sprayer;

"Methods" refers to routine of maintaining, watering and feeding the plant, cleaning pot and stand;

"Materials" are plant food, water, bug spray, extra soil, polish for the stand;

"Market" is the psychological effect on both employees and customers, as well as the public if the plant is visible through a window;

"Management" is determination of who is responsible for oversight of this plant and its care. These "seven Ms" are traditional but I always included the eighth "M" as "Maintenance," lest it get lost among the others. For instance, it's easy to dwell on "Methods" at length, without ever including Maintenance there.

Various Markets In The Chain. A project's "Market," we might add, is not always the paying customer from out among the public. The cabinet maker who makes cupboards is a market for the lumber yard. In a woodworking factory, the cabinet maker's market is the painter who is to finish the cupboard.

So, referring back to our chapter on marketing, the lumber storage area is designed to fill the carpenter's specific needs to make certain kinds of cupboards. The cabinet maker, in turn, fills the need of the painter for something to paint. The painter fills the salesmen's need for cupboards of a popular color and finish to suit specific customer demands.

In the case of the potted plant, there apparently was a *need* for something to soften the harsh bareness of the store. The "profit" could be more cordial relations between sales people and customers. Or a better business "image" would attract more customers.

The point is, *all* "M" factors bear on *any* project, as much with one potted plant as with General Motors' latest array of cars.

One sign of a particularly good interview is to have the executive comment, "You know, your questions have made me look at our business more closely (or in a different way) than ever before!"

This doesn't happen often, to be sure, but the other guy actually seems quite thoughtful and grateful when it does happen! And it stresses how often even the most methodical business proceeds without full awareness, planning and implementation.

Survey Questions A Useful Tool. "Survey questions" are a valuable tool in the initial probe-phase of interviewing. To use them effectively requires some knowledge of an industry (or at least of a similar, closely-related industry, as hardware to housewares, or either to giftwares, etc.)

Six to a dozen questions should involve the "growing edge" or dynamic phases of the industry. Also, these questions should touch on many different phases of the business, i.e., one on cost control, another on marketing, a third on personnel, etc.

Assume you were working the coin-op drycleaning industry (as I did) during its recovery phase in the sixties. Here's a list of questions covering the whole gamut of such an operation, designed to uncover the owner's most effective areas of management:

1. Do you have attendants; what do they do; and how do you train them;

2. Do you maintain the equipment yourself, or have you an arrangement with someone else;

3. What hours are you open, and why; did you experiment with different hours;

4. How much of your personal time is devoted to the business; that is, do you see it as an investment or a job;

5. Are you satisfied with the layout and size of the premises;

6. What means of consumer education have you tried; which worked best;

7. What means do you have for controlling or entertaining children:

8. How do you curb vandalism;

9. What is your most effective source of new business; what are your most effective means of sales promotion?

Actually, these are key questions that coin-op owners were constantly asking each other. Using such questions the writer can tailor a list to probe all phases of any type business that he or she works in regularly.

Two Uses For Survey List. This list is used in two ways. One is to open up new areas, if an interview isn't panning much gold. Every business man, however unsuccessful he may be over-all, has pet phases of the business that he enjoys and in which he is fairly expert and creative. He'll be deft with customers, even though his machinery is held together with baling wire. Or he may be a whizz at quoting you the cost of a day's consumption of paper, even though he's had seven foremen in three years.

Thus, when you finally touch on a pet subject through survey questions, your subject is likely to suddenly take fire, then he or she comes up with a lot of interesting and useful data.

The second use of survey questions is in "cold turkey" calls. Here the writer has no advance information or significant data on a particular business.

The initial interview is exploratory because the business, to visual observation, has no notable features. As in the first instance, the questions probe for what may be exceptional or distinctive about a business.

If the interview still produces nothing spectacular, after the six or dozen questions have been discussed, the writer thanks the business person and leaves.

Survey Can Also Cover Expenses. But such an interview, though not producing a story, is still not wasted for either writer or informant. The writer roughs notes on each question. Then he files them in a survey folder for that industry.

After six or ten survey interviews, there is a sufficient variety of opinions and observations about one or more of these hot subjects to do a "round-up." This is a general discussion, pro and con, of some industry topic. If the questions are well-chosen, it could be a "hot" topic. All main points in the "round-table discussion" are supported by quotes from your survey informants.

Thus, should no story come from a particular interview, there is at least a chance to earn expenses. If a good story does come forth, the survey discussions then provide an added bonus.

However, as a matter of practice, we abandon survey questions to nab the full story the moment it appears. Then, if the interviewee will give us the necessary time, we complete the survey questions afterwards.

Popularity of round-ups waxes and wanes through each decade. Magazines willing to use round-ups are sometimes limited in number. They also vary greatly as to what they'll accept. Here's a critical case where one must know each publication's editorial policies.

On the other hand, surveys provide a limitless source of shorticles on supervisory practices. These are used as fillers with or without reference by name to sources.

When An Interview Dries Up. Sooner or later an interview dries up for lack of knowledge where to probe next. It is almost always fruitful then to ask, "Since experience is the best teacher, what would you do differently now, if you had this whole project to do over again?"

This often helps to obtain a sober review, especially if the project is the informant's pet activity. For, as he first describes the project to the writer, much of his original enthusiasm for the subject may be re-kindled. The entrepreneur projects what was first envisioned. So the above question will then bring on a more seasoned appraisal of what did and does happen.

Once in a while this latter appraisal can prove to be so negative as to neutralize the worth of the project entirely! But the story isn't necessarily killed thereby. It still may be newsworthy, as a pointer to more practical steps to be taken subsequently—even if the story has to be written without mention of names and places.

For instance, I was involved in the coin-op drycleaning industry from its inception. After the pioneering flurry, there was a long period when failure stories out-numbered success stories. Yet out of these "warnings what-not-to-do" evolved the present lucrative coin-op drycleaning industry.

"Growing Edges" Are Most Fruitful. As with drycleaning coin-op, the freelance writer usually thrives most in the "growing edges" of industries. These are where the most new things are being tried. Change and growth are rapid.

Standardization hasn't yet damped-down innovation. And everyone, business man and editor alike, is more open-minded and receptive to all creative ideas.

The writer also enjoys greater personal stimulation as part of such vigorous pioneering. He has a grandstand seat at a great national drama, as he watches a brand new industry or new discipline unfold.

Yet the writer is more than a spectator, for he or she shares in that unfolding by writing about it. By helping spread the news the writer helps foster the new development.

Similarly, whenever a new technique hits an industry (even if it's old hat in other industries) there is great stimulation as well as a lot of fresh story material.

So the alert writer is always hunting for the "growing edges," either in an industry, or as a complete new industry.

Typical "growing edge" experiences for this author have been growth of the motel and mobile home industries from "camps" to their present strength and popularity. We were involved with "piggyback" in trucking, scuba diving in sports, and then snowmobiles. Car washes and domestic swimming pools were fast comers. Circumferential highways were big news for quite a while. "Zero defects" and quality control, inventory control, small plant conveyorizing, employee motivation, all had their peak interest periods.

At the time of writing, it's pollution control, environmental conservation, computer applications, and training the disadvantaged that are fruitful areas for writers. Development of solar energy and all alternate energy sources strike this author as the greatest growing edge in our generation, perhaps ranking with invention of the wheel and of currency and the Industrial Revolution.

Chapter 10

Added Notes on Note-Taking

The experienced writer knows there is no correlation between quantity of notes and quality or richness of their resultant story. Often a few seemingly sketchy notes result in many pages of excellent copy.

Note-taking is affected by a writer's ability to *visualize* processes. Where a process stands clear in the mind, few notes are likely or even need to be taken. But the writer must still be sure there is a note for every salient feature, however brief. Figures and formulae *must* be noted in detail. Though crystal clear at the time given, they can be muddied by later data, especially if the latter differs only slightly.

Moreover, vividness of comprehension fades rapidly. However indelible a mental picture seems to be, the writer should at least sit down and amplify his notes as quickly as possible after an interview.

Where explanation of a process is unclear, it is foolish to keep scribbling more notes in hopes all will become clear when read later. Make the notes an immediate process of analysis or clarification. Slow the informant down to step-by-step elucidation.

Several causes of confusion are possible. It may be unclear whether the whole or a part is involved, or whether past, present or future is the setting. Surprisingly often an informant slips without warning from what's right to what's wrong with a project. Or the tasks of several individuals are confused and inter-mingled. Backtracking when describing sequences can be inadvertant at times.

Finally, never hesitate to read notes back verbatim to the speaker. This often results in the informant volunteering more information as you review them.

You Set The Pace. We remind the reader again—the person interviewed usually has no standards for judging good interview technique. So you set the pace. Major limiting factor is the time an informant is willing to grant you. But don't let a time-limit reduce the quality of note-taking. Whatever you *do* get, get it right!

Sometimes your informant has to grope for the right words. It's natural for the reporter to suggest appropriate words, especially if pressed for time.

But to "put words in his mouth" can distort the interviewee's story, if not his facts. He's likely to veer towards the writer's own preconceived ideas on a matter. The one interviewed often edges away from his own viewpoint, if thus prompted.

The words an interviewee finally chooses may be less accurate than those you might use (and may prefer to use in your story).

Yet *his* choice of words can be a very significant clue to further questions.

For instance, in describing what seemed like a fairly routine procedure, the informant finally won out! You sense real triumph, of more weight than the project itself suggests. It hints there's a bigger, weightier story behind it. This is when mama bear come's arunning!

This is a prime time to plead lack of clear comprehension and a need to review notes, in order to probe the real story in greater scope! Don't hesitate to ask "Was that the turning point in a major program?"

Business People Rarely Know "Stories." Alertness is absolutely vital to business writing. That's another axiom. Business men rarely know a "story" even when up to their necks in it. Having lived with a project daily for weeks and months, many of its details are no longer new to its creator or manager.

Now all the foregoing may have sounded like a too-elaborate method of eliciting a story. Won't questions evolve naturally as the informant's story unfolds? If the informant is a good story teller— yes. But only if!

The opposite is exemplified by Hazel's experience the first time I took her on a field trip into Maine, New Hampshire, and Vermont. None of her Kansas and Washington DC reporting experience had prepared her for "Down East Yankees." Cordial, pleasant, honest, frank—and laconic as Old Man of the Mountain.

Each of Hazel's questions was answered with a simple "Yep" or "Nope." Elaboration came only by detailed questioning. Ask a Down-Easterner to describe something, and you'd get a lengthy ten-word dissertation.

We do not realize, until a similar Yankee-type experience, how dependant we writers are on our informant's usual voluntary description or reasoning, in order to both fill out our details and provide clues to our next questions.

So when the answers are "Yep" and "Nope" a writer has no time to think up questions. On that Down East trip Hazel found survey questions and the Seven Ms a real life-saver.

Multiple Sales From Solid Interviews. Such intensive probing as described for the last several pages do assure the writer of a complete story, of course. In addition, however, such probing provides substance for "multiple sales." This term applies where more than one story, article, shorticle, or pic-cap stem from a single interview or story source.

Multiple selling is one of the techniques that help build five-figure net incomes for pro writers.

The novice journalist tends to cram all information from an interview into one story. Then he or she prays the editor uses, and pays for, all of it. But editors rarely do!

Hence the pro writer pares his information to one simple streamlined story, unclouded by extraneous material.

Then he looks around to see where he can market what's left over—as pic-caps, as shorticles, or secondary articles. These could go separately to the same editor, or more likely would be marketed in several different places. Combined with some data from the original article, left-over notes can make additional stories for other markets.

For example, the basic story you're after might be on efficient layout of a trucking company's new maintenance shop. This was the "lead" that brought you there in the first place (possibly gained from a friendly truck parts supplier).

So the main story of the shop is prepared for a trucking magazine. Part of the story is about equipment for a program training disadvantaged employees in basic skills. But only enough of the training program is described as fits into the shop's design, type and location of equipment, tools, etc.

There's a separate story on the training program itself. The same editor may buy it, or you may find a market in a personnel or middle-management magazine.

In the shop are a lube system and a welding unit used in the training program. Pictures and captions of each in use by trainees could sell to editors of house organs for their respective manufacturers.

Since the building was specifically designed for combined shop-work and training, its details of structure might interest editors in architectural, construction or building engineering fields.

Any new measures to control pollution at this shop could be of interest to the editors in the pollution control field. Special emphasis would be on how the facilities are monitored to be sure they always work right.

Most PR Folk Are Manageable. Something of a bugaboo to the freelance is the PR (public relations) director or person with whom he or she often must deal at big organizations.

The fact is, the PR officer can be anything from a most helpful; expediter to a deadweight drag for a freelance. A writer will sooner or later encounter some who compulsively re-write your story, lest the boss not think they're earning their paycheck!

We have a standard speech for the PR character who wishes to write our story or dictate copy. "Writers don't edit copy," we say, "that's for editors to do. Editors move our copy around, switch some of it into captions, heads, sub-titles, decks and side-bars add their own comments, insert some industry history or other explanatory facts. The editor knows what's best for total presentation of the story. And his or her decisions may even be affected by other articles in a particular issue, especially those preceding and following the one in question.

"So, Mr. or Ms. PR, please review this manuscript for facts alone. Anything more is a waste of both your time and mine."

However the autocratic PR types are rare. Most are genuinely cooperative and helpful. When they get too sticky, let them ok whatever version of your story they insist on. Submit both it *and* your own preferred version to the editor, with a brief explanation then let the editor take it from there.

Pitfalls in Having Manuscripts Checked. Writers and editors vary greatly in their practice of submitting manuscripts to interviewees for final approval before printing.

For editors, there often is a matter of "principle." They resist "dictation" as to what they print (freedom of the press, etc.).

For writers, there is real concern lest the informant get qualms about information given and blue pencil or unnecessarily water-down key points in the manuscript. What one says conversationally often communicates differently in cold type, no matter how accurately the speaker is quoted! There also is the possibility a manuscript will lie around unread on the interviewee's desk. Then the writer must jog the informant, several times even, to spring the manuscript loose again.

Finally there is the very real factor for the writer of added time and cost involved in submitting a manuscript for approval, and revising it after its reutrn.

In general, the better the writer knows the industry and its nuances, the less important is submission for approval. Where the pay rate is marginal, and the cost of submission likely to be high, we often counter submission requests with a version of our rebuttal to PR people's efforts at dictation.

That is, if an informant asks to see the manuscript, we point out that the facts are the only thing over which we have control, since the editor determines the style and presentation.

So then we go over the facts once again with the informant, from our notes. We ask which facts are those he is concerned about having twisted or mis-represented. We then iron these out, to the point of having the basic data dictated, if necessary. This is usually enough to satisfy the informant. Often even this isn't necessary. The informant was only indulging curiosity in asking to see the manuscript, or did so because he or she presumed this to be the proper procedure.

Benefits in Manuscript Approval. However, we're not so sticky as this sounds about submitting for approval. Very often, on seeing the story down in manuscript form, the informant will suggest added points that, by their inclusion, both enrich the story and maybe earn the writer a few more dollars.

On the other hand, approval submission is standard practice with many editors and writers. And it is with us for complex articles in fields unfamiliar to us. But we feel approval-submission is too often a cover-up for sloppy interview and note taking. If interview and notes are solid, the story is half-written when you depart.

Prying Loose the Stagnant Manuscript. The real problem is the informant who does nothing about the manuscript after you send it for approval. He wants to show it to a partner, or his wife, or a couple of buddies. Meanwhile time marches on. In that case we wait a week or ten days. Then we pry it loose by writing or phoning to say that if we don't hear in five days we'll understand the manuscript is approved as is, and will immediately send a copy to our editor at that time.

This usually gets quick action, alibis and apologies—and usually a blanket okay of the manuscript.

Once in a while there's a flat turndown of the manuscript. Usually it is for fictitious reasons. Actually the executive has become apprehensive about letting IRS, his wife, employees or competitors learn something he's been covering-up.

Then there was the independent ice cream executive who gave me a wonderful interview and permitted pictures to be taken. The story was outstanding and rightfully complimentary. But he sat on the manuscript for weeks. Finally, when we were about to submit the copy to the editor (as recommended above), this executive admitted it would be pointless. He'd just sold out to a big ice cream chain.

The sale was being consumated right at the time of the interview.

Don't Put Employees on the Spot. So far, we've treated interviewing as a one-shot event. Get in, get the story, and get out. But a big story usually calls for several interviews, usually with more people than the boss.

In such cases we talk to as many people as time and working capital permit. The first interview needn't be quite so probing, as much of what you need pops up in the subordinate interviews.

Hopefully we start with a run-down on basics by the boss himself. Or a PR director will supply initial briefing. Then we talk with executives or personnel in charge of functions related to the story's subject.

Inevitably there are contradictions between what different individuals tell you. In resolving these, we strive to keep all discussion out of internal company politics. That is, encourage informants to be as factual as possible, rather than rebutting their peers and associates.

To do this, we never quote one member of a firm to another. Suppose we encounter contradiction. We try to introduce one viewpoint as an observation on our part, or a deduction from general industry practice. Then we ask the informant to comment on that.

We acquired this technique the hard way! It used to be fun to see sparks fly! But then we realized that, in controversial situations, the company pecking system asserts itself. If you try stress interviews, the top man's views prevail. Objective thinking of subordinates is muffled proportionate to rank in the pecking order.

Only the real mavericks state their positions under any circumstances. So discretion pays off best in the long run.

Some things we've suggested here run contrary to practices of other very successful pro writers. It is common practice, for instance, to "warm up" an interview by admiring a host's golf trophies. And it's considered wise to not take too ample notes, lest your informant becomes self-conscious and distracted by a scribe's scribbling.

But the business journalist deals with business people. They know what you write will be read by their industry peers. Since business people are generally at ease talking to their peers, they address them over your shoulder, so to speak. It may even help to remind them of this.

Secondly, they *are business* people. Much as they enjoy talking to you, they have a schedule and things to do. So they appreciate it if you promptly get on with the business at hand.

Thirdly, if you are patently business-like in your approach, it wins their respect even if you seem weak in knowledge of their industry.

Finally, the good business man is interested in accuracy. He or she is often personally confirmed note-taker. He or she *expects* you to take notes!

Teamwork Can Be Fruitful. Some freelances work more happily in pairs or teams. Any fairly congenial writers can work together, at least occasionally, if not as a regular thing. Most frequent of these are husband-wife combinations.

Other than strain on compatibility, there are only two major drawbacks to teaming, somewhat inter-related.

First, productivity should be greatly increased over a single person's normal quota, if not actually doubled. Otherwise the teaming is simply providing companionship!

This means that greater geographical area must be covered. Or else it must be more intensively mined. This usually involves digging into unfamiliar industries or new disciplines.

A "discipline," in business journalism, is any phase of business practice that has its own well-defined principles, guidelines and techniques wholly apart from the nature of the business involved.

Accounting, salesmanship, employee training, quality control are examples of disciplines. The *basic principles* of accounting, for instance, are the same, whether in making steel, raising cattle or operating a theatre chain.

Organized Teamwork. Teaming does offer very definite advantages. One is moral support and companionship. Another is incentive, to a degree of competitiveness that raises productivity. Constructive criticism, while events are still fresh in the mind, can be very helpful.

But most useful is the cross-fertilization of two minds shaped by different backgrounds and experiences. Where writers collaborate their differing skills, knowledge and natures often produce the richest, most effective copy. That is, the sales-minded scribe fits well with a nuts-and-bolts type, or a human relations specialist links effectively with a research type who probes methods and systems. Husband-wife or man-woman teams blend male and female viewpoints for good objective balance.

But teams must organize to get the most value from each writer. One method is to split interviews, with each exploring the disciplines he or she knows best. Another is for one to conduct interviews while the other starts taking pictures as soon as possible. Or one will devote time to the chief executive, while the other talks to subordinates or explores the premises for its readily observable features.

Sharing expenses to reduce overhead per story is an obvious advantage of teaming up with another writer. Especially in the Mid-West and Far West, where spaces are wide and expensive to cover, some ABWA members have paired off several times each year. For trips of ten days to a month or more, they share one car and motel rooms (major road expenses).

Each time they hit a new town, they separate each working at his own type of stories. Or while one starts a new interview, the other goes over notes from his last interview, amplifying them while the session is still fresh in mind. The second writer may even dictate a draft of the story into a tape recorder, while waiting in the car or plant lobby.

Sometimes writers "double-team" the story interviews. That is, both ask questions. But they alternate note taking on successive interviews. The note taker writes the story and gets the pay. Such stories are usually richer in data and quickly obtained, because one of the pair is free to think fast without concern for the mechanics of notes.

Double-teaming is excellent for learning new techniques from each other, or for getting fast indoctrination into a field another writer already knows well. It's the method whereby the experienced writer breaks in a neophyte. Especially, it's a good way for two beginners to help each other get a start!

Commercial Client Interviews. A different type of interview is very critical for the freelance writer. This is when starting some writing project for a commercial client, whether PR, advertising, research, training program or whatever.

Audience: Discuss first and fully with your client the people to whom your writing will be addressed—their cultural and economic level, skills and comprehension, age grouping, ethnic backgrounds, reasons why they should be interested in or responsive to your writing. Are they all employees, all customers, all stockholders or all politicians? Or are they a special segment of one of these groups?

Objective: What does this client want these people to do as a result of your writing? Buy something? Do something? Believe something? Stop believing something else?

Measurement: How will the success of your writing effort be measured? Increased sales? Reduced accidents? Better employee morale? Fewer consumer complaints? Lower costs? Less red tape?

Background: What was the cause of the situation and its history.

What, if anything, has already been done by someone else? What were the results?

Obstacles: What have been the obstacles? Labor unrest? Customer prejudices? Unfavorable publicity? Tougher competition? Poor training or quality control?

Program: What are the various steps to be taken, and when? Who is responsible for what?

Help Client Decide. Purpose of this careful initial interview with a client is two-fold. One is to ensure that you, the writer, understand exactly what is wanted. This author has a lamentable penchant for charging into a project before all its basic requirements are clear. It's cost him plenty over a lifetime!

Secondly, the client doesn't always know what he or she really wants. If you don't help him or her think the project through before launching, it can become spongy, time-wasting and subject to counter-accusations when its purpose isn't achieved.

It's quite true there are many clients who know exactly what they want and can be quite explicit in describing it. But too often a small businessman particularly is reacting to an impulse to "do something" about a situation without having thought it through. Then, when he sees a writer's efforts aiming off the mark, the client changes his mind in mid-stream. The project is aborted, or has to be completely revised.

We usually cannot foresee all eventualities on any project, and it certainly pays to be flexible. But preliminary exploration of the basic factors listed above can save plenty of wasted time and money.

"Village Watchman" Data. To conclude this chapter on note-taking, we cite one Sir Josiah Stamp who ran England's internal revenue system for 16 years up to 1910:

"The Government are very keen on amassing statistics," said Stamp wryly. "They collect them, add them, raise them to the nth power, take the cube root, and prepare wonderful diagrams.

"But you must never forget that every one of these figures comes in the first instance from the village watchman, who just puts down what he damn pleases."

When you include data in your notes, verify their source whenever possible.

Chapter 11

How to be a Scanner-Snagger

Business writing fluency is often tethered to one firmly-set post—the "readership survey." The relative merits of readership surveys are constantly disputed. But they never can be completely ignored! For readership surveys are solidly entrenched in business paper publishing by the nagging demand of advertisers for proof of each magazine's acceptance by its readers.

These surveys are made of carefully chosen cross-sections of a publication's subscribers or recipients, to balance large and small firms, cities vs towns, and geographic spread. The actual survey may be done by mail, or in person, or sometimes both ways for better validation.

The process is to show articles and news pages from a recent issue to the person interviewed. He or she is then asked to check one of several boxes, a set of which is keyed to each page shown.

The boxes might be captioned as follows:
- ☐ Do you remember the headline and subheading?
- ☐ Did you read the first few paragraphs?
- ☐ Did you read halfway through the article?
- ☐ Did you finish the article?

More boxes and questions about reader reaction to subject matter may follow. But the above are of primary concern to editors.

Of some concern to us, of course, are similar questions on recall of illustrations. But, as business *writers*, it's the "how-much-did-you-read?" questions that vitally concern us.

Business People Are Scanners. The pay-off question is, are we writers "scanner-snaggers?" Do we catch and hold the attention of rapidly-scanning executives, as they doggedly and impatiently weed through foot-high stacks of third-class mail?

In their reading, business people learn to skim for core data. How well-educated they may be does not matter. They might skim skillfully or clumsily. But, at all costs, skim they must to the best of their ability. For the next wave of reading material comes in the morning with the impersonal regularity of ocean breakers.

The two basic elements of scanner-snagging are: (1) The actual merit of the data presented; (2) The ease with which it is grasped and assimilated. The latter is the concern of this chapter.

Courses in rapid-reading are available by the dozen these days. Even more urgently needed, perhaps, are courses in a style of writing that may be read more rapidly.

Rapid-readers skip along key words like footstones in each shallow sentence stream. If forced to erratic hops and jumps, or too-frequent puzzled pauses, an impatient bound to the next page quickly results.

Therefore the writer, to get read, makes sure all footstones are there, are visible, and are in easily-reached order.

"Scan-Level" Editing. Editing or revising copy should be at two levels. One is routine grammar correction, tightening sentences, substituting dynamic words for drab ones, and so on.

Then there is the "scan level" of editing. Revised copy is reread rapidly, for sense at scanning speeds. Here is where the roughness shows up. There's a break in the pace here, backward twitches of the eye there, an abrupt need to re-read a clause or sentence for better grasp of it.

Scan-level editing is shifting word order, moving phrases around, changing punctuation, or even substitution of different words. It is all for the single purpose of promoting faster reading and quicker comprehension.

Sometimes scan-level editing requires striking out entirely a bit that, on first draft, seemed desirably dramatic, cute or intriguing. But excision is necessary, because that bit proves to be a slippery rock that brings the scanner to a dead halt with one foot in the water.

Negative Incentive For Brevity. A near-fatal irony of business journalism has been its prevailing payment by the word, the column-inch, or the page. It is the most negative incentive for concise writing one could imagine! Many writers develop superb skill at constructive verbosity.

It is true, of course, that writers do not always have the best editorial examples to follow. For many editors, with blank pages to fill under deadline pressure, often are equally prolix.

These practiced word-fountains rarely edit or write for publications that are regularly subjected to readership surveys. The first hundred words of such verbiage is usually enough to shunt busy scanners to the next article, or even to another publication.

Example of Editing. The following example cluttered my first draft of this book: "The folder that contains the notes for this chapter is by far the fattest of all in my file."

This is typical word-fountain writing. It is typical of an unedited first draft. It is the over-riding weakness of writers who pride themselves on their capacity for single-draft production.

This sample sentence dawdles over "folder" and "notes." It's redundant around "fattest." And at the end a reader can be excused for asking, "How's that again?"

The footstones in this sentence are: "Folder . . . notes . . . this chapter. . . fattest. . .my file." These key words by themselves make quicker sense than did the original sentence.

Yet, with secondary words stripped away, the word "folder" shows up as superflous. For this sentence is not to describe how notes are filed. It tells a reader the chapter's material is substantial.

Now let's omit "folder" and flesh out the key words: "Notes on this chapter were the fattest in my file."

But the sentence following this one concerns the chapter, not the file. To further smooth it for rapid reading, it could run: "The fattest notes in my file were on this chapter." This version of the sentence not only speaks its piece clearly. It even leans into the next sentence.

Thus the final footstone of one sentence reaches firmly to the first footstone of the next. This should be consistent practice, I believe, except for positive reason to do otherwise. Such a reason would be referral back to an earlier thought or paragraph, or picking up another facet of a central theme.

When sentences are not meant to link, two things are necessary. The first sentence must clearly complete its thought. The following sentence must promptly show to what new topic it does refer. Often it is better to start a new paragraph regardless how short this makes the preceding paragraph.

Business Writing Not Self-Expression. All this is simply sound composition, as taught in any good writing course, but in a new frame of reference, which is scanner-snagging.

Yet so many proven rules of composition seem to go by the board today! People strive too hard to be different, to be free of restraint, to express their personhood, or release their psyches, or whatever. Or else they're simply too lazy to work at making writing easily readable.

This is their privilege. It's still a free country.

But this brings us right back to that tetheringpost of readership surveys. If writing doesn't snag scanners, no matter *how* creative and self-expressive it may be, it just is not going to get read by even a simple majority of desperately busy business people.

Business publications strive to hold readership in the entire market to which they are addressed. Any such market is almost certain to have scanners in the majority. Therefore copy written for these markets must be scanner-snagging.

This does not mean a writer's personality is swallowed up in bland anonymity. *Time, The Wall Street Journal* and *Business Week* are popular publications with distinctive styles that are firm and consistent.

Yet personalities of original writers clearly flavor each article (except where obviously written by a committee). Choice of words, phrases, similes, even idea development, all tend to remain those of the original author.

Scan-Level Sharpens Personal Style. Practice in scan-level writing, therefore, does not drastically change a writer's personal style. This was vividly demonstrated in my own experience during my ten years as an editor.

Galina Terr was my managing editor. Each month she polished and prepared for type-setting the rough or second-draft copy written by me and two other editors, plus at least a dozen writers.

For all of us she dramatically sharpened and smoothed the quality of our writing. Yet Galina was always able to retain the personality of each writer intact in the final product. So much so, in fact, we often were unaware of the extent of her editing, until the published version was checked against that submitted to Galina.

Writing for pace may seem unduly laborious and time-consuming, especially to one who has settled comfortably into a gushing style of word production.

However, just being constantly aware of the urgent need for a scan-able product can deepen a writer's sensitivity to pace, in both writing and reading.

For sensitivity to scan-level writing can be cultivated through one's reading. Each time you must stop and re-read any sentence for better comprehension, take time to analyze why it isn't clear. Then try to re-punctuate, re-arrange re-word, or split up that sentence for greater clarity.

This is one of the most valuable exercises any writer, of whatever discipline, can practice. He or she should do it habitually and persistently.

Each Writer Has Many Styles. It's a common misconception that each writer has only one style of writing. Too many scribes believe "this is *my* natural style, and I can't help it."

But do you talk to six-year-old Debbie the same as to Grandpa, who at age 75 can still break 100 on the golf course? Is your communication with Junior, the model airplane champ, the same as with your spouse of many years?

Of course not! We instinctively shape our speech to the person or persons being addressed. The same should hold true for our writing.

Hence the greatest problem with business writing styles is inability of the writer to visualize the persons being addressed. Once we personalize and emphathize with our audience, style almost takes care of itself.

I tell elsewhere about having to re-write a story for Swan Cleaners of Columbus, Ohio. They wanted something for customers to read. I was so intrigued about the story's obvious interest for drycleaners, I failed to even register in my mind their consumer-readability requirement.

The first version came out pure drycleaner-ese. The second hit the button as a consumer piece. But neither version presented any difficult style problems.

With one I mentally addressed my drycleaner down at the corner. For the later version I was telling the story to the lady next door.

Yes, it is true we have speech and writing mannerisms unique to each of us. But when we are attentive to our audience, these personal touches are grace notes that decorate and freshen our message. We pick and choose those most suitable to our audience.

True style is the joining of ideas and vocabulary that you believe your audience can absorb most readily, based on *their* backgrounds, experience, education and current state of mind.

A Few Stumbling Blocks. Distrust of big words has been prompted by the "fog index" of Rudolph Flesch and other easier-reading exponents. Yet big words should not be evaded merely because of length. When the sense of a word fits precisely, with no reasonable alternative, use it, without qualm or quiver.

Most business people today are literate enough to cope rapidly with big words, provided they don't clot together in clumps.

Three big words in a row are sure stumbling blocks, regardless how readily each is understood by itself. Two less-familiar big words will also stub the pace.

Such clumps can be broken several ways. Re-arrange the sentence. Substitute one smaller word, especially for the middle word of three. For "corporate management hierarchy" try "levels of corporate management." Insert another smaller word into the series. Punctuate more.

Hesitation occurs when a less familiar word splits a natural word group or a phrase. For instance, consider the phrase "small imaginary circle."

"Imaginary small circle" scans more readily. Small circles are easier to visualize than imaginary circles. It's a choice. You either imagine a small circle, or small an imaginary circle.

A subjective decision? Yes, certainly. Arranging words and phrases must be largely subjective. Moreover, after you juggle a sentence around a few times, you can lose all sense of feel for it. Sometimes you have to move on, and try again later.

Description Is Being Precise. Very often a word or phrase that gives trouble is descriptive. This is because, however accurate, the description is not germane to the thought of the sentence.

Time magazine was long noted for vividly trenchent adjectives and adverbs. Today these are used more sparingly, and only if they do not slow the reading pace.

"Dapper, mustachioed Doakes" is relevant if his actions are neatly and handsomely executed. Or sharp contrast may be effectively dramatic, if "Doakes' " involvement is messily devastating.

But should a description be irrelevant, a reader's prevailing mind-set towards dapper mustachioed men could intervene. However fleetingly, personal feelings derail the basic thought of the sentence.

It strikes me we often strain too hard at description just for description's sake. Color is thought to be provided by many adjectives and adverbs. Yet the real need is to replace drab key words with more vivid words.

But we don't do this simply to add color, either. Don't just replace "said" with "stated" simply for variety, unless the speaker actually was positive and authoritative.

The substituted word or phrase must be more precise than that which is replaced. Good word substitution always progresses from the vague and general toward the precise and specific.

Degrees of urgency, for instance, are communicated by replacing "run" with "trot," "lope," "hustle," "dash," "hurtle," "charge," etc.

If a writer is precise in choice of key words, the writing will be vivid enough without adding many modifiers. Careful attention to verbs alone can electrify a manuscript!

The Hypen Goes "Boo." Pace is improved at times by hypenating words. I myself am the bane of hypen-hating editors who insist I refer to "editors who hate hyphens." If a hypen speeds the reading, I hypenate.

But not indiscriminately! For instance:

"Each morning we have ham and eggs."

"Our ham-and-eggs launch each day."

In the second version, the hyphenated words create a single image which would fuzz in fast reading without the hypens.

Of course I'm safe with certain hyphenations because they already have wide acceptance; "year-to-year figures;" "out-of-state coporations;" "next-to-last group." (For the last, try "penultimate" on your audience sometime).

But compare the following. "Any stain-causing metals must be removed" versus "Any metals that cause stains must be removed." Or "This wheelchair-bound patriarch leads a full, active life" versus "This patriarch, though bound to his wheelchair, leads a full, active life."

At scan levels of reading, properly hyphenated phrases scan easily. Their counterparts slow the pace at each descriptive clause.

Readers Are Key To Style. "Study a magazine's style before submitting manuscripts," we are often instructed. "Then follow that particular style in preparing your manuscript."

This advice usually is not explicit enough for business writing. Any logically-structured, clearly-written manuscript is likely to be acceptable style—*if* the facts therein are truly newsworthy, informative and accurate.

When a business editor says "study our style," he or she is likely to really mean "note carefully the nature of our audience."

In cross-section, what degree of knowledge and experience do they have? How well informed are they about their own industry events and background? Can they be expected to know the disciplines basic to their industries: chemistry, geology, psychology, salesmanship, finance, or whatever?

What are the prevailing influences—consumer-orientation, union-stressed, government-controlled, environmentally-structured, etc? Are they in manufacturing, distribution, transportation or service?

The writer must then use terms and expressions familiar to the large majority of this audience. Words, expressions or concepts not likely to be familiar, yet vital to the story, should be clearly but simply defined at first usage.

If this can be done in a separate sentence or paragraph, a scanner who knows the definition already, breezes by to the next step in the story. However, the paragraph following a definition must, of course, link neatly back to the paragraph preceding the definition.

Beware, however, of variations in meaning *within* an industry or organization. I once did an analysis of the bill-of-lading procedure at A-P-A Trucking Co., North Bergen NJ. This involved tracking the several copies of each invoice to their final disposition.

Various departments referred to different copies as "bill-of-lading," "B/L," "Invoice" or "Pro" (for process paper). *But* in some departments a term might refer to a different copy from usage in other departments. The same term might refer to the whole multi-copy packet, or to only a single sheet from that packet. Therefore it was necessary each step of the way to make clear exactly what a term referred to, no matter how often it was used.

Publications Are Either Parochial Or Universal. Unfortunately the writer often finds, or has cause to suspect, editors themselves really don't know or understand their audiences. Many editors talk down to, or up to, their readerships. Sometimes they even talk right past them in blind fascination with their own thoughts!

This is most true where office-bound editors get into the field infrequently. Or they meet only the most successful, most aggressive or most sociable of their readers, at industry conventions or meetings.

Such lack of editorial rapport is detected by a freelance writer in the coolness or indifference towards a specific magazine shown by businessmen during interviews. It is even evidenced by a business person's more frequent reference to rival papers.

Most business magazines are edited for narrowly-defined industries or disciplines. A parochial spirit rightly pervades each magazine's content. Editors and writers are absorbed in the welfare of an industry or discipline. Readers identify with the paper and its staff, like "blood-relatives," as one businessman aptly put it. Such a magazine is often referred to as "the bible of the industry."

On the other hand, magazines that serve multi-faceted industries, must be more "universal" in nature. That is, they address themselves to a complex universe of business people with many differing interests. Such industries often contain within themselves vigorous competitive elements that wither any hint of real unity at each succeeding industry crisis. Transportation, food and housing industries are prime examples.

Some editors and publishers may be unclear in their own minds, or even unaware, whether their approach should be universal or parochial. They truly edit "by the seat of the pants."

Styles May Be Evolving. More often than not magazine styles are evolving in new directions, usually from parochial toward universal status. This means the former blood-relative rapport with readers must be supplanted by a mental posture of scrupulous fairness between competing elements. Dependability as a complete news source then becomes a paper's prime asset.

This shift is a traumatic experience for editors and writers alike. It results in editors who don't seem to know their own minds from one day to the next in regards to manuscript evaluation. Perhaps the greatest cause of accepted-manuscript mortality is changes in audience-identification by editors and their publications.

My last editorial stint involved merging two parochial magazines into one universal publication. This was for two industries that were rapidly merging, even while simultaneously splitting into new specialty disciplines.

Core of the new magazine format was general information of concern to all readers. This was written at the newspaper level.

Special-interest material fished from this main-stream was presented in language unique to the special discipline each item involved. Side-bars explained terms and concepts likely to be unfamiliar to general readers. Thus knowledgeable scanners could breeze through special material without wading through explanations of the basics. Yet a general reader did have handles by which to grasp the material, if it interested him or her.

At the other end of the scale was material directed at the relative novice in the field—new entrepreneurs, absentee owners and students. This material dealt with fundamentals in educational style.

Each type of writing had its own physical format, to permit visual identification. A scanner could thus pass over whatever his experience suggested would be of no interest.

This merger shaped up as an exciting challenge in editing. But the publication never really got off the ground. At the last minute, top management with Jovian aplomb merged a third universal-type magazine and its personnel into the program. More personalities and different ideas were jigsawed in. A crazy-quilt monster was born. Even so, it died slowly!

Study What Style? Any freelance studying this magazine for style, however, would have been confronted by three distinct styles. Each style was geared to a specific audience. And, though not common, multiple styles are not unusual. Therefore it behooves the writer to concentrate on the audience.

Finally, the point of my experience is that many magazines have no permanent styles to follow. Most are evolving most of the time, either to meet readership crisises, or adapting to the latest fad, or simply due to a change in editors or publishers.

A freelance writer, therefore, had best concentrate on writing simply, clearly and logically. This done, a competent editor can readily refine the copy into current style. A good manuscript is always easy to edit for style. A poor manuscript is difficult to edit for any purpose.

There are many manuals of style. I'm familiar with only a few. But to compare even them is futile, for each impacted my own style at quite different stages of development and need. My current favorite is *"Writing With Style"* by John R. Trimble, published by Prentice-Hall. Trimble shames me with the clear conciseness of his own writing.

For help with simple clear, logical writing, I suggest 71-page pocket-sized *"The Elements of Style"* by William Strunk Jr. & E. B. White, published by MacMillan Paperbacks.

It's brief enough to really be studied carefully. It's easy reading. Instructions are precise and well-illustrated. Even where a writer occasionally disagrees with the authors, one is still greatly challenged. And repeated reading invariably clears a memory dulled by today's smoggy bureaucratic jargon.

Style Includes Empathy For Audience. But, back to audiences again. A publication's audience can never be overlooked by the writer. Choice of language must be weighed for the mental images likely to be called forth in their readers' minds.

It is unwise, for instance, to refer to business tactics as "tricks" or "schemes" (i.e., "It was a good trick for filling the hall"; or, "Doakes' scheme paid off in more shopper traffic.")

Most businessmen are ethical and socially responsible. They wholeheartedly support codes of ethics developed for their industries. Many individuals flinch, therefore, at possible inferences of chicanery, however innocently intended by the writer.

Likewise business journalism differs from the norm of newspaper reporting. "Yellow-journalism" or muck-raking per se, or dramatizing events all out of proportion to their significance are usually risky for business writers.

This certainly doesn't preclude exposure of real evils in an industry. Business papers have frequently been the first to expose industry cancers, often at considerable financial loss in advertising, and even at physical risk to their personnel.

Certain news-type business papers do feature controversy as an "air-cleaning" measure. Controversy even becomes a game at times when industry individuals stir up a fuss "just for the Hell of it."

If the freelance is reporting controversy, first make sure there's a real market for the reports. Especially if payment is on acceptance only.

For controversy is subject to many nuances and influences not readily determined by a freelance, who lacks real inside knowledge of an industry. Power politics, personalities, divergent philosophies, competition, economics, association pressures, union/management conflicts, changing social structures all affect news values.

We don't say steer clear of controversy. We merely warn you, be sure you'll get paid!

Front Page Copy Is Usually Positive. As a matter of practice the positive elements in an industry or discipline make better front-page copy in business magazines than do positive events reported in most public news media, with their general murder/fire/robbery syndrome.

Editors and publishers of business papers are most concerned with building the industries of which their publications are a vital part. Their prosperity is directly linked to the health of those industries.

But what is positive reporting for a given industry? The same positive story for solar energy researchers could be negative, even threatening to manufacturers of coal-fired, oil-fired or nuclear power equipment.

Yet the good editor of a coal, oil or nuclear publication would print solar energy news anyway. Then positive recommendations might be added for off-setting or dealing with this new competition.

Empathy Provides Credibility. We must always beware of presenting techniques that are not applicable to a given publication's industry.

When I edited a drycleaning magazine, one freelance doggedly sent me articles for years on merchandise inventory-control, mark-up and gross profit.

But a drycleaner's major inventory problems are with customers' garments. They're entirely different from handling stocks of new merchandise. Several times I carefully explained this to the gentleman. And still his inventory articles came in three times a year like clockwork, during the full seven years of my tenure.

In time I visualized him as a robot, programmed and left running unsupervised, until a tube or transistor should finally give way and turn him off forever.

Don't Stall—Blurt It Right Out! One basic rule in scanner-snagging was almost omitted from this chapter. It's in every textbook, every style manual on news reporting. It seemed to me virtually a cliche! Yet I'm violating that rule in this paragraph right now.

The rule is—get to the key point in your first dozen words. Whatever reason there is to write the piece in the first place, spill it right now, at once.

My decision to repeat the rule came after shop-talking with a veteran editor. He was discussing manuscripts from writers he uses regularly.

"When I get George's manuscript." said this editor, "I go immediately to the third page to find out what his story is all about. With Don, I go right to page seven or eight.

"Mary does get her message on the first page or top of the second. But Bob always has it in the first paragraph neat and clear.

"I rarely touch Bob's copy. It often goes to the printer as is. But with Don's I automatically throw away the first six pages, then edit the rest. Don's story is always there alright, all of it, but it tags along like the caboose on a mile-long freight!"

A Psychological Quirk, Maybe? As an economic proposition, why does Don waste *time* writing those first six pages? On *every* manuscript? Not only time, but six sheets of paper, plus the carbon copies, plus two extra postage stamps, all go down the drain with *every* manuscript.

In a year's time this can really mount up!

Inability to launch out purposefully in an article may actually signal some psychological quirk. Practice *can* establish a habit of getting to the point promptly. But the writer may never do so comfortably, until he or she has determined why it is so hard to do so.

For instance, I've observed that writers who are habitually slow getting into stories are also slow getting into interviews. They platitude about the weather, the economic situation and golf scores, while interviewees impatiently wait to get on with the business at hand.

Such a writer might ask himself or herself, "Am I *always* averse to stating things bluntly, even in conversation? Do I always beat around the bush? Do I feel brief statements or short accounts are a form of cheating? Or does brevity seem bluntly rude, somehow not worthy of me?"

This doesn't call for deep introspection or psychiatric treatment. It simply means realizing fuzzy starts are part of one's instinctive make-up. Such a writer, in other words, doesn't start from neutral, but must learn to shift from reverse to high gear.

Both practices often stem from lack of enough preparatory thought. Yes, a reporter should be something of a blotter, receptive to all he or she hears. But, before the interview, it is well to review in one's mind, what one already knows about a story situation and about the interviewee. Then even during the interview lead-in lines will often begin to form themselves.

And if Don would just jot on scratch paper what he thinks his key point is, he'd have less trouble getting off the ground. Actually he's using those first six pages to think out his story.

No scanner will ever be likely to fumble along with a writer all the way to the key point. So tell it right now at the start—or forget the whole thing.

Chapter 12

Manuscript Make-Up

Physical Appearance of Manuscripts. Every writing textbook deals with how to set up a manuscript. The reader doubtless knows the first page should have the writer's name and address in the upper left corner, the word and picture count in the upper right.

If necessary, the rights offered are also spelled out in the upper right (in what is often called "the rights ear"). Under the new copyright law it is sufficient to put "Copyright—Joe Doakes—5/15/79.

New Copyright Rules. New rules on copyright that came into effect the first of 1978 upset traditional dealings between publishers and writers. It used to be that a publisher automatically bought all rights on purchase of a manuscript. Now the writer or author automatically retains all rights, except those expressly granted the buyer of the manuscript.

For the business writer the copyright is of little prolonged value, since news, including case histories, is generally in the public domain. However, interpretive work is covered by copyright, as is material the author desires to syndicate, include in a book or manuals, or otherwise sell to a second or foreign market.

Many features of the new copyright law will have to be tested in court. Therefore we refer you to the latest authority on copyright at the time you read this book. What we might say now could be obsolete in a year!

Dating Advisable. Of late I've concluded it's advisable to also type in the date a manuscript is mailed. This can jog an editor who lets it lie around too long.

Dating is less important where the writer has a good continuing relationship with an editor. But if most of one's production is sprinkled among many markets, much of it on speculation, dating can be beneficial.

Natural objection, of course, is need to retype a fresh first page, if the manuscript has to be re-marketed. But most times first-page-retyping is necessary anyway. And how many manuscripts, actually, does one have to re-market? If re-typing first pages is a serious chore, you just aren't making it as a writer.

Cover Sheet For Speculative Articles. Some writers have a special "cover sheet" printed or mimeographed to go with their manuscripts. This is usually a half-page, on colored stock, that carries name, address, phone number, rights offered, word and picture counts and date actually mailed.

There also can be notations whether the manuscript is speculative or on assignment, and if the latter, assigned by whom. If the writer's own record system calls for serial numbers on stories, that number also goes on the cover sheet.

Space for the story title and deck is clearly set forth, sometimes in a hairline box in the middle of the sheet. (A "deck" is an expanded sub-head that usually explains the key point, or why the story should interest the reader). Some writers even provide space for a full abstract of the article's key points.

This cover sheet has several advantages. For one, less information irrelevant to story content crowds the first page of the manuscript. Usually name, address, title and deck at most are enough on the first page.

The cover sheet has an added advantage of permitting a little promotion copy, such as geographical area covered, disciplines specialized in, experience and background, membership in professional organizations, etc.

Promotion is out of place on the manuscript itself. Presented in a typed cover letter, it engenders impatience if repeated often. Moreover, editors pay scant attention to cover letters. But modestly included at the bottom of a cover sheet, a promotional message may be properly repeated ad infinitum.

Finally, the writer can retain his carbon of the cover sheet in permanent files for record-keeping, long after the manuscript carbon is destroyed. Also the editor can return the original (or a copy thereof) with his check, to show exactly what is being paid for. This is especially useful when a check covers several manuscripts.

Titles Are For Editors To Edit. Story title and sub-title (or deck) are placed a quarter to a third the way down the first page of a manuscript. This leaves room for the editor to scratch them out and put in his or her own versions. It's also space for an editor's instructions to the printer.

A writer should never be offended if an editor consistently changes his or her titles, sub-heads, or decks. You create them according to how the particular story strikes you. The editor re-writes them according to his knowledge of industry trends, to fit the latest publisher's crusade, or because of personal bias or quirks. Reason for change can even be as simple as too much similarity of a title to that for an article on the facing page.

Insertions Or Instructions In Margins. Editor's do like wide margins on each typed page. This is for instructions to printers, true. But also they make room to write or type an inserted paragraph vertically along the margin. Or sometimes the paragraph is typed on a narrow slip of paper, which is tip-pasted to the margin, then folded back over the page.

For regular clients, I make a practice of suiting width of copy to a publication's columns. That is, I count the average number of letters in a published line, then set my typewriter margins accordingly.

For instance, for one account the column width averages 55 letters. So I set the margins for 52 letters, allowing three letters beyond the margin release.

On my typewriter, this gives a left-hand margin of 1½ inches, and an average 1 3/4 inches on the right. I'm not particularly scrupulous about filling or over-running lines, but they average out well.

Different typewriter types, as well as the printer's various line spacings will produce different results, of course.

When the publication has skinny columns in print, I set my typed lines to double the letter count of one narrow printed column.

These tailored typewriter lines have at least two benefits. They help the editor to see where he's coming out on copy length. And they help me control my paragraphing, as it may appear in print.

Typed copy as double-spaced in manuscripts looks much less dense than the same wordage will look in print (unless the printed text is "leaded," or widely spaced between lines).

But massive printed paragraphs really repel scanners. Moreover, long paragraphs inevitably get complex. They tend to encompass more than one key point per paragraph. And they harbor long sentences.

Therefore, with *my* type margins set to column width, I try never to write any paragraph more than six lines. Moreover, I strive to mix six-liners in with plenty of two-, three- and four-line paragraphs.

Pages Do Get Lost. *Every* page of a manuscript must be sufficiently well identified to enable it to get back with the rest, should it get separated. This is one detail especially worth spending time on, however boring or time-consuming.

A key word or two from the story title and your name should be shown, as well as the page number. Suppose I have a story about algae control in Lake Carnegie. I type in the upper left corner of each page "Algae In Carnegie—Palmer—7." The number is page seven of the manuscript in this illustration.

I don't write "algae" only. For the editor may also have other material in hand about algae. Using "Carnegie" alone might get confused with something on Carnegie Hall, Carnegie Tech, or even Charley Carnegie.

My name is on *each* page because the editor may have another report from someone else on a different facet of the Carnegie Lake study.

If writing about something with a name common to many places, you should include the city for closer identification on your carryover pages.

In a single issue, for example, we once had stories about three different firms all named "Dollar Cleaners." In such case, the carryover slugs should be "Dollar, Omaha—Palmer—4," "Dollar, Atlanta—Palmer—10" and "Dollar, New Haven—Palmer—5," etc.

Body Type Gets Mixed, Too. In a story on a Topeka sporting goods dealer, I told about his screwball idea for a "tornado-proof" roof for his boat display shed. A week later, back in Nashville, I got a story on a dealer's boat display there also.

The Nashville story was printed first, with the screwball roof idea in about three inches of type inserted into it. A later issue carried the Topeka story, with its last three inches taken from the Nashville manuscript.

Two other dealers were visiting the Nashville dealer when I dropped in to explain. I never had a chance! They simply laughed at me and went off to lunch together. I left a note of explanation, but never got an acknowledgement.

Such transpositions of copy are quite easy in the publication process. Copy pages get shuffled at several stages of manuscript-handling. Copy can be mixed at the print shop. Or columns of proof-text can be misplaced in "dummying-up" pages.

Anyway, badly-burned once and slightly-scorched several other times, I now try to put something on every page or two of my copy that hopefully will warn the editor if his body type gets scrambled.

I repeatedly refer by name to the person interviewed, or to the firm or the city. This can be done most gracefully by scattering quotes wherever appropriate (i.e., "It cost over $1,000," explained Berger, "but is worth every penny!"). Besides sparking up the story, quotes always help ensure the article all comes out in one piece.

Use A "Comfortable" Paper. Choice of paper for manuscripts causes more argument among writers and editors than one might expect!

Formerly I swore by erasable bonds, despite their higher cost. One can type at high speed with them, confident of easy correction of errors. And they make a neat crisp-looking page.

But erasable paper, in my view, also has drawbacks. One is cost. Another is higher incidence of paper cuts, deep and painful slices into one's fingers. These are due to the razorlike edges of these papers.

Also a drawback is high reflectance, common to all heavily-coated papers. Glare is a very real irritant and fatigue factor, to the writer and editor alike.

Reading and editing manuscripts is a chore most likely to be done away from the editor's office. This is because so much work material can be carried in a thin brief case or even a manila envelope. It's also because editors are more free from interruptions away from their offices and able to concentrate on their manuscript reading.

Thus manuscripts get read and edited at home—as well as in restaurants, bars or lounges, in reception and waiting rooms, on trains, planes and buses, in cars and in motel rooms.

Lighting varies from dazzle of a morning sun off clouds below your plane to dim pseudo-candles in some rococo eatery.

The editor is tired or tense, hoping to get all these manuscripts read in one sitting. Or the reading may be aided by a mug of beer or a martini. In any case, a hard-to-read manuscript gets the poorest attention—and glaring surfaces contribute greatly to hard reading.

Mimeograph Paper Easy On Eyes. I've now settled on a good grade of 20-lb white mimeograph paper. It's uncoated surface has a minimum of glare. The surface takes good clean type impressions. And erasures are not a real problem on good mimeo bonds.

Pale colored stocks can be used, if the typewriter ribbon is kept relatively fresh, and type is cleaned frequently. (Not that one should ever be lax with white paper either!) Green tints are reported to cause the least strain to the eyes.

Colored stocks cost a little more than their white equivalents. A 16-lb colored stock shows through less underlying copy than in white, and costs less than 20-lb. It's best to test what's available to you locally before investing heavily in a particular grade of paper.

Most editorial offices now run manuscripts through their copiers. This is for protection, should the original get lost. It also provides extra copies to cut up and re-arrange in production.

But some brands of copiers have trouble with certain colors or shades of color. So one might at least test tinted stocks on a few different copiers. Your stationer can give you information on this. Also more and more copiers are available to the public for such test at libraries, schools, post offices, stationery stores, etc.

Chapter 13

Seat of Pants to Seat of Chair

The first axiom of freelance writing, stressed by every scribe who makes a living at it, is: Don't *ever* talk out a story—shut up and start writing!

Otherwise the writer will be like the boxer who "leaves his fight in the gym." Enthusiasm for a story is quickly exhausted by too much preliminary discussion. You just plain get bored with it.

Many a promising writer never makes the grade because he or she "talks a good game," instead of settling down to work. This applies especially to many long-time writer's club members.

A second axiom is: Don't waste time gloating over that big story you just put in the mail. You're done with it! Keep moving! Precious work hours slip away while you indulge yourself.

Save the critique and the blow-by-blow account for leisure hours. While still at your desk, resolutely reach for notes on the next story, or start lining up your next interviews. Keep moving! Keep moving!

All writers bog down on occasion. Some bog down at the start of every new article. And every writer has a favorite device or two for getting going.

The consensus seems to be that action sparks creativity. A writing coach bullied James Jones into producing *Journey's End* by keeping him active with words. Whenever her proteges seemed unable to further their own work, she made them stay at their typewriters copying articles from magazines.

Somehow this starts the sub-conscious mind working creatively. Pretty soon something bubbles to the surface. Then a writer can turn back to the creative job at hand.

Breaking Out of the Doldrums. A Survey on "How to Break Out of Writer's Doldrums" was once conducted among the members of Associated Business Writers of America. Following are some verbatim responses.

"Keep my work organized toward a minimal goal," said Bill Abbott of Tampa Florida. "I tell myself over and over, I *must* keep at least ten stories in the mail, ten stories in hand for writing, and ten stories listed for interviews and pictures. Call it my "Rule of Ten, Ten, and Ten!"

"These three groups often get temporarily out of balance—as do budgets and bank accounts! But just organizing them is mentally helpful. It gives me a guide, a goal. It keeps me busy and interested."

To save time and keep up production, Abbott did two other things. He concentrated his efforts, and he avoided cold notes. For the first, he found momentum most helpful to either interviewing or writing. So Bill would bunch his interviews, possibly spend a week just interviewing. Then he'd settle down to a stretch of writing.

"While interviewing," he said of cold notes, "I make it a point each night to review my notes. I expand them, then work out an angle, an outline or sequence. Thus when I sit down to write the story, the job is almost one of copying!"

The key to Bill Abbott's system, of course, is keeping ten manuscripts in the mail. We'd suggest, however, that his quota of ten *never* include any manuscript over six months old. If half your ten circulating manuscripts are old, you're in trouble. Their payout is never as good as for fresh manuscripts.

The "unbalance" Bill referred to is caused by market conditions. The manuscript market is usually open widest in late winter and spring. Then an alert writer has to really hustle to keep ten live manuscripts out. This is because sales run well above a writer's average at that time.

Likewise the market usually opens moderately in the fall, again with notable step-up in turnover. Summer months and early winter months are slow-to-dead for many freelance business writers, in many industries. This cycle is directly related to increases and decreases of business paper advertising in those seasons.

Therefore it behooved Bill Abbott or any other writer to build inmail inventory to higher levels during slack months. His target might be 15 to 20 manuscripts in circulation for February through May. Otherwise there's a natural tendency to slack off at that ten-manuscript level. This would result in lower-than-possible sales when the market picks up.

Frequent Change To Maintain Pace. The late Larston Farrar was a prolific business writer in Washington, D.C. He contended writers go stale quickly, then *need* frequent breaks. But Larston found change of subject or type of writing refreshed him more than a coffee-break!

Larston would have several projects scattered over his desk, his work table and a chair or two. Whenever he bogged down on one project, even temporarily, he'd quickly swing to another.

Even if "locked on collision course with a deadline," Farrar would often switch jobs for a few minutes, just to "jog my thought patterns."

"Most writer doldrums are self-caused," warned Farrar. "The writer pities himself, one way or another . . . put upon by bookkeepers . . . disappointments . . . trip-up in a good editor relationship . . . departure of editor friends . . . all cause him to get discouraged.

"If the writer can do one, or three, or ten projects a day, large or small, and line up more for the next day, he's too busy to worry about jackasses who persist in not recognizing his genius!"

Test The "Greener Pastures." A different psychological gambit came from Alameda, California. "When doldrums move in, try selling merchandise on commission for a week," urged George Burnley wryly. "I absolutely guarantee this will send the most indolent of our fraternity scurrying back to typewriter and camera!"

"Try writing an article on 'How to Cure the Doldrums," suggested Frank Zdy of San Diego, California.

"If total daily 'sick calls' into business offices every morning is any yardstick," he added, "freelances have a very small corner on the doldrum market!

"My defense is to combat inaction with activity. . .after a couple of do-nothing-fruitless days, I'm off on a field trip, a change of scenery, a whole new set of challenges (I still swallow hard on the interview approach). . .Long before the end of a field jaunt there's the urge to head home and start work on the material gathered!

"I vary the routine. For variety I do the entire photographic process myself: shoot pic, develop negs, enlarge prints. Add interviewing, research, writing and marketing, and you have all sorts of combination choices!"

Ask Yourself Why. Main hazard in "varying the routine," in the author's experience, is continued avoidance of a particularly sticky job! Sooner or later one has to face the beast down and conquer it.

Sometimes the best solution is to sit down and ask oneself "*Why in the devil am I dodging this job?*" Then make a decision and act.

Do I feel something is unethical about it? Contact the vulnerable person and clear it up.

Don't I have the key facts? Get the facts *now*, or else pare the story down to what true facts you *do* have, or else junk it—but do it *now!*

Am I committed to something that will cost me more than I can get out of it. Write down on your scratch pad the least costly procedure to ethically follow then do it.

A similar suggestion came from Fred DeArmond of Springfield, Missouri. "The worst doldrums come from acute preoccupation with personal affairs that have nothing to do with writing," fretted DeArmond.

"Two devices help this. One is to give intensive thought to the personal problem, hit on a course of action, then act. For good or ill, the action clears the mind.

"The real block is when a delay *must* ensue. Then I take time to sit down and ask myself, "Have I done *everything* I can for the present? If not, do what's still incomplete. Then stick this business in the abeyance file. While it cooks, get going on a piece of work. At least try to—sometimes it works!

"Second device is to simplify my own life. Rental property, farming, sideline businesses, all are sources of constant frustration and time-consuming interruptions. They follow Robinson's Law by swelling tumor-like 'til they take up all your time!"

Anticipate Brighter Hours. To George Toles of Hamburg, New York, "Inertia is the occupational disease of the freelance writer: no boss, no set hours, no sharply defined deadlines!

"There is no Shangri-La in this business—nor in any business. Roll with the punches when dark hours come. Concentrate on anticipating brighter hours. Remember, you're not alone in the doldrums. We all have to fight our way out!

"When you seem to labor with poor results, look back at your earnings record over the last few years. Note the peaks and valleys, and how they still seem to average out at the end of the year!

"If everything you tackle is sheer drudgery, take a few hours off—don't try to lick such moods. It'll prove a good investment; you'll return in better spirits.

"But don't let it become a frequent habit, or pretty soon you'll find yourself out of business!"

Incentives And Atmosphere. In Albuquerque, New Mexico, Edna Wood Grier's anti-doldrum device paradoxically is to put herself under pressure!

"I've tried saving money for luxuries, but this just doesn't work for me! I must be committed to paying a pound of flesh on a fatal day of each month. I'll certainly never be able to afford the doldrums!

"Best spur is the deadline . . . if I promise an editor, that does it. But it doesn't work when I just promise myself to finish a story on a given date.

"I also whip myself into a writing frenzy by simply reading market lists!

"Finally, leaving pages of final copy untyped at night makes it possible to pitch-in promptly next morning. Soon I'm in the swing of writing again."

Maintaining good habits appeals to Allen Sommers in Philadelphia. "Work a regular schedule as if you had to report to a boss," he insisted. "That's one reason I established an office downtown . . . designed specifically for work, a conducive atmosphere.

For me, working at home is a chore. Even when locked away in a den, there are distractions. Most writers *love* distractions. They find every excuse not to work. Hence the proper surroundings of a business office encourage better work habits. And these mean greater income and growth."

Ideas Are Like Puppies. Your author suspects writer-doldrums *can* be due to *either* too little or too much self-discipline!

Certainly the case for a strict writing schedule needs no more elaboration. It's perfectly valid. At your chosen writing period, whether 8 a.m., 1 p.m. or midnight, you confront the typewriter just as punctually as any time-card slave!

Incidentally, that mid-night reference is not a gag. One freelance-writer-friend was a drawbridge tender at night. He whiled away empty hours in his lonely high tower by writing business articles. Interviews were done during two or three off-duty daylight hours.

However, most of us writers suffer *too much* trying to be masterfully-disciplined thinkers. We grimly tell ourselves, "Now for the route sales story. Gotta chain my mind on it. Now what's for the opening?" Then your mind squeaks erratically like a whistletoy in the baby's grasp!

Why? Psychologists say we are healthier if we vent strong feelings. Strong emotions or thoughts generate a psychic energy, they say, that plagues us until released or burned out by a related activity. For instance, since murder is anti-social, we take a fast walk to dissipate anger, chop wood, or box three rounds in the gym, to restore our equilibrium.

I suspect creative thought generates similar irrepressible psychic forces. Just try to cram a creative thought back into some mental cupboard because it is irrelevant to your topic of the moment!

It'll whine and yipe like a puppy, until one can hardly concentrate on the job at hand. And crowding a whole litter of rejected creative thoughts into the mind's closet is like trying to keep a passle of four-week-old puppies in a shallow basket.

Respect Irrelevant Creative Ideas. I suspect that, whenever creative portals of our minds are opened, every ignored infant inspiration comes tumbling out, however irrelevant to the matter at hand.

So, as a writer bends determinedly over the typewriter on a fresh project, six thoughts pop up, none dealing with the story at hand. And over succeeding hours they scramble up again and again puppylike, regardless how often you shove them back down.

My eventual solution involved a stack of small scratch pads. On the first pad I scribble down as fast as possible the first idea that pesters me. This could be for a different story, a repair needed on the porch, something to write my aunt, a matter for the church men's meeting, etc.

The next intruding idea goes on a fresh pad; the one after on a third pad. I've had as many as seven pads lined across the back of my desk on a particularly creative (disturbed) morning.

All details for each subject go on the same pad. I keep scribbling as long as thoughts flow easily. But I don't push them. The moment creativity dries up on one of the puppy ideas, I go back to the job at hand.

If later another idea waddles out of my mental basket, I again stop long enough to set it down also on a pad. Usually after the first big flurry of the morning. I can settle down to a day's steady work, with perhaps one or two pauses to elaborate on the ideas.

Once the payoff job is completed, however long it takes, the writer can go back to studying the pads. Often they hold a surprising amount of good data to be worked into several projects (not necessarily writing). Some of it may even be ready to undertake immediately.

Unfulfilled creativity throws up tremendous mental roadblocks. It causes a vague fatigue, indecision, procrastination—and writer's doldrums!

Writing notes on pads temporarily satisfies the subconscious mind that its fruits are being recognized. For the creative mind is as vain as an opera star! Or rather it's like giving recognition to an obstreperous youngster. Once convincingly recognized, such a child often becomes quite manageable!

Give Your Mind A Chance. Back of this theory is advice psychologists and self-improvement consultants give about worrisome problems. They say to study all the facts of a problem thoroughly, then sleep on

it. A solution, or at least better understanding will come with the dawn.

But we don't half suspect the great capacity of the sub-conscious mind! It probably can deal with many problems and concepts, not only while we sleep but all the time.

We all have those days when several problems that bugged us for a long time suddenly all get solved at once. We usually just think we're especially sharp that day, or lucky. But actually, if we look back, we'll find we gathered in a lot of facts the few previous days. The subconscious mind had a lot to mull over before that "lucky" day.

Therefore, when the story doesn't jell, review the data. Look at them in relation to similar stories, for what's different. Study them for significance to the industry or market. Think about them from every angle. But don't write. Sleep on it! Be prepared to write in the morning.

Avoid putting the notes back in the file without study. Give the sub-conscious mind *something to mull over,* and set a positive time to write after the mulling-over period.

Organize With Half-Pages. There are times when notes simply refuse to organize into an acceptable story.

That's when I type out the details of each major point of the story on a separate half-sheet of paper. For this I cut discarded manuscript carbons in two, use the blank backs.

Somewhere along the way the story outline finally shapes in my mind. At that point I can fit these expanded half-page notes and remaining notes together into the final story. If not, I continue "fleshing out" each point and detail until all are down on the half-sheets.

When the notes are exhausted, I spread the half-sheets out on my desk, kitchen table, card table or the floor. Then I juggle them, until they arrange into some logical sequence.

Invariably I discover one of two things has happened, sometimes both at once.

First, there will be several points or ideas that don't belong in the basic story at all. I've been trying to stuff them in where they could never fit! These are probably a "cat and kittens"—a basic article, plus one or more independent pic-caps or shorticles.

Or secondly, one or more vital pieces of information are lacking from the basic story. It won't hang together without them. In this case, I either (1) Hunt up the missing data, or (2) Whittle out the salvageable pic-caps or shorticles, and abandon the basic story. This is because sometimes it's just too uneconomic to track down what is missing.

Sometimes a single facet of a story so intrigues the writer, he can't mentally get past it to the remaining story. In this case, one way to get started is to write up the intriguing segment, without even waiting to organize the story. Once the mind is purged of what may even be a minor point, the other facts will fall in place.

This is not suggested as orderly or normal procedure. It's simply a device to halt vacuous glaring at an innocently passive typewriter.

Once written, the scribe may find this segment is a separate item anyway, that does not belong to the main story.

Physical Tricks Can Help. Sometimes a physical trick helps one get started. One is to move to a comfortable chair and start handwriting on legal-size yellow pads. The mental menace of an expectant typewriter at times arouses only defiance in the writer. Its temporary avoidance can un-dam the creative flow. Then as handwriting proves too slow to keep pace, you move back to the typewriter, almost with impatience.

Hand-composition often gives a brief change of pace, too, when locked into a deadlined article that cannot be dropped for even a few minutes.

Is The Story Distasteful? A more serious obstacle to getting started is that a story sometimes is actually distasteful to you. But you have a commitment to the editor, possibly even an advance payment. And you had no idea originally of what would be involved.

To get off the dime, don't write. Phone the editor promptly. Describe the problem, the facts and your aversion. See if there is a compatible angle that he'll accept. Don't waste time on correspondence—you'll bog down all along the line on *all* your work until the matter is cleared up!

This may result in a smaller article and lesser fee, or even total abandonment. On the other hand, you'll feel better, your mind will clear, and you won't waste time avoiding the typewriter.

We personally remember a broad assignment for a laudatory analysis of a housing development, which proved prone to all sorts of shoddy practices. Also the requested description of a pricing system that concealed vicious consumer gouging. The result, after consulting the editor, was a scaled-down piece on architectural refinements on-ly.

Very often prompt consultation with the editor will result in conversion to a "crusading" type article, though possibly your facts can only provide the editor a stepping stone to launch into something greater than you can cover from your area.

Make Yourself Creative Time. One deterrent to easy creative thought is the scheduled interruption. Mail comes at 9:45 a.m.; the laundryman is due at 1:30; and you get the kids at 3:15.

It's easy to think nothing important can be accomplished in the time prior to such interruptions. So the time between is fiddled away.

One solution, of course, is to do something about the schedule. We learned to ignore the mail until noon (most of the time). Laundry is set on the porch with the money, and we ignore the sound of the screen door. (Kids are no longer a problem).

But another alternative is the "lot system." In business a "lot" is the quota of pieces to be produced in a given time, such as per hour or every two hours. It is usually a standard amount.

However, the writer can set himself or herself a new quota or lot to be accomplished by time of each scheduled interruption (including coffee breaks).

Very often the lot system can also crack a mental logjam on a large assignment. Tell yourself that by mail-time, you must have the story outlined and two opening pages at least roughed out. Or you want that story polished by time the kids come home.

The lot or quota is suited to the time interval, of course.

But make it as specific as possible. Then try to do just a little bit more in the available time.

Somehow it's always easier to get going on this little segment of work, than wading into the big job, even though the latter starts with the very same process.

Kind of like a dog gnawing first on a corner of a very tough bone.

Chapter 14

Photography for Business Writing

Most business articles need illustration, usually by photographs. Others can be greatly sparked up with illustrating. Some articles almost *have* to be "picture stories"—mostly photos or drawings with long captions and little body text. The latter include a majority of "how-to" pieces.

Hence a freelance business writer faces several alternatives:

(1) Leave illustrating to the editor or client. This is often done where the writer chiefly supplies expertise, or availability at the scene, and the client has a photographer or artist on tap for illustrating.

(2) For each story, the writer can hire a local professional photographer to take the necessary pictures.

(3) The writer can work with a photographer as a team. Such teams very often are relatives—husband and wife, parent and son or daughter, etc. There are several such teams in Associated Business Writers of America.

(4) The writer personally takes his or her own pictures.

In the latter case, there is further choice: (1) send exposed negatives out to commercial photo-processors, or (b) develop the film, send only selected negatives out for enlargement; or (c) develop film and make enlarged prints oneself.

Continuous debate as to which alternative is most practical has never been conclusive. The factors seem to balance out quite evenly on a subjective basis.

Therefore personal inclination and circumstances become the deciding factors. If photography is fun, a creative outlet for you, then do it. But try to do it profitably.

This brings up another axiom of business writing—*the more illustrating the writer can do on his or her own articles, the fewer stories are necessary to "make a living," because of higher gross and net income per story.*

Anybody Could Do It At Home. No writer should reject out-of-hand, as being beyond one's capability, the idea of doing his or her own photography or darkroom work!

Basic photography *is* simple. It's little more difficult than baking cake from a cookbook recipe, or sanding and painting a table from step-by-step instructions.

And simple basic photography is all you do need for 95% of all business articles.

The following are most of the factors involved in choosing the best alternative for you:

Leave Illustration to Client
Advantages
(1) When you have all you can do in time available to produce the necessary wordage, it's best for another to do the illustrating;
(2) You don't have to "start at the bottom" with a new skill;
(3) Unnecessary to guess what illustrations a client might prefer.

Drawbacks
(1) Lose control of half your story as produced;
(2) Not realize maximum dollar return from a particular job;
(3) Miss an opportunity to see whole story visually as well as verbally (which often enlarges writer's comprehension);
(4) Some photography can only be done on location.

Hire A Local Photographer
Advantages
(1) He or she is presumably technically skilled and fully e-quipped;
(2) Sees things pictorially, graphically, usually gets more vital, more dramatic views than an "amateur";
(3) If you work together, the photographer can start shooting while you are still interviewing;
(4) Can take unposed or candid shots while you engage informants;
(5) If alert, he or she will often pick up points to beef up your story:
(6) Increases impact on interviewee—a "team" is always more impressive;
(7) Reduces one's own distraction from juggling photo equipment and notebooks;
(8) Spares you visits to photo-processor, or the time your own processing would take;
(9) Some writers *need* to work with other people as moral support;

(10) Many writers need the prod to keep moving, of a photographer paid by the hour or guaranteed so many 8x10s per day's shooting.

Drawbacks
(1) Expensive, sometimes costs lion's share of a story payment;
(2) Photographer can miss or distort key points in striving for dramatic or arty pictures;
(3) Not always available, often requires second visit to a location;
(4) Speculative shots are limited, due to high added cost;
(5) "Notetaking" shots to help with descriptions get too expensive;
(6) Trying to synchronize photographer and interviewee can be distracting and time-wasting;
(7) Constant scrutiny by a companion, especially if a stranger, can be un-nerving to some writers;
(8) You lose freedom to stall and to study a situation carefully, with a photographer alongside like a taxi-meter ticking.

Team Up With a Photographer

Advantages
(1) This has virtually all the advantages of hiring a photographer;
(2) Writer and photographer get to know each other's capabilities, habits and weak spots. Each learns to work with and around the other most efficiently;
(3) The photographer learns the writer's fields, becomes extremely helpful in contributing points observed during picture taking that the writer may have missed;
(4) You can review difficult stories together, compare notes and observations;
(5) Such a team shares many expenses, which holds down each individual's operating cost.

Drawbacks
(1) Together you two have to make twice as much money as one alone. This means working a territory that provides material enough to keep you both going full time.
(2) Unless a relative, the scheduling problem is always present, especially on rush jobs;
(3) Team-mates have an obligation to each other—each has priority on the other's time. This inhibits one in taking assignments that exclude the other;
(4) Synchronizing workloads is difficult, as one or the other can

94

too often be kept idle in waiting. (In a true partnership, such as with relatives, overhead tasks can be apportioned to balance workloads, even on a flexible basis, if necessary);

(5) There is less freedom in marketing, in that agreement must be reached on speculative efforts.

Take Own Pictures—Use Commercial Processing
Advantages
(1) The writer keeps more gross revenue on each story, by doing more of the total labor on it;

(2) Having your own equipment with you, you're always ready for the unrepeatable shot;

(3) Scheduling is completely flexible as to time, distance or destination;

(4) You get the picture as *you* see it;

(5) Most interviewees still marvel that "you take your own pictures, too!";

(6) You can switch to photography while you wrack your brain for more questions or a fresh angle;

(7) You can photograph scenes or objects inexpensively, to aid subsequent description of styles, arrangement of parts, location of equipment, etc.;

(8) Illustrating your own work gives great satisfaction (did it *all* myself).

Drawbacks
(1) Commercial processors are undependable as to both quality and service;

(2) Much time is spent over photo equipment, purchase or supplies, and mailing, or pick-up and delivery, of film and prints;

(3) Poor eyesight may handicap you in trying to get sharp pictures;

(4) Photo gear can be a nuisance, awkward to lug, easily mislaid, vulnerable to theft;

(5) Interviews are more complex in blending note-taking with photo-taking.

Take Pictures, Develop Film, Send Out For Enlarging
Advantages
(1) Even less outside cost, so writer is paid for more of the total labor on a given story;

(2) Can get "rush" pictures faster;

(3) Can "force" (over-develop) negatives taken in dim light, to "save" a picture;

95

(4) On trips, can develop negatives before leaving town, to be sure exposures are correct.

Drawbacks

(1) Takes time from writing;
(2) Can be smelly, messy and cluttering;
(3) Requires close concentration, absence of distraction;
(4) Cost and maintenance of more equipment and supplies.

Do All Photography Yourself

Advantages

(1) You get paid for all the labor on each story, at lowest out-of-pocket cost;
(2) Fewest stories required to "make a living";
(3) Produce prints of exact contrast and cropping desired;
(4) Highlight or subdue small areas at will (commercial shops do "custom printing" too, but at doubled-prices);
(5) Do truly rush jobs, especially overnight or over weekends, when commercial shops are closed;
(6) Makes a welcome change from hunching over the typewriter;
(7) Doing own prints make for more skillful handling of the camera;
(8) Less expensive (dollarwise, not timewise) to put in extra shot or two, giving client more choice.

Drawbacks

(1) Requires small room, large closet, or light-tight nook;
(2) Smelly—as with stale tobacco odors, the breath exudes chemical odor after darkrooming. Hair, skin, clothing are permeated with it (good ventilation does reduce but not entirely eliminate the odor);
(3) Can cause eyestrain when darkrooming in volume;
(4) One may get absorbed to uneconomic extent, which is okay if recognized as partially a hobby;
(5) Takes a lot of time away from writing, figuring average four to six satisfactory 8x10 prints enlarged per hour, at best;
(6) Requires a patient, indulgent family, or a remote darkroom, or living alone.

Chapter 15

"A Little How-To On Photography"

So much for pros and cons. If the reader wants no part of photography, this chapter is of little value. From here on we assume the writer at least considers doing part or all of the photo process.

However, this is no place for detailed instruction in how to take good pictures. There are good manuals on photo technique at all skill levels available in any good camera store. Also helpful and stimulating are the photography magazines.

"Arty" or mood photography is for photography buffs! There's a whole separate marvelous world of literature for them, and it also has no place in this freelance business writing text.

Therefore these chapters are simply guidelines for a business writer chiefly concerned with photography as a means to improve net annual return from writing.

A second purpose in these chapters is to acquaint the writer with "what goes on" in photography, sufficiently to aid communication between writer and photographer.

Camera Is A "Light Valve." The mental block that deters most writers from photography is the apparent complexity of a professional camera—all those knobs, levers, buttons and numbers!

Start by looking at a camera this way: *a camera is simply a valve for controlling the flow of light.*

A photographic film is sensitive to light within a certain range of brightness. Light brighter than the upper limit of this range makes developed film jet black. Light more dim than this range's lower limit will not even register on the film. Moreover, a film's sensitivity range is much less than that of the human eye.

Serving as a light valve, therefore, the camera shutter admits only the proper amount of light that a given film can handle, can digest, so to speak. The closer to optimum this amount of light is, the more perfect the resultant negative and print.

There are two ways to control light flow to the film.

Changing the aperture (size of shutter-opening) determines the *intensity* of light that reaches the film. It's like raising or lowering a window shade.

Varying the shutter time or speed (the period during which the shutter is open) regulates *how long* that light strikes the film.

Together intensity plus duration control the total light that acts on the film.

If the aperture is doubled in size, but the time interval is halved, the film actually receives the same amount of light as before. If aperture and time interval are both doubled, four times as much total light reaches the film. If aperture and time interval are both halved, the film receives only one-fourth as much light as before.

Controls For Sharp Images. Why are *two* controls necessary? Why not use only the aperture-adjustment or only the time-regulator.

Both are necessary because they affect a compromise between: (a) need to "freeze" movement in the scene, to avoid blurring of images; and, (b) providing adequate "depth-of-field." This is the span of image sharpness from front to back of the scene photographed.

For instance, shrubs in front of a house might be important to a writer's story. Keeping these within the depth-of-field ensures their images are sharp in the photograph. Of much less importance would be background mountains, which aren't pertinent to the story, and would be allowed to blur beyond the depth-of-field.

Clarity or sharpness in the depth-of-field increases with distance from the camera to a point of sharpest clarity, then diminishes slowly beyond that point.

From point of sharpest focus, one-third of the field of satisfactory sharpness lies closer to the camera, the other two-thirds behind the focal point. Therefore focusing should usually be done on some object or point *one-third* the way into the important part of a scene, rather than at a midpoint front-to-back.

But back to freezing motion for a moment. Under most conditions the writer will encounter exposures as fast as 1/50-second to 1/500-second are necessary to freeze moving objects. However, to "stop" speed such as hummingbird wings takes special equipment beyond any normal practical need of a business writer.

Exposure for a still scene may be as slow as necessary, lasting many seconds or even minutes.

For sharp pictures, when a camera is hand-held, exposure needs to be at least 1/100-second. Otherwise a photographer's own body movement can jar a camera enough to blur images in the negative. Such blurring movements usually include breathing or pressing the camera trigger.

Blurring may not show on prints of "contact" size (same size as negative). But on enlargements the effect is as though one's glasses needed changing, or as though the scene were observed through the bottom of a glass tumbler.

For the several ways of steadying a hand-held camera at slower exposures I refer readers to camera manuals.

Speed Vs Depth-of-Field. However, for a specific amount of light needed for perfect exposure, if shutter speed is increased to freeze motion, the aperture must also be opened wider. The extra light thus admitted makes up for the shorter exposure.

But this also reduces depth-of-field. That is, when a shutter opens widest, the picture will be sharp only slightly in front of and behind the focal point. Portraitists use this fact to show a person's features clearly, while blurring the background.

If the shutter is closed down to its tiniest opening, then a picture will be sharp from immediate foreground all the way to "infinity" (i.e., as far away as the camera can record).

Preserving Depth-of-Field. Sometimes light is too limited to allow exposure speed that both stops action and preserves enough depth-of-field. In that case there are some alternatives.

For instance, if motion is toward or away from the camera, instead of across its field of vision, shutter speed may be reduced to 1/25 second, or even 1/10 for slow movements. That is, change of camera angle may avoid blur by getting into the line of movement.

Another tactic is to snap the shutter just as motion hesitates at a reversing point. Examples would be when a machine driveshaft completes its stroke, or a laborer's shovel is flung outward. In the latter instance shovel movement is frozen, sharp in detail, while earth flying from it is blurred. Blurred dirt supplies the feel of action where detail is unimportant.

However, if proper depth-of-field is not obtainable at a necessary combination of aperture and time, then moving the camera back may be the solution. For depth-of-field deepens rapidly as distance between camera and object increases.

That is, should camera and object be only five feet apart, depth-of-field may be only ten inches at a given aperture. At the very same aperture, but with 10 feet separating camera and object, depth-of-field may increase to four feet, and at 15-foot distance, same aperture, depth-of-field becomes 14 feet. In each case, two thirds of the sharp field lies behind the focal point.

Of course moving the camera back results in the object covering a smaller portion of the negative. Therefore the sharpest possible negative is necessary to permit substantial enlargement of that smaller figure. This requires a rock-steady camera, usually through use of a tripod.

Most camera bodies have depth-of-field scales on them, usually in conjunction with their focusing devices. These indicate depth-of-field for any aperture at any distance.

Some Films Are "Faster." Short of using flash equipment, the final alternative is to change film for one of "faster" rating. Different films vary in their sensitivity to light. Their "speeds" or degree of sensitivity are indicated by manufacturers' ratings, expressed in numbers. Fast films commonly used as this is written have a speed-rating of "400." A "slow" film may be rated at "64" or "100," with popular color film at this writing rated at "64."

Since light intensity is what a film registers, then aperture and shutter speed adjust the intensity to what the specific type film can handle. When they are unable to do so, it is possible, though not always practical, to switch to a film with a different range.

"Fast" film can be used at surprisingly low light levels. It is suitable for "candid" or available light work indoors, for dawn and sunset lighting, and even for underwater photography.

Drawbacks to fast film are largely four: (1) It can be too fast for bright outdoor scenes, especially at high altitudes. Light-colored filters may be needed for noonday shots.

(2) Capacity for true color values is somewhat limited. That is, reds and oranges in clothing or decor tend to come out darker in relation to other colors. Pink in white people's skin comes up darker than life in relation to hair colors.

(3) Fast film also tends to "graininess." This is a pebbly effect in solid areas, which becomes increasingly pronounced on enlargement and fuzzes image outlines. Grain is reduced, but not eliminated, by use of "fine-grain" film developers and careful development.

(4) Fast film is more expensive.

"Slow" films are preferred for their ultra-sharpness, for more faithful color rendition and for lower cost.

Clean Lens Makes A Difference. I might add right here that a lot of blame on films for poor color rendition and for lack of sharpness should be cast instead on dirty camera lenses!

The exposed outside surface of a frequently-used lens needs cleaning at least monthly. Use a special detergent and tissues available at camera stores. These do not harm the bluish coating that lens makers apply to filter some red tones out of sunlight.

The detergent not only removes dust, and finger marks, if any. It clears off the tough skim of tobacco smoke, for which lenses seem to have special affinity. Nicotine's yellow-gray density can cut film speed by as much as one-half, if allowed to accumulate.

For each picture taken, therefore, the photographer must estimate how much of the scene front-to-back needs to be sharp, as well as how fast is the movement that needs to be frozen. (Not all movement requires freezing. If detail in the blurred area is unimportant, blur may even add a feel of action to a picture. Blur can also make unavoidable background or foreground objects less distracting.)

An "exposure meter" helps choose the right combination of time and aperture. This meter measures the average light intensity of a scene. Then a dial or guage is adjusted to show a range of combined apertures and times to select from for that particular light intensity.

It's often possible to choose among two or three combinations. But most will be rejected, either because the shutter speed is too slow to freeze action, or the aperture is too large for the depth-of-field needed. Good modern cameras do have "automatic" exposure meters that reduce your calculations. But if you don't understand *what* they are doing for you, much of your photographic effort can result in endless frustration.

Supplying More Light. But suppose the exposure meter says *no* suitable combination is possible under the available light? ("Available light" is a photog's term for the range of illumination existing at the scene).

Then the photographer resorts to artificial light, flood lights, or flash units of various designs and makes. These all are assigned "guide numbers" according to their relative light intensities, to aid in selecting proper apertures. The number of feet between the subject and the light (not the camera), divided into the guide number gives the proper aperture.

That in a nutshell is the function of a camera as a valve or spigot for controlling light flow to film. There are only these four factors to understand: film speed or rating; shutter speed or timing; aperture sizes; and depth-of-field. All are reduced to numbers requiring only simple arithmetic that you can do quickly in your head. Or scales and charts are available to avoid even most of the arithmetic.

Focusing No Mystery. Cameras must be focused, of course. But focusing needn't overwhelm the novice photographer. These are only two types of focusing devices.

By one method the camera user sees a "split-image" in his

viewfinder. That is, the upper half of the scene appears dislocated right or left from the lower half. By twisting a knob, the upper half is moved into its proper relationship to the lower part of the scene. The camera is then in focus, ready to shoot.

Or focusing may be done on a frosted "ground glass." Here the entire scene will be blurred. Turning the knob sharpens the image, until it reaches the focal point. At this point the image is remarkably sharp and clear, due to the nature of the ground glass.

Users of ground-glass focusing like it because they can compose the whole picture as they focus. Main drawback is that a strong light behind one's head makes it hard to see the image on the ground glass.

This is no problem with split-image focusing, which is also more convenient for folks with poor eyesight.

Special magnifying devices are available for either type focusing, if impaired vision is a serious problem.

Cameras have knobs for moving film, sockets for flash units and cable releases, delayed exposure timers, etc. But these are specific to each camera model and are best studied from their manuals.

Chapter 16

What Camera to Buy

The preceding semi-technical discussion was not meant to be even basic "how to" guidance. The reader should go to photo manuals for that. Our real purpose was for background to equipment selection, chiefly the camera.

I hope I was explicit enough for the reader to forget any idea of an "inexpensive" fixed-focus camera with little or no adjustment in aperture or shutter speed.

You *can* take excellent pictures with such cameras. Pros can even do amazingly beautiful work with them, simply by knowing how to compensate for their inadequacies.

But, as a light valve, such a limited camera is like a water pail compared to a faucet. It will do some parts of the job quite well, but is totally inadequate for most work.

Nor is the Polaroid camera, despite its amazing capabilities, suitable to business press photography (true at least as this is written). The film has a single range of light intensity. And making enlargements is complex, costly, and not yet satisfactory in quality.

Until recently most publications did not accept Polaroid shots as being too "soft" and lacking in detail. The barriers are breaking down as Polaroid quality steadily improves. But confining oneself to Polaroid work is still far too limiting in terms of available markets.

Most medium-priced cameras on the market today are quite adequate for press work. Moreover, cameras as a class are more durable and troublefree than the vast majority of consumer products. In terms of technical adequacy, a good camera is a "best buy" for the money invested.

Bigger Still Better, To Start. I would urge the novice to begin with a camera using #120 or #620 film. These give twelve exposures per roll of film, each negative being 2¼ x 2¼ (9 cm x 9 cm) in size.

Many photo buffs will argue in favor of cameras using the smaller 35-mm negatives. These open to wider apertures, admitting more light as needed, and they have proportionately more depth-of-field. They are much handier where flash light is inadvisable or impractical.

But 35-mm cameras *must* be handled with great precision, especially if 8x10 enlargements are to be the end product.

The 2¼-square negative is much more "forgiving," especially for the novice. Blur from movement or not-quite-sharp focus doesn't become so pronounced on enlargement. Graininess in fast film is less bothersome, as are dust or scratches on the film.

Contact prints from the larger negatives, used in "proofing," are easier to study and mark for enlargement instructions. (A "contact" print is the same size as the negative). Portions of the bigger negative can be enlarged more satisfactorily than from 35mm sizes.

Buyers of color transparencies also *prefer* larger sizes, except where used in slide presentations.

You do change film twice or three times as often with #120 or #620 film, as with 35-mm. But this is an advantage as often as a problem.

For instance, most jobs don't require a whole roll of film. So the 20 or 36 exposures in the smaller camera must be completed before the film is processed, or else part of the film is wasted.

Moreover, with only twelve exposures to the roll, it is easier to group a class of shots on one roll, then change type of film for a second type of subject matter. A store interior might be photographed in available light with fast film. Then close-ups of garment fabrics, wall paper, jewelry, etc., could be grouped under special lighting on slower film, to obtain better color values.

However, switching film speeds is a bit esoteric. You *can* do all your business writing photography with film of one type.

At best, there's a trade-off in benefits and drawbacks between the 35-mm and 2¼-square negatives. But with the latter the novice will be more comfortable and more successful in getting saleable prints consistently.

One Year Payback Possible. Figure to spend at least $300-$500 (1978 prices) on basic photo equipment. How much would you pay a photographer in a year if your total output was illustrated articles? You could make back your whole investment in a single year of active photography, for what hired photography costs. This could include $200-$400 more for film and commercial processing the first year (estimated as of mid-1978).

You can buy your camera second-hand from a reputable camera dealer. Many little-used but sound cameras are traded in constantly, as photo buffs upgrade their equipment. It'll cost $100 to $250 (at 1978 second-hand prices).

Reject any camera the case of which shows dents or abrasion

that evidences hard usage. Examine the lens closely for scratches or dull spots. If in doubt, clean the lens or ask the clerk to do so. (Dirt often looks like a nick or small scratch).

Run through all shutter speeds, listening for progressively faster clicks or buzzes of the shutter. Hold the camera so you can see the shutter aperture when the trigger is released at 1/10 second. Note if the opening is symetrical (not necessarily round) at every aperture.

Next run a roll of film through the camera. Buy one, if the clerk doesn't have an old one for the purpose. Note if the film moves smoothly and if the exposure counter catches and releases with precision.

After you've done all this, you can be reasonably sure of a sound camera.

If you are yet dubious, and if the store won't make you a guarantee, take the camera on trial. Go to a photo-buff friend immediately. Have the latter run through a couple rolls of film, chiefly testing all the adjustments on typical scenes and exposures.

Then have the film processed at once and study the negatives with a magnifying glass. Images should be sharp and detailed within the depth-of-field. If unexplained black or gray areas show, especially at the edges of a negative, suspect a light leak in the camera. The dark areas will show up in the same places on different negatives of different scenes.

Give Camera A Chance, Get Acquainted. Once purchased, unless some overwhelming reason dictates otherwise, don't change cameras for two years at least. And stick to a single type of film, except for compelling reason to switch.

This is because, as one noted instructor rightly said, "You don't really *know* a camera, or a film, until the shutter has clicked a thousand times!"

Cameras have many intricate parts that in their fitting together create individuality for each camera (just like an automobile). You need to get familiar with the "personality" of your individual camera, to the point where use of it becomes second nature to you.

Many variants in cameras and film have very valid reasons for them. But most are designed less from basic need than to boost sales of photo equipment and supplies.

One will do very profitably with a modicum of equipment and supplies. With a $500 investment (1978 dollars) one can handle 98% or 99% of what $5,000 worth of photo gear could do in average business photo-journalism. Depending on how much photography one does, the scale of diminishing returns starts between $500 and $1,000 investment.

Six Essential Pieces. The beginner should start with six pieces of equipment.

First is the *camera,* equipped with a lens of *normal* "focal-length" (distance between lens and film). Most cameras come so equipped. But still check with the clerk to be sure you don't pick up one with a special lens.

An *exposure meter* is the most important accessory. Late model cameras even have exposure meters built in. Many meters control aperture settings automatically. These are all handy, but expensive. Also the user must still know when to "over-ride" a built-in meter under certain conditions.

All exposure meters are easily adjusted for any film speed rating.

Next most vital accessory is a *flash unit* or strobe light. This is synchronized with the camera shutter. Pressing the shutter trigger automatically fires the flash at the instant the shutter is wide open.

A small flash unit the size of one's hand will throw ample light for at least 15 feet. It will be good for 30 or more flashes of uniform intensity, though the wait between flashes gets progressively longer. These units are re-charged from house current, requiring several hours or overnight for a full charging.

Such units can also be used directly off house current, either when run down or to conserve their charge for mobile shooting.

More powerful and expensive flash units are powered by heavier batteries good for 1,000 flashes or better. These will throw useful light up to 50 feet indoors. Batteries for such units are usually carried on a strap worn over the shoulder.

Another accessory is a *tripod.* This is a three-legged support with collapsible legs. At full height it should be rigid enough so the camera mounted on it doesn't move when the shutter trigger is pressed carefully.

A tripod enables sharp pictures to be made at shutter speeds slower than 1/100 or 1/50-second. Other benefits are explained in photo manuals.

How few photographers now use *sunshades* on their cameras still surprises me! Sunshades block out incidental light that strays into the lens at sharp angles.

Our own eyes are lenses. We protect them from incidental light by visored headgear and by squinting, in addition to natural shading by our eyelashes. But cameras can't squint. So stray light bounces into the lens itself, some of it slipping through the aperture to faintly "fog" the film.

This results in a faint gray cast to the finished photo. The effect is as though seeing the photo through slightly dirty water, as all the white areas aren't quite pure white.

Sunshades are to be used *all* the time under *all* light conditions, not only in bright sunlight. Even indoors the mirrors, pictures, polished tables, waxed floors, shiny furniture and equipment, all bounce incidental light into the camera lens.

It's really easier to use the sunshade regularly from force of habit, than to decide each time whether one is necessary.

Another rarely-used but important tool is the *cable release*. This is a 6" to 12" flexible cable with a push-button at one end. The other end attaches to the camera's shutter trigger. The flex of the cable absorbs much of your hand's thrust, even while it activates the shutter trigger.

Careful use of a cable release permits shooting pictures at slow speeds, without causing camera motion that blurs the negative image. In such cases, the camera is rested on a tripod, table or solid object, or is steadied against a post or door jamb.

These six items are listed in descending importance—camera, exposure meter, flash unit, tripod, sunshade, cable release. But to me they *all* are indispensable.

Other Accessories Handy To Have. In addition, it certainly is convenient to hold the camera in a carrying case, with a strap around your neck. The strap removes worry about dropping the camera. It also makes it easier to climb around, as is sometimes necessary.

The case protects the camera against sharp knocks. You use it right in the case, with the case front dropped like a drawbridge. Knobs and levers all stick out through special openings.

You will also prefer to have a larger case in which to lug the camera and accessories to or around the job. All except the tripod, which usually stays in the car until you need it, unless you know in advance you'll use it a lot. These cases come in many sizes, shapes and fittings.

Extra Lenses Are Handy. There are other items one can do without, but which at times are handy to have. In fact, many photographers will argue the wide-angle lens belongs up there with that first six items.

A wide-angle lens is essential for taking in all of a squarish room, or wide exhibits and displays from narrow aisles at conventions, or store windows from sidewalks—wherever one can't back off far enough to use a normal lens.

However, if the photographer is careful enough to analyze the important features of such wide scenes, an entirely satisfactory photo can be made of its important features alone.

Thus the wide-angle lens may actually not be all that vital. It can be an excuse for unimaginative photo composition.

Moreover, a real good wide-angle lens can cost nearly as much as a normal lens and camera together. An inferior wide-angle lens distorts badly around the edges. Crop out the distortion and you might as well have used a normal lens.

A telephoto lens is useful for taking large-image pictures of objects you can't get close to. It is frequently used with available light to get candid shots without distracting convention speakers or equipment operators.

Usage of various lenses varies widely with type of work. Generally I use the wide-angle lens about 10% of the time and the telephoto for 2% of my shots. But on some rare occasions I've used one or the other exclusively.

One or two lens filters are handy to bring out clouds in your pictures. They also increase the contrastiness of the pictures, or give more snap to monotone scenes. Filters are tinted discs that fit in front of the lens. Their tints may be yellow, green, orange or red, depending on the effect desired.

A polaroid filter will reduce obnoxious reflections in store windows, picture glass, lighted billboards, fish tanks, silverware, or whatever.

A "slave unit" enables you, without connecting wire, to flash an extra light at a distance from the camera. This unit has a photo-electric cell that is triggered by the regular flash unit on the camera.

Older Cameras Are Back-Ups. I myself carry a spare 2¼-square-film camera, as well as a spare small flash unit—as insurance. The camera is usually unloaded so I can insert color or black-and-white film as needed.

The spare flash unit gives me a reserve of 30 flashes. I normally use the professional-type 1,000-flash unit referred to earlier. But two of the smaller 30-flash units can carry a beginner through a full day's shooting.

On major assignments, I still carry a 30-year-old 4x5 press camera in the trunk of the car. It has a normal lens available, but usually its 90 degree wide-angle lens is installed. Since an 8x10 enlargement is only double this camera's 4" x 5" negative, I still get my very sharpest pictures with old "Jumbo."

Moreover, Jumbo is reserved for color work for those few clients who insist on transparencies no smaller than 4x5.

But Jumbo is pretty much a luxury, used for two or three pictures a month at most. No novice photographer needs one. I simply couldn't part with Jumbo, because we started serious freelancing together 25 years ago!

Occasionally I make 35-mm color slides on some assignment. I used to rent a suitable camera for however long I needed it. If I programmed the picture-taking carefully, that time could be short. But my color work has increased to where I now have my own 35mm camera for slide work.

Color Photos In Greater Demand. I've said little about color, so far. Color work is not difficult, if you use the exposure meter carefully, set your apertures and speeds accurately.

For color is less "forgiving" than black-and-white photography. The latter actually has some latitude for error in exposure, and you can compensate for error in the darkroom. But for color, the exposure has to be just right. Otherwise the color values become "unreal," even though the images are still perfectly clear and sharp.

To protect oneself on color work, it is common practice to shoot an identical scene three times. Make one exposure at the setting indicated by the exposure meter. Next open the shutter aperture one notch for slight over-exposure. Then shut it down a notch below the first setting for slight under-exposure.

One of these three exposures is almost sure to be perfect.

The market for color photography in business writing is small but growing. A major demand is for color shots suitable as magazine covers. But a few publications now buy stories illustrated in color, especially if color adds to comprehension of the subject matter.

Industrial, commercial and organizational clients are also using more color, especially in their exterior house organs and in their stockholder reports.

Color Market More Critical. Advertisers, using color for years now, generally patronize the big commercial photographers. But sometimes a writer runs onto a one-chance-only shot or sequence that has advertising appeal. One such break for me was when two big power shovels were scooping a large crane out of roof-deep mud, after the latter slid off its log matting! The shovel manufacturer was delighted with the picture sequence.

Prices for accepted color transparencies run steeply upwards from double that of black-and-white enlargements.

However, acceptance is also more difficult to get. Color printing is expensive for publishers. So editors tend to be the most critical and demanding in their color illustration purchases.

In profitability, therefore, color work is likely to be a trade-off with black-and-white, at least until considerable experience is gained. That is, you sell fewer color transparencies out of total output, than your sales percentage of 8x10 black-and-whites.

Early color work couldn't sell unless transparencies were at least 5"x7" is size. The market has since gradually backed down the scale, until even 35-mm transparencies are now largely acceptable.

But you still encounter many clients who are sticklers for the larger sizes.

I've refered repeatedly to transparencies because most photo-journalists prefer them to color prints. Simple reason is that they cost less to produce, yet the quality is highly acceptable to clients.

Photography buffs can and do process their own color work, especially when providing fast services. But color processing is meticulous business. More steps in the process each have closer tolerances in time and temperature, than do black-and-white film and paper. There are far more chances for error.

I therefore do not recommend color processing for the business writer, unless working at least 50% in color. The exception, of course, is the photography buff.

What Size Enlargements? When ordering black-and-white enlargements from commercial processors, the question of size is important. Many editors specify 8x10s (8" by 10" enlargements) unconditionally. But others will accept 5x7s without a quibble.

Some of the former, moreover, will accept 5x7s *after* they become familiar with your work. This is because 8x10s are often required merely so an editor is assured of having a reasonably large image after cropping out irrelevant parts of some pictures.

Editors with art departments that re-touch photographs naturally prefer the larger prints as easier to work on. Eventually, whether 5x7 or 8x10, a picture is most likely to be reduced in size as it finally appears in the magazine. But many magazine covers are illustrated with photos enlarged from 8x10s.

So if you are careful to fill each 5x7 print with significant subject matter, it will usually be quite marketable. This means the images in the picture are big and fill the scene. Everything not relevant to the message of a photograph should be omitted by the photographer, not the editor. Thus the latter gets the full impact of the scene shown.

"Custom Finishing." Commercial processing for a 5x7 usually runs about 25% less than the charge for an 8x10. "Custom finishing" prices are double standard rates, as a rule. "Custom" finishing means extra care taken to bring out every detail latent in the negative. The method is described in a later chapter under "darkrooming."

However, note that a custom-printed 5x7, at roughly 1/3 more cost than a standard-printed 8x10, *can* be a "better buy" than a custom-printed 8x10.

Early color work couldn't sell unless transparencies were at least 5"x7" in size. The market has since gradually backed down the scale, until even 35-mm transparencies are now largely acceptable.

But you still encounter many clients who are sticklers for the larger sizes.

I've referred repeatedly to transparencies because most photojournalists prefer them to color prints. Simple reason is that they cost less to produce, yet the quality is highly acceptable to clients.

Photography buffs can and do process their own color work, especially when providing fast service. But color processing is meticulous business. More steps in the process each have closer tolerances in time and temperature, than do black-and-white film and paper. There are far more chances for error.

I therefore do not recommend color processing for the business writer, unless working at least 50% in color. The exception, of course, is the photography buff.

What Size Enlargements? When ordering black-and-white enlargements from commercial processors, the question of size is important. Many editors specify 8x10s (8" by 10" enlargements) unconditionally. But others will accept 5x7s without a quibble.

Say a 5x7 costs $1.50, an 8x10 runs $2 at regular prices. Custom work on each then would be $3 and $4 respectively. The custom-printed 5x7 *should* be a better picture than the standard 8x10. The custom-printed 8x10 would still have an edge on the custom-printed 5x7, because the larger size is easier to work on. How much edge depends on the individual processor.

Yes, 8x10's Do Sell Better. A psychological factor also weighs in favor of 8x10's. Editors *are* swayed by print size. I learned this by practical test.

Back in the Fifties, when doing my own darkroom work, I once decided to experiment with providing only 5x7's, instead of the 8x10s I had uniformly sent out up to then.

These smaller prints had just as good quality as their predecessors, because I worked quite hard at making them so, often re-doing a print several times to get it just right.

After persisting for a year, I audited the results. For that year my *average* sale of photographs dropped to almost exactly one less picture per story. I promptly switched back to all 8x10s. And sales of pictures immediately snapped back to the former level per story.

All other factors during that period were unchanged—same clients, same number of stories, same territory, same productivity, same writing loads.

Of special interest was the editor who always swore photo size was immaterial to him. "I'll use 4x5's, if their quality is right," said he. Yet he cut back the deepest in buying my 5x7s, then boosted purchases quickest on my return to the big ones!

A further cost advantage with 5x7s, increasingly important these days of soaring postal rates, is shipping. The 5x7 takes a smaller envelope. A manuscript can be folded once around the photos to protect them. This requires less weight of cardboard stiffener in the envelope. Finally the smaller envelope takes less of a beating in the mails, and no one tries to fold it en route.

Working With Proof-prints. When *you* take pictures but send all processing outside, you work with "proof-prints." Each proof-print is a single 8x10 collective print of all exposures on one roll of film. The picture from each exposure is "contact" size (same size as the negative).

Unless every exposure was right on the button, these pictures vary widely in quality. Thin or transparent negatives produce dark prints, opaque negatives result in too-light prints.

But proof-prints aren't for showing your friends! This one-shot printing of a whole roll is the cheapest means of showing a processor how you want your enlargements.

A red grease pencil (china marker) is used to indicate what you want to show or omit on each print. The marking is done right on the surface of the print. Such marks will wipe off readily with tissue, if you change your mind.

To "crop" a print is to indicate what parts you want omitted from the enlargement. On the proof-print, you draw a straight line where the edge or edges of each enlargement should be.

If you are cropping off a substantial part of a scene, it may be advisable to mark an "X" in the part to be omitted.

When cropped, the part to be enlarged should have the same proportions as 8 is to 10, or as 5 is to 7. Otherwise the processor will go by the larger dimension. Then your print will include more than you intended.

For an 8x10, the area you mark for enlargement, whatever its size, should be one-fourth longer than it is wide. For a 5x7, it should be 2/5ths, or 40%, longer than it is deep.

Variations In Cropping Prints. But suppose only one side of the contact print needs to be carefully cropped for enlarging. This may be a wide meaningless expanse, like a floor, ceiling, lawn, sky, pavement, etc.

Then just make a slightly wavy line with the grease pencil across the end of the proof-print that is to be cropped. The processor will automatically crop to whatever distance makes a neat 8x10 or 5x7.

Or you may have a square negative and want the whole square enlarged to 8x8 or 5x5. To indicate this, make a small square, with grease pencil, in the proofprint margin, or in a light area of the proofprint.

Individual negatives on roll film should never be cut entirely apart. With 2¼"-square film, leave at least every two exposures together. For 35-mm film, at least three exposures should connect. (These fit flat in a #10 envelope).

This is because connected negatives are easier for the processor to handle in enlarging. Some processors even charge extra for handling single negatives from roll films.

Proofprints of connected exposures should be connected the same as their negatives, for ready identification. But you obviously won't have all connected exposures printed. Send them all along to the processor anyway, still attached to mates that *are* to be printed. But mark rejected-proofprints across their faces with a big "X" in grease pencil.

Use A Magnifying Glass. A good magnifying glass will pay for itself many times over. For one thing, it will give you an idea how details will appear when enlarged, by studying proofprints under the glass. Often details look different when enlarged. This is particularly true of facial expressions.

Many times the magnifier helps choose between duplicate negatives (for whatever reason taken). Or you can determine whether a person's eyes are partially closed. The glass also sometimes reveals that a negative which seems sharp actually will on enlargement be slightly blurred.

The magnifying glass helps to identify people on proof-prints. It has often enabled me to read, or at least distinguish between, name badges of conventioneers. You are able also to read a sign or placard you didn't notice when taking the picture, to decide whether it belongs in or out of the final print.

Handling Rush Orders. Proof-prints are not always necessary or advisable. You may be happy with square enlargements, for instance, from square negative exposures. You can then order enlargements on delivering the undeveloped film to the processor, if reasonably confident the exposure will be normal and printable.

This is common practice on "rush" jobs, since it eliminates one whole step.

Or you can order proof-prints as usual, while at the same time requesting rush enlargement of certain exposures. There are tiny numbers in the negative margin opposite every exposure. If you make a record of each exposure, you can order proof-prints for the whole roll, plus "rush" enlargements of, say, exposures #3, #7 and #12.

You would still order proof-prints of the whole roll because that's easier and cheaper than separating nine exposures out for proof-prints.

I do make one strong admonition for dealing with processors. *Put explicit instructions in writing—always!* Don't rely on verbal instruction. Don't be vague like "Give it the usual, George." Sometimes George has a new employee, or part-time help, who doesn't know what "the usual" is.

The average successful processing shop is an organized madhouse. Good processors very rarely mix orders, to be sure. But when they do, it can be a real nightmare!

Finally—it is not necessary to deal with a processor in your home town, though usually desirable, all things considered. Service by mail can be both practical and satisfactory. Sometimes, even with postage, it can be less costly, compared to car mileage and parking meters, or bus fare to a local processor.

The big advantage *is* avoiding frequent trips to the processing shop. The biggest drawback to mail service is time lapse, especially if you need rush work done.

Biggest advantage of the local processing shop for the novice photographer, is guidance on how to improve pictures. Quality of this guidance depends on the personality, experience and cooperativeness of the processor.

Chapter 17

Photo Processing Pay-Out

Economics and convenience usually tip the scales in favor of a writer's taking his or her own pictures—barring strong personal reasons for not doing so. Or the writer may hire photography only in those cases where compensation warrants the cost.

But, as suggested earlier, the economics and convenience of developing one's own film, or of printing the enlargements oneself, are more debatable. They depend much more on personal circumstances.

Basically the question is: "Can you spend the same hours *more* profitably researching and writing *more* articles, than in processing film and pictures? Or does the best net return for time expended come from doing your own film developing or darkroom work?"

Generally speaking, if in your area the writing is there to be done, in quantity at reasonable rates of pay, it will rarely be worth a writer's time to operate a darkroom. This is speaking on strictly a dollars-and-cents basis.

Two major considerations for maintaining your own darkroom are: (1) if you just can not get good processing, or can't get it at reasonable prices; or (2) when the amount of profitable writing is sufficiently limited in your area to make the darkroom the more profitable alternative for part of your time.

When travel-trailering, I operated a darkroom because processing was too undependable from one city to the next, while using the mails via our forwarding service made for too long a time lapse.

Developing Film "InSitu." But developing one's own film, then sending it out for processing is something else again. I'd say it's a toss-up whether the writer should do his own.

If film has been carefully exposed in the camera, then developed at the temperature specified, for the correct time interval, the result will equal that obtained from a good commercial processor. Film development is the truly "cook-book" phase of photography.

Bear in mind, a special darkroom is *not* necessary to developing negatives (though admittedly more handy). Therefore negative development isn't so "anti-social" as darkrooming. That is, the person developing film doesn't need to disappear for hours behind a closed door.

Compact one-quart or half-gallon light-tight developing tanks are used in full daylight. Chemicals are poured in and out of the tanks through light traps in their tops.

The film does have to be threaded into the tanks in complete darkness. With practice this can be done in 60 seconds in a dark closet.

Or a "changing-bag" may be used. A changing bag looks like a black laundry bag with sleeves into which you thrust your arms the wrong way. The changing-bag can be used in full daylight. (It also can be hell when your nose itches or beads of sweat roll off it).

So film development is the least expensive, least time-consuming, most foolproof step in total photography. Besides it's fun to see what comes out!

Developing Film On-The-Road. During seven years of barnstorming, I carried a film-development kit in the car trunk. Unfailingly, film exposed each day "on the road" was developed that night, in my motel room or in the travel trailer. Thus I *knew* I had all my shots before I left town.

This kit consisted of two developing tanks, three half-gallon plastic containers of ready to-use chemical solutions, several small packages of fresh chemicals, a thermometer, a timer, the changing bag, a cord and clothes pins. Later a small electric fan was added to dry the film reel of each tank between loadings. Also it hastened the film's drying.

All this nested neatly in a top-opening cardboard case with handles. It was about the dimensions of a medium-sized suitcase (a one suiter). Actually it was the container our tank-type vacuum cleaner arrived in.

Bart Rawson, then editor of *Commercial Car Journal*, still tells of finding me in a non-airconditioned Chattanooga motel room after one day of solid photography. Heat off the parking pavement outside made my room's doorknob too hot to touch.

Bart still swears I was stark naked, persistently disregarding a perfectly respectable pair of jockey shorts.

In three hours that evening I developed six #120 rolls and two dozen 4x5 sheets of film. Initial rinse was in the tanks. Final rinse was in the bathtub, with frequent changes of water.

Developing temperatures was held in bounds by stowing chemical containers in packed ice buckets (belonging to the motel).

A small plastic dishpan might have served as well for this. But nowadays you can set the solutions in front of the airconditioner, if necessary.

One word of warning—always handle chemicals in the bathroom, or over a vinyl floor. They can stain or bleach carpeting and upholstery. I always carried an armful of newspapers to spread wherever necessary. For drying film, a cord from the shower head to a towel rack held negatives over the tub to dry, suspended by clothespins.

Darkroom For Enlarging. For printing enlargements, a darkroom *is* necessary. A compactly-arranged 4'x6' space *can* serve as a crowded darkroom, and for one person working alone, 5'x7' is quite adequate.

Unless a person lives alone, it is rarely practical to use the kitchen or a solitary bathroom as a temporary darkroom, Interruptions are too frequent and too urgent. And too great a strain is thrown on the most loving and charitable family.

A full-time pro business writer can produce 30 to 100 saleable photographs per month. This represents one to three full days printing in the darkroom each month.

Such a short ration of production-time makes the *temporary* darkroom a questionable project. Time spent setting up and removing equipment, including curtains, blackout blanks in windows, ventilation devices, chemical and rinsing trays, etc., becomes wholly uneconomic if it is a frequently-repeated process.

Set-up and take-down can represent a half-day of "overhead work" (unproductive hours) for each printing session. Do this for three one-day darkrooming stints per month and it tots up a day-and-a-half of overhead time.

So you eventually try to darkroom all in one straight session, just to get done and get back to normal. This inevitably results in a couple of 16-hour days, plus another day or two of zombie-existence while you recover.

Meanwhile the family tries to function around your equipment. "You just gotta wait, dear, I can't open the door yet!" "No bacon today, dear, you know it smokes up the enlarger lens!"

To top it all, you lose the prime advantage of being able to rush prints out. Very seldom would you set up a temporary darkroom just to rush through two or three prints.

Where To Put A Darkroom. Even if you are blessed with two bathrooms, it may not be practical to occasionally tie one up as a darkroom. Bathroom fixtures do not accommodate darkroom equipment too readily.

Best array I've seen was mounted over a large tub. One shelf at waist-height held the enlarger and paper cabinet. A lower shelf 5" above the tub was taken by trays of chemicals. Then prints were slipped into the tub for final rinse.

Main objection I found was constantly stubbing your toes on the tub-side, and some light reflection from white fixtures.

Look the house/apartment/mobile home over for a corner that can be sacrificed to darkrooming. Prime requisite is to be close to a water source, and have electricity available. Don't hesitate to consider how partitions could enlarge or enclose the area.

Large closets, dressing alcoves, ends of hallways, corners of porches, basements, attics are all possible locations. A large closet back-to-back with a bathroom involves a minimum of piping.

For instance, as I sit at my desk (in what was a bedroom) I look at a clothes closet, 7 ft. wide and 2 ft. deep. It backs up the bathroom to minimize piping. With a narrow door (30") and 7 ft. of partitioning I can make a darkroom 7' x 4½'. There'd already be a heat register in one end. A fan with a light-trap goes in the outer wall, as does a small air conditioner.

The cost would be minimal. If the house (mobile home) were sold, it would take little effort to restore the closet as before.

If you look, you might be surprised at what space is available for a darkroom.

Basic Darkroom Equipment. Basic darkroom equipment is the enlarger. This is a sort of camera in reverse, that is, the light is inside. It passes through a lens and shutter to the sensitive surface of the paper outside.

The negative is placed in a special holder with the lens and shutter below and the enlarger lamp above it. This shutter has aperture sizes similar to a camera shutter.

The largest aperture in the shutter passes enough light through the negative to enable the image to be focused sharply on an easel below. After focusing, the light is shielded, the enlarging paper is placed in the easel, and the exposure is made.

Prior to the exposure, the shutter aperture is made smaller according to the density or opaqueness of the negative. This is to control the length of time of the exposure. Timing usually ranges from 10 seconds to a minute, depending on how much "dodging" or "burning" is necessary.

"Dodging" and "Burning." You "burn" a small portion of a print that will otherwise be faint, to bring out details that might be lost with only normal exposure to light. This is frequently necessary for white faces in an otherwise dark scene, or for window and door areas of buildings.

During burning, a shield is interposed between the lens and the enlarging paper. (A shirt cardboard serves nicely). A hole in the shield permits a small beam of light to pass, carrying a small section of the image on the negative.

This hole is held over the section of the print to be burned. It prolongs the exposure at just that point alone as much as ten times the overall exposure. Meanwhile the rest of the print is shielded by the cardboard.

A frequent use for burning is to bring out clouds. Study of your negatives will often show light outlines of clouds in the dark parts representing the sky. These rarely come out in routine printing.

But if you cover the lower part of the enlargement, so the sky gets exposure three to ten times as long as the earth part of the scene, you often get beautiful cloud formations that give life to a print.

On the other hand, to "dodge" a print, one does the opposite of burning. With a little spatula, or disc of cardboard on a thin stiff wire, the light is shielded from a small area that otherwise tends to become too dark with normal exposure.

Often you cut stiff paper into fancy shapes and stick the wire through them, in order to dodge irregular areas.

"Custom Finishing" Maybe! Burning and dodging are the major ingredients of "custom finishing," for which one usually pays double to three times the standard enlargement price. As can be seen, both take time to be done right, often on a trial-and-error basis.

But burning and dodging by the photographer himself can save many a shot that would otherwise lose its key point or dramatic impact in the usual commercial processing.

Actually, you sometimes can get limited burning and dodging included at regular prices on commercial work. This is by arrangement with your own processor, especially if it is a small local firm.

The processor's determining factors are how much extra work is involved and how much he wants your business.

In enlarging, the actual exposure takes a fraction of the time required for inserting a negative, cropping and focusing. Hence an added 20 seconds of burning or dodging on top of the basic 10-second exposure isn't all that much.

On the other hand, if negatives are badly over-exposed they require long enlargement exposures. Then, to burn in spots on one of these could take up to ten or fifteen minutes more. For those you can forget custom treatment, without paying extra.

To request this extra work, you mark the proof-prints previously described. Areas to be burned in are slashed with red grease pencil, thus: / / / / /. Dodging is similarly indicated by small circles:
∘∘ ∘
∘ ∘ ∘ ∘ ∘
It's my experience that processors, when their business is slow, often do some voluntary burning and dodging to beguile customers. But as soon as business picks up, this "frill" is by-passed.

Darkroom Arrangement. Darkroom enlargers usually operate vertically. They require three to five feet above a supporting table or shelf. The height depends on the size or portion of the negative being enlarged.

This is because enlargement is achieved by moving the negative and lens up away from the easel that holds the paper. The further apart negative and easel are, the larger the image on the paper.

The darkroom is illuminated by a red or greenish-yellow "safelight" of very low intensity. Its candlepower is so slight, you must hold printing a few inches away from the light to read it.

This light is usually over the developing tray, to enable you to watch and control development of paper. Paper emulsion is insensitive to faint red light. Fast film is sensitive to this light, and must be developed in total darkness, until the last few seconds when it can be briefly inspected.

It is best to have a special timer in the darkroom, similar to a cooking timer, but calibrated in seconds. This measures length of exposure. In emergencies, when my timer conked out, I have used the second-hand of my watch, held up to the safelight. That induces acute eyestrain quickly.

A light-tight container for storing enlarging paper is needed. This will hold the three to seven different grades of paper you will use. Several grades are necessary, since negatives differ in contrast and require paper sensitive to these degrees of contrast.

A contrasty paper or negative has lots of bright whites and dark blacks that need to be toned down in order to look natural. On the other hand a "soft" scene is close to a monotone. It requires contrasty paper to lighten some areas, darken others. Photo manuals explain this in some detail.

Two to four non-corrosive chemical trays must be large enough to move 8x10 prints around in them. These are usually 11"x14" and about 2½" deep.

The first tray, for development, should be shielded from the enlarger. This is so you can make a second exposure while a prior print is developing. Print development normally takes one to two minutes.

Second tray is a "stop bath" to halt developer action abruptly. This gives you positive control of your developing. Third tray is for "fixative" to hold the picture permanently at that stage of development.

Prints are transferred from tray to tray by tongs, one for each tray.

Rinsing is done in a larger tray, with fresh water running through it from a special jet nozzle. Rinsing can also be done in still water changed often, if the prints are shuffled frequently. Obviously this is time consuming.

Print drying is best done in an electric dryer. After the enlarger, this is your most expensive piece of equipment. Your alternative is to squeegee prints onto stainless metal sheets for drying by air, often aided by a separate fan.

The later process is labor-wasting and time-consuming. The metal sheets are not all that cheap either.

Ventilation Must Be Positive. Ventilation of the darkroom is critical. In a small space especially, the air can become quite fetid and stupifying.

"Fixative" is the most pungent chemical. Therefore the exhaust duct should be above and behind the fixative tray. Moreover the exhausted air outside ought to be directed away from neighbors. (Photographers can walk the street and know who's darkrooming where by whiffing an odor of fixative).

Because a ventilation system must be carefully light-trapped, you can't depend on natural air currents. The principle of a light-trap is to cause the air to move through a U-turn or S-turn, in which there are no reflective surfaces. The fresh air intake may be an always-open entrance to the darkroom, so long as it also makes a U-turn.

There *must* always be well separated openings for intake and exhaust, to avoid sucking chemical-laden air back into the room.

Changes in air current direction through U-turns in both intake and exhaust cause turbulence. This radically slows air flow. Therefore some forced draft is usually necessary, generally provided by a small fan.

It is desirous to control the temperature of darkroom chemicals, though not so critically as with film development. In the South I *have* produced satisfactory prints at room temperatures of 100 degrees F. and more. But it takes juggling of paper grades, exposure times and development times. You can waste a lot of paper, especially as the temperatures change. Or you can use an awful lot of ice cubes!

Therefore a small air conditioner is useful to keep both you and the chemicals at better operating levels. It has to be of smallest size, or it won't work efficiently. Otherwise, it's better to draw your incoming air from an air conditioned room in the house.

This unit should chill incoming air only. It should not recirculate room air. For chemical fumes play hob with the innards of most air conditioners.

On the subject of processing film and print, the preceding should be enough to provide the reader with questions to ask the experts, if desirous of pursuing it further.

Get The Feel Of Photography Anyway! But photography is something you don't just read and talk about, and then come to satisfactory firm conclusions. You have to get the feel of photography to really know and judge it.

It would handsomely pay any business writer, who is uninformed about photography, to take at least the most elementary course in it. This is provided such a course does make you handle the equipment, process the film and paper.

You will then be reasonably able to guide yourself into practical, efficient photographic operation. Most such courses provide the equipment. If a camera is not provided, the instructor will probably be able to recommend one, either to purchase or to rent.

There are many truly inexpensive adult evening courses in photography offered at high schools, colleges, YMCAs, photography schools, and even photography clubs. For openers, ask your local photo dealer where these courses are, or watch the papers for them. They are generally advertised just prior to registering.

Should you decide after such a course not to do any photography yourself, you still will be more conversant with the problems and basic criteria of commercial photographers. You thus will be a far more skillful purchaser of photographic services, as well as more informed seller of their products.

Chapter 18

Other Illustrations Are Possible

This chapter is for the business writer having no talent, or no training at least, for sketching or mechanical drawing. As with photography, it is a mistake to assume one is incapable of making acceptable floor plans, or simple elevations (vertical views) of buildings or equipment.

This is because certain simple drafting tools have virtually removed freehand work from mechanical or industrial drawing.

But, why bother with drawings anyway?

Sometimes it's almost impossible to describe in words the relationship of physical objects to each other. Even if these relationships are very clear in the writer's mind, they may be hard for a reader to visualize.

Arrangements of equipment, furniture, fixtures, wiring, plumbing, ducting, gearing, leverage, etc., are often too complex to depict with routine photography. Yet arrangement is often vital to comprehension of a story.

Yes, you *can* do it with photographs, if you use many, carefully keyed to each other. But will the editor want to run so many pictures? Will he or she care to have long explanatory captions for each picture? And if so, will the pay be profitable to you.

The Chinese cliche is that one picture is worth a thousand words. Many times, however, a single drawing is worth a dozen pictures, in terms of accurately getting the message across. A drawing also has the merit of costing less in materials than so many pictures—about equal to one photo print, in fact.

Know How Editor Values Drawings. The catch to all the above is that too many editors put an absurdly low value on the time a writer invests in a drawing. Some editors even have the gall not to pay for any drawings they use.

Hence you'd better know your editor before showering him with drawings or sketches.

One tip-off is the number and quality of drawings already appearing in a magazine. If they are non-professional in character yet quite understandable, the editor is probably publishing sketches pretty much as they come in. 123

Most often this is the practice of editors who have no staff artist or use no outside drafting service. But to send such an editor a really crude sketch is a waste of time. He'll simply ignore it, due to his expense in having it re-drawn.

But if your drawing is neat, well-proportioned and legibly lettered, this editor is likely to use it. He'll pay as though it were a photograph either by unit price or by the proportion of a page it occupies. Since editors who use drawings tend to play them up, especially floor plans and workflow diagrams, this can often be quite remunerative.

If a magazine prints elaborate or artistic drawings, check with the editor. He will probably welcome a rough drawing, so long as it is intelligible. His art department will make the finished drawing from that.

In any case it is important to be able to give the editor a rough draft in at least proper proportion and clearly lettered. The editor's artist shouldn't have to puzzle over details of even a rough sketch. Otherwise the wrong message might be conveyed in the final drawing.

Graph Paper and Templates. For the business writer two inexpensive drafting tools almost eliminate need for freehand drawing. These are graph papers and templates.

Graph paper is lined vertically and horizontally to form squares of uniform size. Various papers come in a variety of sizes and styles. Of the lines forming the squares, every fourth, or fifth, or tenth line may be heavier than the rest. This is to make calculating dimensions easier and quicker.

For instance, a popular graph paper has squares one-fourth inch in size, with every tenth line marked heavier. If you make each square represent one foot in actual dimension, then each heavier line would mark off every ten feet. If each square equals five feet, then the dark lines equal 50 feet.

Suppose, in the first instance, you draw a room 45 feet long and 18 feet wide. Lay your ruler along a heavy horizontal line near the bottom of the paper. From your starting point (representing a corner of the room) draw horizontally across four heavy vertical lines, plus five squares. This represents 45 feet.

Then, from the same starting point, draw vertically across one heavy horizontal line to within two squares of the second. This equals 18 feet.

Against the shorter wall is a desk 7½ ft. from the corner. It measures 3 ft. by 5½ ft. Count off 7½ squares from the corner on the graph. Then draw a line across the next half square on through five more squares, for the long dimension of the desk. At right angles draw out three squares from each end of this line. Then close the oblong on the fourth side, to indicate the desk.

If your building, or garden plot, or highway cloverleaf, or whatever, is too big for a quarter-inch-to-the-foot scale, you can make each square represent any distance you wish, 2 feet, 5 feet, 20 feet, 100 feet, etc.

Draft Can Be Inked Over. Once the pencilled drawing is satisfactory, the pencilled lines are retraced in ink. A regular drafting pen and india ink make the smoothest, blackest lines. However, there now are a variety of ballpoint and even felt-tipped pens that will do more easily and quite satisfactorily. Use a ruler with a raised edge so ink doesn't run under it to create blobs on your lines.

There also are spools of narrow black tape, in varying widths, that many professional artists now use for lines on drawings—quick but more expensive.

Your inked drawing on graph paper can be quite suitable in many magazines for reproduction as is, without re-drawing. Squares and heavy lines on graph paper are printed in green or blue-green that normally does not reproduce. Then only your black drawing comes through. Or else the graph paper lines reproduce so faintly as to make a background for the drawing that actually dramatizes it.

It is preferable to use different pens to make lines of at least three different thicknesses. Heaviest lines might show boundaries, walls, partitions, posts, or usually any immovable object. Medium-thickness lines indicate furniture and equipment. Finer lines are for lettering and for detail on equipment, etc.

After doing a few drawings, you develop your own sense of emphasis by line thickness. Variation in lines for emphasis becomes comparable to underscoring or overtyping for emphasis in manuscript writing. For instance, your story involves a certain group of machines. The drawing is to show its relationship to other units. This special group may be drawn in heavier lines to catch the eye immediately.

Graph paper by-passes the T-square and special drawing board commonly used in drafting rooms. This is because the graph lines do all your "squaring" in advance.

Coming in large pads with heavy cardboard backs, the graph paper is held firm until detached. The pads can sometimes even be propped at a slight angle for easier working. If the backing is not stiff enough, tape a sheet or two of corrugated cardboard to it. Or you can make a drawing easel of thin plywood.

If you can't refrain from bearing down with pen or pencil, insert a couple sheets of heavy wrapping paper under the graph sheet you work on. This will prevent grooving the next sheet underneath. Otherwise the grooves from an earlier drawing may show up in the reproduction of a later product.

Templates and Lettering Guides. So much for straight lines. A variety of templates deal with curved or irregular lines of whatever description. Templates are flat pieces of plastic. They have holes and curved or shaped edges around which you run pencil or pen to get the desired lines.

The most readily recognized templates, of course, are lettering guides. Some of these are even available in dime stores. But art supply stores or good stationers will have the widest selections in all kinds of templates.

Of the lettering guides, only the smallest-sized are likely to be useful for your drawings, unless your whole sketch is large scale. It helps to draw a faint pencil line on which to perch your letters, to be erased after letters are inked.

Lettering can be typed for drawings, if its scale permits. (A quarter-inch-to-the-foot scale usually qualifies for elite type). Typing should be sharp, even and black, without smudging or erasure. Lettering can be typed on separate strips.

For easier cutting into narrow strips, the lettering is typed at the left margin of a sheet of paper. The strips are then rubber-cemented to the surface of the graph. If carefully done, there is little hazard of these strips coming loose.

However, I do not recommend use of lettering templates for the average drawing. It is quicker and, if neatly done, acceptable to letter a drawing freehand. Nor is this difficult. The author has atrocious hand-writing, yet has had many sketches published with carefully hand-printed lettering.

If you've done no lettering before, study an alphabet of simple-style type, then imitate it.

Poor freehand printing usually results from trying to do it cursively like regular handwriting. Cursive writing is done with the wrist and forearm in motion all the time.

But for the best printing, each stroke is a separate motion. My forearm must rest on a firm base in order to control wrist and finger movement. There are times when I even hold the right wrist with the left hand. This is because intense concentration sometimes causes the writing hand to jerk, ever so slightly, but enough to wiggle a straight line.

Concentration can also make one perspire, imperceptibly perhaps, but enough to smear. It's a good idea to always have a separate clean sheet of paper to lay under your arm and wrist. I use white mimeo paper for this (as being readily absorbent).

Lettering should generally be in upper and lower case. Tests have proven it easier and quicker to read than words in all upper case.

Special Templates Helpful. There are many kinds of plastic templates on the market. Most have very specialized uses. So, for lack of space, I'll describe only those most useful to me. Anyway, just out of curiosity you'll find it fascinating to examine for yourself a store display of templates.

Next to the ruler, my "circle template" is the most useful drawing aid. The plastic sheet has 44 circles (actually discs) cut out of it, ranging from 1/16" to 3" in diameter.

Each circle's perimeter has markings to help position the center of the circle. Centering is quite simple on graph paper, by aligning these circle markings with the graph lines.

In addition, the four corners of this template are each curved to a different radius.

A separate "store plan" template is scaled ¼" to 1'. Two "house plan" templates are respectively scaled ¼" to 1' and 1/8" to 1'. These are used chiefly for marking out doors and their swing directions. Also for certain irregular shapes such as toilet stools, lavatories, sinks, etc.

With practice, these templates aid in the swift outlining of furniture, appliances, equipment, etc. However, one does get pretty deft at outlining oblong pieces by following squares on the graph paper with a triangle.

All the above templates reside in my desk. But I carry the most wierd-looking in my camera case. It resembles a mad scientist's doodle during a ladies' tea!

I sometimes use it rough-sketching on location. The size of my hand, it is a combination of ruler, French curve, protractor, two triangles and six circles. It has to be kept in an envelope, to avoid entanglement with photographic gear. This template's outline, and two irregular holes in it, are all curved. Each curve gradually changes shape along its entire length. Thus, somewhere on the template, there is sure to be a short piece of curve that will fit any given need. You may have to shift the template several times to compose the whole curve that matches some irregular shape. But the curves are all there.

A "right triangle" is less important with graph paper than when drawing on blank pages. In the latter case, the triangle is used with a T-square to make accurate rectangles.

However, the triangle is still handy with graph paper. With it you can draw vertical, horizontal or diagonal lines in rapid succession without swinging a ruler around. I use two different-sized triangles for this.

In addition the triangle has angles of 30 degrees, 60 degrees and 90 degrees. These suffice for many drawing purposes where the exact angle is not critical to the story. For instance, streets or pathways meet at an angle, a plank rises to staging, piping slopes to a tanktop, etc. It may be only necessary to show their relative positions and their angles may not be critical.

For exact angles, a "protractor" is used. This is a half-circle, with one straight edge in which a center point is marked by a notch or small hole. Numbers for degrees of angle are marked around the curved portion.

Presume you have drawn a straight line, to which you want to draw another at a 67 degree angle. The protractor is placed over the drawn line so that line passes beneath the small center hole and also under "67 degree" on the curved perimeter. Now a new line drawn along the straight edge of the protractor will intersect the first line at 67 degrees.

Rough Drafting. Obviously drawings are rarely finished on location. This means you develop techniques for sketching roughs that can later be readily translated into finished work.

If you try to draw roughs to scale on graph paper, you're way ahead when ready for the finished sketch. Your lines might be wavy, crossed out, smudged with coffee and grease-stained. But you do have something from which to make a tracing.

Back home again, you lay a second sheet of graph paper over the first, then tape the corners to a window, so light shines through both sheets to help in tracing. Now you can use a ruler for tracing over the lines carefully. Or eventually you learn to prop a sheet of tempered glass at a slope and put a light behind it.

Especially if you wear bi-focals!

If the rough sketch was fairly accurate in dimension, you may even trace at least the major portions of the finished sketch with a pen. This reduces the amount of intermediate drawing to be done in pencil.

128

But whether you draft on graph paper, wrapping paper or the side of a shipping carton (I've used 'em all), the following technique applies equally.

Grid Keeps Proper Proportion. Your aim is to keep the whole drawing in proportion. It is done by establishing a "grid." This is a pattern of regular squares or blocks into which a space divides evenly. Such a grid is imaginary, but is easily visualized.

Start by looking for fixed points of reference—in the room, the factory, the field, or whatever is being plotted. These points are items of known measurement or distance from each other, and are set in some regular pattern.

If a room has posts or pillars at regular intervals, you're "home free." Measure the distance between two or three pairs of posts, to be sure they are evenly spaced. Then fill in your sketch first with all the posts.

The person interviewed can usually be counted on to supply key distances or dimensions with some certainty. But every now and then he or she won't have the faintest idea of measurements.

A carpenter's tape could always be handy to have along, of course.

However, in the dim past as a Boy Scout, I once learned to use body measurements. When walking briskly, one pace for me is 36" or three feet. So 100 feet is a bit over 33 paces, and so on. Pacing will take care of a majority of the necessary measurements.

For other measurements, I know my shoe is 11" or a bit less than one foot. From the base of my palm to the pinky tip is 6". Widespread fingers are 9" thumb tip to pinky tip. Elbow to index finger tip is 18." Armpit to palm knuckles is 2'.

Outstretched arms span 6', nose to fingertip being 3'. Floor to groin is 30", to tip of sternum (breastbone) is 4', to chin is 5', to eye level is almost 5,6".

Whether I'll cope so readily with metrics remains to be seen. One needn't be dramatic or grotesque in making these measurements. Many can be made as casually as standing alongside a machine or resting a hand on it.

A secretary once talked all the time I was measuring her office, then was startled when I came up with the measurements. When I explained how they were obtained, she only commented, "Well, I did think you were awfully restless!"

Double Check Blueprints. Often a business man will do a big favor by supplying a blueprint. He may even let you take it home with you, or keep it.

If so, you should never, repeat, *never* leave the premises without checking the blueprint against the actual installation!

In the first place, nothing is ever installed exactly the way the blueprint calls for it. Secondly, the blueprint may antedate a dozen changes in layout and even structure.

To belabor the point, I have *never* in 40 years of business writing been handed a blueprint of a building or land plot that fully agreed with details as they actually existed. I still remember a drawing made from a blueprint showing pillars 20' apart. After a near nervous breakdown, I learned they were spread to 24' spacing, because a different type roof girder had been substituted.

For machinery and equipment design and placement, a print will be even less accurate. A shop owner once bet me a luncheon that drawings for his lathe assembly were correct to the last detail. Then he himself found the lamp moved to the opposite side to give the operator more hand clearance.

So we had a real friendly lunch.

If you do obtain a blueprint, it will almost always be necessary to scale it down for your drawing. Quite often you can divide the blueprint scale by four and come up with ¼" to 1', suitable for your graph paper.

Look For Girder Supports in Walls. However, let's get back to plotting the sketch. Suppose there are no posts out in the room. Then look for girder support pillars in the walls. These look like protruding sections of wall, but are actually casings around vertical steel supports for ceiling girders.

They'll stick out 6" to 2' from the wall, and measure 18" to 3' across. Also they usually occur at regular intervals, whether you can see them all or not.

You'll soon learn to spot girder support posts. They jut at awkward points into rooms and offices, or else partitions are butted into them. Often equipment or furniture is shoved against one, or nested in its angle with the wall.

Measure between a couple pairs of such support posts to determine their span. Check to see if posts on end walls are at different spacing than on side walls. Then mark on your sketch all posts you can see, afterwards filling in the rest, because you can be sure they exist. Draw faint lines between the centers of opposing posts, and you now have your "grid" of identical squares (or oblongs).

Now start with one square. You first sketch in whatever is directly on an imaginary line between two posts. Do this all around the square's imaginary line. Then fill in the middle space.

You'll find it absurdly easy, for very little is left to go in the middle spaces. Keep on doing one grid square at a time. When done, your whole drawing is in reasonably accurate proportion.

Other guides can be lights at regular intervals, linoleum floor squares, heat or air conditioning vents, windows, ceiling or wall joints, etc.

But suppose you're in one of those places built in nine installments over two centuries, with absolutely no symmetry whatsoever to the structure.

This is when you look for wall elements that appear to be opposite each other. They could be windows, doors, or a window opposite a door, a fire extinguisher, partition, vending machine, ventilator, etc., etc. Just use whatever you can to create your grid.

The important thing is always to be able to fill in along imaginary lines first. This is what keeps a drawing from getting distorted.

Grid-making applies outdoors also. Light poles and fences often provide the repetition desired. Doors or windows on a long building will do likewise.

If necessary, pick out tall trees, smoke stacks, or church spires off the property—anything to fix an imaginary line along which to work. If the best-situated object is wide, select a detail as your fix point—one edge, a special rock, a crack or weather stain, anything you can keep in view.

But beware of moveable objects, like the ladder that was shifted 20' while I was at lunch! I spent over an hour figuring out why one side on my sketch simply refused to piece together!

How To Mail Drawings. The real problem with drawings isn't making them. It's mailing them.

I work pretty hard at scaling a drawing so it will fit 8½"x11" paper, just so I can mail it flat. If it must be larger, I sometimes am able to fold it once around a thick manuscript with several pictures, to avoid a crease. (Problem is that a crease is likely to show on the published reproduction).

Or if you can arrange a relatively bare space across some fairly central part of the drawing, then a crease through there may do no harm. (If you inadvertantly crease or groove a drawing, you usually can iron it smooth again from the reverse side. Do this on a smooth firm surface.)

Otherwise I use a mailing tube. Good stationery and art supply stores carry these in several sizes. Or I make them by rolling any light cardboard into two or three thicknesses, then taping it.

When the drawing is mailed separately, it must be thoroughly identified, both with your name and address and as to the story it belongs with. Also the manuscript must clearly state that a drawing is coming separately.

Finally, send the drawing the same postal class as the manuscript. Otherwise they might arrive a month apart on the editor's desk, during which time anything can happen.

Drawings Have Other Uses. Sketching supplies a welcome change from typewriter pounding. Also sketches give new perspective to stories. Do the drawing *before* you write the manuscript. It'll stir new questions in your mind, make other points more clear. You may phone the interviewee afterwards for more information, prompted by what the drawing says to you.

Previously I suggested photography as a means of stalling while thinking up more questions to ask a difficult subject. The same applies even more so to sketching, if the story logically lends itself to a sketch. Even if you never intend to make a final drawing, sketching permits you to reasonably tarry around the premises. This very likely will generate more questions to be asked.

Almost anything said so far applies to two-dimensional drawing, particularly floor plans and layout. Elevations (vertical surfaces) are done similarly, creating some sort of grid to keep all in proportion. Frankly, I've done few elevations, except as schematic drawings in which proportions are less important.

There also are many different management-engineering diagrams that some business writers will employ. However these apply to specialties. The presumption is that, if you are versed in the specialty, you are already familiar with the diagrams. Basic texts on methods-study and workflow will show and explain such diagrams.

The reader will have to investigate three-dimensional drawing on his own. It's beyond the scope of this book.

I have made and sold a few laboriously-worked-on three-dimensional drawings. This was with the aid of "how-to-draw-in-ten-easy-lessons" type booklets.

Perspective is the real beast to be tamed in three-dimensional drawings. Perspective is that quality that makes everything look increasingly smaller the farther it is from you.

The key is to establish a "horizon vanishing point" for each drawing. Then keep that point always in mind with every line you draw that moves away from the viewer. Then you can come up with a reasonable three-dimensional image.

But it's at this point I usually reach for the camera. *I* can't make a buck struggling with three-dimensional artwork! For you, maybe yes.

Chapter 19

Education and Training

One young but quickly-successful business journalist we know had a degree in Business Administration, with Journalism as his minor. We understood at the time that his alma mater urged journalism students to take their majors in disciplines about which they intended to write.

That is, would-be poets, novelists and dramatists should major in those literary arts. On the other hand, would-be medical writers ought to major in pre-med courses, while aspiring economics writers should have degrees in economics.

Thus "journalism" graduates would launch into adult life with some practical working knowledge, as well as a craft skill!

His journalism professor later denied such a policy, stating this young man was a special case. However, we still think the Business Administration degree is a sound, practical idea! For this young man's intended career had been business writing and publishing from the beginning.

The rewards of business journalism are in direct proportion to a writer's knowledge of business disciplines in general, plus familiarity with the various industries about which he or she writes.

Bottom pay-rates go to "human tape-recorders." These are writers who dwell on the most obvious and superficial material. They scurry among billboards, store windows and merchandise displays, without ever really learning the principles of advertising and promotion.

They dutifully quote informants verbatim, without verifying data historically by research or by observation. They learn very little from the information they process. These are the "amateurs." They never really make a decent living at business writing, no matter how frantically they scurry!

By contrast, the pro writer scoops up only that superficial material that is convenient to his search for more sophisticated subjects. Often this material serves chiefly to cover expenses when the big story conks out.

Because the tape-recorder material is so obvious and easy to get, crowds of amateurs are bustling around to get it. Competition is fierce. Editors are swamped with the superficial. Pay is peanuts because so many amateurs are grateful just to be published at all.

Therefore, a successful business writer, to reach the better-pay markets, is constantly educating himself. This is both with formal study and classwork and indirectly by reflection on work processed as he or she goes along.

Four Education Areas, Business writer education covers four main areas. The first, and most important, involves how to market manuscripts or writing services. He or she needs to be constantly probing for new markets—and learning about them.

One reason is intensely pragmatic. Most accounts are limited (budgeted) as to what they can spend. One editor is able to buy only so many stories per year from your locality. His editorial budget is further limited, in that whatever has been allocated usually must be pro-rated geographically and by topic.

The writer is likewise limited in his capacity to produce. Therefore a steady increase in income comes mostly from methodically finding better-pay accounts and dropping cheaper ones. (More on this in a later chapter).

The writer's market place is in constant flux. Each editor's needs ebb and flow with changes in the industry, in economic conditions and in publication policy.

Lucky is the writer who has one or two good-pay accounts to absorb a sizeable chunk of his work year after year. But he's also very vulnerable! When such a bread-and-butter account does shut off, he'll probably have to scrabble to replace it. For dependance on key accounts usually makes a writer quite lax in his overall marketing.

In 20 years of freelance business writing, I've never had the same editor or client as top-pay account two years in a row. Only two accounts have twice been top-pay, but not in consecutive years.

The typical full-time freelance business writer's income will derive 75% to 80% from about six industries (including up to a dozen magazines within those fields). The balance of his income will be scattered among a dozen or more industries, with one to three sales per year in each. (This applies to the full-time freelance without retainers or other contractual arrangements).

This is because the writer gradually gains competence in those six industries. Writing in greater depth generates more volume and higher pay rates. These, in turn, increase desire to probe those industries. It's a really beneficial spiral!

But then comes the new editor. If he's grateful for his predecessor's cozy arrangements—fine! But the new editor too often desires to sweep clean with his or her new broom. Anything and everything his or her predecessor did is automatically anathema!

So then the writer, if he cares to, must prove his worth all over again. Sometimes it takes a year or two, or even more. Often the editor must first learn more about the industry to fully appreciate the writer's competence.

Or the publisher decides they should put that freelance money in staff travel, or enhanced artwork, or heavier magazine promotion. The editor is told to hire an assistant or two, and to forget freelances.

Economic conditions, whether national, or internal to an industry, also affect the rate of manuscript rejections. So do the individual fortunes of the publications. Thus a freelance writer *can never presume a market will be permanent.* That's an axiom!

Writers Can Be Taken For Granted. Finally, many editors tend to take their steady contributors for granted. Their pay rates do not rise commensurate with the improving quality and depth of the material. At such times a writer needs to be independent enough to damp down or cease his flow of material, as leverage on the pay rate.

I had one classic example of a business paper that I sold extensively—every other year. I'd complain about deteriorating rates and lax payments for a month or so each time. Then I'd stop sending manuscripts. After a lapse of six months or so, a plaintive query from the editor would arrive, as to why no manuscripts were coming in (despite my earlier flurry of complaints).

After an exchange or two of correspondence, including a rate adjustment, the manuscript flow would resume. Then a year later the whole process would be repeated.

All of which means the writer needs to constantly be prepared to substitute another field for one of his six majors. Not that six is a magic number. But six is a good average. Both Hazel and I found six about all we ourselves each could keep up with in depth at any one time.

Therefore, up to 10 percent of our writing effort has been toward probing entirely new fields, even though the return may be less. We want to know what's out there! We like to have a few more editors already familiar with our names and quality of work, against the time we may need them.

Thus, when a major account suddenly dries up, the writer can move fast to develop its replacement. Since editors rarely tell you in advance of policy changes, there's inevitably a time-lag before new markets start paying off.

Learning New Disciplines. Okay. We've claimed marketing as the prime area for self-education of freelance writers. Areas two and three are somewhat interwoven.

Area two is learning new disciplines and increasing knowledge of familiar disciplines. "Disciplines," you remember, are sectors of business practice, such as accounting, salesmanship, shipping, etc.

Many business writers get their start as specialists in one or two disciplines. This is especially true of those who launch into writing after retirement, or have been moonlighting in familiar specialties.

Understanding the basic principles of various disciplines is necessary to credible writing. This is why we thought the degree in Business Administration was so helpful to the young man cited earlier.

There is good reason for the term "trade journal" having given way to "business magazine." The number of disciplines now involved with any good operation in any industry has multiplied greatly since World War II.

Take drycleaning, for instance, which still epitomizes the small business with two to a dozen employees.

In one year's time a good drycleaner might possibly call on specialists in accounting and taxes, finance, advertising, public relations, employee training, layout and methods engineering, decorating. He could deal with representatives of two or three unions; with technical salesmen; with maintenance mechanics and boiler inspectors; and so on.

In today's business world, it no longer is enough just to be able to press pants, or bake cakes, pilot a tug boat or sell cosmetics. Every business is a complex bundle of interwoven disciplines. The basics of these disciplines are similar, but the *differences* from one industry to another are what make the real business stories.

Learning New Industries. Area three is increasing our knowledge about specific industries. We admire, for instance, the dogged self-discipline of Robert Latimer! For years on end, he read through at least one business magazine each week-day night. It starved his leisure reading, but as a result Bob knows his industries more than superficially. (Of course, we do suspect that to Latimer these magazines are leisure reading, because he himself identifies with the people in the industries).

There needs to be method, however, to the reading and study. Otherwise our efforts are too haphazard to produce maximum benefits.

We learn quickest by going from the known to the unknown.

That is, start with what we already know, then try to continually enlarge the boundaries of that bit of knowledge.

This is done "vertically" by increasing knowledge of a particular industry. It's done "horizontally" by taking what you learn about a discipline in one industry and finding its parallel in a similar type of industry.

For instance, I first stumbled onto an elaborate inventory control system for sporting goods at Rich's department store in Atlanta. A patient and very lucid department manager helped develop an excellent two-part story for *Sports-Age*.

With this as a jump-off point, I spent a couple solid evenings at the public library. I looked up "inventory control" in at least a dozen business handbooks and textbooks. By the end of that week I had a fair grasp of the *basics* and terminology of the subject.

As a result, though I'd never written on the subject before, I developed saleable articles, after suitable interviews over the next six months, on inventory in office supplies, a supermarket, a truck dealer, a hardware wholesaler, an ice cream manufacturer, and two more sporting goods dealers.

These, in turn, became the take-off for articles on control of tool and parts departments at several trucking companies, thence into similar departments with several farm equipment dealers.

Hazel's similar experience was through study of waitress training at Hot Shoppes in Washington, D.C., for *Restaurant Management*. This led to study of training methods in several different kinds of food services, and then into similar programs for motel maids, plus giftwares and jewelry sales people.

Often a discipline can be quite minor. Take the "want-book," for instance. This is simply a notebook or copy book, in which a merchant and his employees note whatever stock is low and should be re-ordered before exhaustion.

I quizzed hardware dealers about their use of want-books for about six months. This produced an excellent round-up article on the subject. It also lead into a number of larger articles on fast-moving lines, seasonal buying, etc.

Also I learned enough about want-book use to employ it as a survey question in a dozen other retail fields in which I was not well versed.

As an "expert" on the want-book, I could use that knowledge with confidence as a probe into new industries. I needed only to ask how basic want-book use principles applied in each new industry. With a foot in the door, other articles soon materialized in the process of interviewing.

Sometimes a new technique provides this kind of a self-education tool. Back in the fifties, there was a big flurry of converting gasoline engines to use of LPG (butane or propane gas). Since the gasoline engine is similar in design for most applications, the conversion process was also quite uniform.

I first encountered LPG conversion in a truck fleet. So I initially reported the technique in several versions to truckers. Next I reported case histories of truck conversions in several industries for magazines serving those industries.

This then led to stories on LPG conversion of lift trucks within factories and warehouses of several industries previously unfamiliar to me. Farm equipment came next. And this whole field opened up for me through LPG conversion, was lucrative for several years after. LPG conversion was also my introduction to the gas industry, in both LPG and natural gas.

As when learning about "inventory control," I resorted to the library for the basics of LPG (nothing there on want-books). Of course the conversion techniques were too new then to appear in the libraries. But the nature of and differences between butane and propane could be learned. So also could the production, marketing and economics of LPG be ascertained, that made it attractive to some situations and not to others.

Learning Disciplines a Deliberate Process. The more methodically and extensively one studies a discipline, the more quickly a return can be made on the investment in time and cost.

I have accumulated reference books that seemed to have continuing value as refresher material. I keep manuscripts that set forth basic knowledge of techniques or industries. Over a period of 40 years, I've taken two or three correspondence courses, and attended three dozen or more seminars or workshops of up to a week's duration. All were taken chiefly to round out knowledge and understanding of one or more disciplines.

Must Grow As A Writer. The fourth area for self-education on the writer's part involves his or her own technical competence. Since that is largely what this book's all about, the details are discussed throughout. Here we stress that self-education as a journalist must also be deliberate and persistent. For lack of growth *as a writer* is the rather startling handicap that we see many journalists inflict on themselves!

It *is* easy to get immersed in the pressure of grinding out copy to keep the vital backlog built up. It's quite tempting to dash a first-draft manuscript in to the cheap editor who "doesn't deserve any better."

The question is, can I the writer, for whatever reason, afford to let my techniques slip. If I don't *practice* doing my best on the shoddy publication, can I "make out" by practicing on good pay magazine?

My work is my professional image in whatever magazine it appears. Moreover I have obtained some good-pay jobs from business men who read my stuff in cheapie magazines.

You never know who's looking!

Chapter 20

Learn How Industries Differ

Credibility is the big bugaboo for the business writing freelance. He or she is addressing an audience far more experienced and in many ways more knowledgeable about the industry than the writer. To be effective, the writer must understand at least the key elements of an indstury. Otherwise the writer is an easy mark for biased, twisted or even deliberately false information.

There are a number of helpful things to look for in studying an industry. For instance, its over-all make-up, its major components and power centers, its competition and its allies, its strength and weaknesses, are all revealed by the character of the associations and magazines that serve that industry.

Take the laundry-drycleaning industry, for instance. Its Siamese-twin nature isn't so apparent to the man in the street. Yet two major associations, American Institute of Laundering and National Institute of Drycleaning recently negotiated a merger. This is despite a prior history of fierce, competitive independence. Wash-and-wear fabrics and coin-op self-service revolutionized what is now called "textile maintenance."

One laundry and two drycleaning magazines reflect the earlier independence. Another already-merged magazine foreshadowed the association merger.

These associations and magazines represent the "professional" or traditional services, in which the customer hands over garments and linens for complete processing.

But even while the pros are merging, they are engulfed by competitive and divisive elements.

Coin-ops are represented by their own national association and a couple of magazines. The professionals do make some bows in their direction, but usually in terms of pro-owned coin-ops.

Rental groups are the opposing adversaries. Here the business both supplies the garments or linens and does their processing. The major rental groups—linen supply, uniform rental and diaper service—each have their own associations and special magazines.

Learn Sub-Group Distinctions. Why is it important to know of these distinctions within the textile maintenance industry? Because they affect the way each segment operates. Management factors and techniques differ for each group.

For instance, coin-op has a minimum of labor, yet its proportion of labor cost devoted to equipment maintenance is the highest of any sub-group.

On the other hand, the rental groups all deal with inventory problems. Though their labor costs are highest in textile maintenance, the purchase, maintenance and manipulation of inventory is still their major problem.

These distinctions are important to know because many firms in the laundry-cleaning (textile maintenance) field offer two or even all three types of service. If the writer is not aware of the differences in the nature of each service, he can write some very distorted stories!

Yet the textile maintenance industry is actually relatively simple, because its outer limits are fairly cleancut. It's a sort of world of its own.

Now take hardware, for instance. Competition ranges from drug stores to department stores, discount houses and mail order firms. The independent hardware merchant must keep an eye on them all.

Here the writer is likely to delve into paint, plumbing, lumber, housewares, appliances, giftwares, fencing, well-drilling, hobbies, sporting goods, electrical goods, garden wares, lawn care, etc., etc. Each of these separate lines also has its own independent retailers.

These lines vary substantially from each other in one or more of the following: normal turnover, quality range, mark-up, styles and fads, labor, installation cost and complexity, warranties, sales cost, warehousing, shopwear and breakage, pilferage, etc., etc.

To look at the hardware store as a whole, the writer needs some understanding on how the separate lines blend and balance out.

Learn Operating Ratios Quickly. One of the first elements to grasp about an industry new to you are its typical "operating ratios." These enable a writer to judge whether or not he's dealing with a good operation, and in what areas it's most effective.

Operating ratios are business costs stated as percentages of total sales. If the annual labor cost was $60,000 against $180,000 in sales, then the labor operating ratio was 33.3%. If, in the same firm, repair of building and fixtures was $3,600, then the maintenance operating ratio was 2% of sales. If it cost $24,000 to maintain a truck and driver, then the delivery operating ratio was 13.3% of sales.

Comparisons between similar businesses, or measuring against industry standards, is done through these percentage ratios. Comparisons are too unwieldy for dollar figures to be used, where sales volumes differ widely.

Therefore every industry has its "normal" operating ratios. These may be formally published by a business magazine, a trade association, or some industry accountant, or they may simply be rule-of-thumb generally accepted around the industry.

Most industries of any size do have state and even local associations where industry ratios may be obtained, or at least discussed.

Investment Ratios Significant. Another guage for the writer to learn is "investment ratios." Most familiar is the ratio of "Net Profit to Investment."

A merchant says his firm made "5% profit on sales." What does that mean, to the writer or to anyone else? Is it good or bad?

Suppose he used $50,000 investment in facilities and average merchandise inventory to produce $100,000 in annual sales. Then that 5% or $5,000 profit on sales would actually be a 10% profit on his investment.

But if only $25,000 investment in facilities and average inventory was needed to produce $100,000 sales, then the same $5,000 is a 20% return on investment.

One reason for decline in traditional "family laundries," for instance, is that the necessary investment often *equals* annual sales. That is, the ratio is 1:1, or one-to-one. Hence, 5% profit on sales is also 5% return on investment. An investor could get that same 5% return more safely in a savings account, or good stocks or bonds, than in a family laundry—and be spared the management headaches to boot.

Business men, of course, are often unwilling to reveal their operating or investment ratios for publication. But they will refer to some ratios confidentially. And it helps the writer greatly to know their significance, because ratios are usually quoted to make a point about efficiency of operation.

Ratios For Lines, Departments. Ratios apply to segments or product lines of a business also. And here business men more readily consent to publication.

However, if a sporting goods dealer remarks that snowmobiles return him 35% on his investment, beware! Does this ratio include *all* invested costs of promotion, warehousing, display and maintenance or repair service necessary to market the snowmobile line? Or is he fudging on strict allocation of costs.

Each specific line of merchandise or service has its own unique characteristics, including return on investment. Therefore, except for the purest of specialists, business performance is a blend of several or many investments.

Hence every business story hangs on one central peg, however invisible. That peg is the effect on "investment return!"

This thing, this method, this person, that I describe in my article—how does it or he or she affect the firms' return on investment? Is the return increased, reduced or simply maintained?

Not All Investment Is Dollars. Now there's a subtle variant here, especially for the smaller business man! Too often he literally invests his blood, sweat and tears, instead of cash! For instance, he may labor an extra three hours daily at some chore that investment in a machine could reduce to thirty minutes a day.

Investment in that machine might truly reduce his return on total cash invested. But if it spares him a heart attack, it's still a better investment in the long run. Eventually it even leaves him in better cash position by eliminating medical expenses.

Therefore, the writer needs to realize that some investment returns are social or personal, yet fully as valid as cash profits. The important matter is to identify them for what they are! Many changes do not affect cash position but do enhance human or social values connected to a business.

Turnover And Percent of Capacity. Two other ratios are common terminology in many industries. One is "turnover," the other "percent of capacity." Each, where applicable, directly affects both operating ratios and investment ratios.

The first applies to how often an investment "turns over" in a given period, usually a year. Say an automobile dealer stocks 10 models at any one time, at an average cost of $3,000 apiece. Then his inventory cost or investment will be $30,000 at any given time.

At the end of the year the firm sells 100 automobiles, constantly replenishing inventory with new units. Total cost of all 100 cars is $300,000. But the firm never had more than the $30,000 invested in inventory at any one time. So the turnover was "ten times," or $30,000 divided into the $300,000.

But suppose the same dealer felt the wide variety of models and styles require a richer display, necessitating an inventory of 20 vehicles to sell the same 100 units per year. Now his current inventory is $60,000, and his turnover is reduced to "five times."

Another form of turnover is the ratio of units processed by a facility in a given time. A luncheonette may need "seven turns" to make a profit in a high rent district. This might mean seven customers per stool served between 11 a.m. and 2 p.m. (Details differ with hours open, clientele, prices etc.).

"Percent of capacity" refers to some standard of normal capacity. For a motel, it may refer to total number of rooms, or total number of beds, possibly including rollaways. (One of those tricky statistics we writers get booby-trapped with sometimes)! So a motel owner says he needs 80% occupancy to break even. If he means rooms, that's not bad; but if he means beds, he's in trouble!

Fabricating businesses likewise need to make clear their basis for percent of capacity. Is their capacity estimated for one normal shift, or with overtime, or two shifts, or round-the-clock operation, and is it for five days, or six, or seven?

"Economic capacity" is also a factor. You read a certain steel company is at 89% capacity. Does that include the old Klunkerville shop? It can't make a nickel profit unless prices are sky-high. So it's deactivated most of the time.

Chapter 21

The Hot-File

A productive freelance leads a kaleidoscopic life! He could interview an office supply dealer and an ice cream packer in the morning, then a motel operator and a truck fleet supervisor in the afternoon (if he's having an unusually good day).

These are not only different industries, but even four different *types* of business! Their major concerns and emphases all differ, as indicated by a wide variety of operating ratios.

Hence the blank stare of a motel owner was quite understandable the day I introduced myself as reporter for Ice Cream Trade Journal. It's hard to keep track of *everything!*

Bane of the average freelance's life is trying to recall quickly all the facts and subtleties of various industries and disciplines. It's one reason we each found it practical to concentrate on a half-dozen or so.

For me this problem resulted in what I eventually came to call the "hot-file."

This hot-file is a collection of two dozen to 50 or more manila folders. Each represents a topic on which I feel need to keep up-to-date. It can be a new industry, a new (to me) discipline, a recent development in a familiar industry, or even some social or economic trend likely to affect business. Examples of the latter are militant consumerism, air and water pollution, or the energy crunch.

Into each folder goes every scrap of pertinent information that I encounter in either my work or my reading. Clippings are from industry magazines, *The Wall Street Journal, Business Week, The Harvard Business Review, Time* and the daily newspapers.

If the information can't be clipped, I make an abstract and file that.

I also abstract data from books, whether my own or from the library. Although time-consuming, this abstracting helps fix the data in my mind. It may even cause me to reflect a bit on the topics abstracted. Then, while I may not remember the details exactly in the future, I'm more apt to remember their existence!

Red-Line For Fast Scanning. In filing these clippings, all the key phrases or data are underlined in red. This means that to refresh my mind on a subject, I can yank out a hot-file folder and rapidly scan the red underlinings.

Sometimes I come across a lengthy passage that is helpful, but doesn't warrant copying or abstracting. Then I leave a 3x5 card in the folder telling where this passage may be located. The card will also have the briefest of abstracts of that passage, just enough to recall it to mind.

I also use 3x5 cards for cross-referencing. If I come across an article on quality control, for instance, it goes in the industry file if strong on the industry, with a cross-reference card in the quality control file. If it is basic to quality control with only examples from one or more industries, the story goes in the quality control file with cards into the various industry files.

When deeply involved in a subject, it helps to get a simple textbook, or even a syllabus on it. By "syllabus" I mean the expanded outlines in paperback that flood bookstores. We used to call them "trots," designed to help students review subjects and cram for exams. By now the syllabi have multiplied so that one can be found for almost any discipline.

Ideally, I go through a syllabus with red pencil, underlining whatever I think could be useful in current stories. And ideally, I should note in the margins other sources of information on the underlined points.

As a practical matter of time, this gets done only on the hottest subjects, at the time of their greatest interest.

Mastered Discipline A Good Entre. I must risk unduly belaboring this point. When a writer masters, or becomes well-acquainted with some discipline that cuts across many fields, he or she has good entre to businesses, and also the prime key to multiplying knowledge.

For instance, for one client I did a major research project of isolating those quality control techniques from defense and aerospace industries that might be applied to the laundry/dry-cleaning industry.

Once identified, these simple basic quality control techniques are found to apply in some way in all industries. So now, as a reporter, I can investigate quality control practices in every industry I contact. In this "age of consumerism" a frequent interview-opener is "what new quality-control measures have you instituted for warranty assurance?"

And, because I approach new industries from my own firm base of quality control, I can get interviewees to relate everything they discuss to these basic quality control principles.

Therefore I'm usually getting my story on quality control wherein I am knowledgeable. But at the same time I am learning the new industry to which it applies.

It has been my experience that by trying to interview from a firm knowledge baseline, I usually produce manuscripts worth at least 50% higher in price than when I hit an interview in "cold innocence." This is true even while learning a new industry at the time.

One reason for this better manuscript is that many successful business men don't know why *all* things they do seem to work out, or why other things fail. Many reach their successes purely by trial and error, plus having the natural instinct to cut their losses quickly on bad decisions.

When the writer is knowledgeable about disciplines, he is able to "flesh out" stories. This is through describing or suggesting the basic principles involved. Thus knowledge about disciplines will add value-wordage to many stories that pays off in higher fees. Moreover such knowledge is used repeatedly. It rarely is a one-time pay-off!

Weeding and Questions Important. We said the hot-file varies from 24 to 50 folders or more. This is because it is deliberately weeded every three to six months. If a newly-investigated industry proves to be too low-pay or otherwise unrewarding, the folder on it is pulled. It goes out into our storage shed, for possible retrieval if circumstances change.

Also, if some highly volatile situation settles down so that little or nothing new is occurring, its folder may also go to storage.

As a result the file is truly "hot" all the time.

One other thing going into each file is a list of questions I'd like answers to. This doesn't mean I dash right out after answers. But I find that by thinking situations through to the point where the questions flock to the surface, I become alerted to them. Then, as I go about my regular work, I keep stumbling over many of the answers, simply because I'm "sensitized" to them!

Very often some of these questions can be asked when an interview lapses, or an interviewee is relaxed and loquacious (providing your main story is safely in your notebook).

We'd like to claim this hot-file is meticulously up-to-date. In truth, clippings, notes and abstracts collect in one "To Do" folder. Then on a rainy Saturday or some quiet evening, I get out the red pencil and ruler, to go through the whole "To Do" folder underlining key phrases and data. Then the items are sorted to folders they belong in.

This usually results in poring over the contents of three or four folders at the same time.

Leads For Creative Story Ideas. For the creative writer, the hot-file produces inexhaustible story ideas. This is because the collection of information from various sources reveals trends to be exploited while new. It exposes biases, myths and misinformation to be carefully refuted. It also shows the blank spots or vacuums where nothing has been discussed or published. These all spotlight ripe areas where some research or plain digging in the field can prove very fruitful for a writer!

Many folders prove to be abortive. I assign folders to any subject that suddenly seems "hot." Often this results in what I term "clusters": A cluster is a group of very closely related topics.

For instance, when I was immersed in coin laundry/dry-cleaning, it was logical to get interested also in coin vending of all kinds. So a separate folder was built up on coin vending.

Much in the coin-vending folder at that time proved to be on the subject of "in-plant lunchrooms" using coin-operated food dispensers. Eventually I made a separate folder on this, and then went on to write a few stories on the subject. These lead into other stories on in-plant feeding not involved with coin-op.

In the end I never did write on the subject of coin vending by itself, as represented by that one folder. Yet it was the link between coin-op laundry and in-plant feeding. Undoubtedly this coin-op cluster would have spread further, if I hadn't been interrupted by a major project.

Well, we've set forth the hot-file principle, even while admitting to its somewhat haphazard use. Its greatest merit is providing order or method to the learning process. Moreover it supplies a way to work from the known to the unknown. Finally it's a rich source of story ideas when assignments run dry.

Chapter 22

Editors Have Problems, Too!

Just to keep things in perspective, it's time to talk about editors and their problems. This will make more intelligible our later discussion of writer/editor relationships.

Also, many writers, especially those with limited local markets, often edit small trade journals, house organs or newsletters on part-time basis. For them we may shed light on editing cost constraints.

Let's first look at a typical (and actual) operating ratio chart for a modest-sized business magazine. Its net advertising revenue (that is, after commissions to advertising agencies are deducted) was slightly over $700,000 for one year.

NET ADVERTISING REVENUE 100.0%

    CIRCULATION (subscription) COST 9.1%

Printing Expense..28.9%
Paper & Wrappers... 9.0%
Postage (magazine only)................................. 7.0%

    MECHANICAL EXPENSES 44.9%

Advertising Sales Compensation............................. 8.1%
Advertising Office Salaries................................... 2.5%
Advertising Branch Office 0.9%
Travel & Entertainment 1.3%
Telephone & Telegraph... 0.7%
Promotion & Research... 1.8%
Artwork 0.2%
General Advertising Expense................................. 2.1%

    ADVERTISING SALES EXPENSE 17.6%

Editorial Salaries... 7.8%
Travel & Entertainment 1.0%
Manuscript Purchases....................................... 1.0%

Artwork & Photography Expense 1.8%
General Editorial Expense 1.5%

EDITORIAL EXPENSE 13.1%

OVERHEAD EXPENSE 2.6%

GENERAL & ADMINISTRATIVE EXPENSE 4.0%

NET PROFIT BEFORE TAXES 8.7%

Notice how "Mechanical Costs" overhang the other cost groups. It's more than total editorial and advertising costs combined.

The printer's bill alone is double total editorial cost. And if the printer raises his price just 4%, the dollar increase will be more than this paper's total manuscript costs.

A 10% boost in paper costs will do the same, as would a 15% postage boost.

We mention just printer, paper and postage because they are cost items over which a magazine publisher has the least control. Yet they represent nearly 45% of total cost.

Data for Staff-Written Paper. We discuss them merely to show manuscript purchasing in perspective. This is a magazine that claims to be mostly staff-written. From the *editor's* viewpoint this claim is correct, because his three major contributors are technical experts from within the industry.

Factually speaking, these technical contributors are freelance, for they are not on the publication payroll. A writer is not "on payroll" until the employer regularly deducts tax withholding and social security payments.

Altogether the technical experts account for an average $350 per month out of normal $600 expenditure for "manuscripts." Another $100 is consumed by news clipping service fees. Therefore only $150 per month usually remains for the dozen or 15 non-contractual freelance articles bought each year.

Editor Turns to Freelances. But then a field editor resigned from this group of papers. He was not replaced. Instead the editor undertook to fill his needs through freelances from all over the country. The time formerly devoted to supervising the field editor was now turned to cultivating a "stable" of professional freelances.

Of course the freelances appreciate the opening of another

market for their professional services. But the editor was most pleased to have gained some flexibility in his budget!

The next chart shows what happened. Dollar figures are *monthly* averages for each cost item. (Editorial salaries involve staff shared with two other publications.)

	Before		After	
Editorial Salaries	$4,550	7.8%	$3,560	6.1%
Travel & Entertainment	590	1.0%	700	1.2%
Manuscript Purchases	600	1.0%	1,690	2.9%
Artwork & Photography Cost	1,027	1.8%	875	1.5%
General Editorial Expense	875	1.5%	817	1.4%
TOTAL EDITORIAL EXPENSE	$7,642	13.1%	$7,642	13.1%

Most editors are expected to hold their costs at or below a specified ratio to net sales. Some even get modest bonuses based on savings attained below the targeted ratio.

Ad/Ed Ratio Controls Cost. This editor's monthly budget was $7,642 against a monthly advertising sales figure of approximately $58,300. If advertising fell off by 5%, the editor presumably cut his expenses by $382 per month. For an advertising drop of 10%, his cut would be $764.

Some editorial cost falls automatically with an advertising sales drop. This is because most business magazines hold to specific "ad/ed ratios." That is, total editorial pages are kept at a specified percentage of advertising pages, whatever the latter may be. The ratio most frequently applied is 2:1, with editorial matter at one-third of the total number of pages. Ratios for different publications vary from 1:1 to 3:1, or from 50% to 25% editorial.

As the number of ad pages drops, the need for editorial pages shrinks proportionately. Automatically this reduces editorial costs for artwork, engravings and a few miscellaneous items. But not proportionately, however. For the showpiece articles in the "front of the book" will continue to get the lion's share of the artwork, as does the magazine's cover.

Before changeover to freelance utilization, over half this editor's budget was in salaries. For short-term cost control, salaries are virtually "fixed" costs. Therefore the *non-salary* expenses must be cut at least *twice as deeply,* to achieve the requisite editorial expense drop in ratio to advertising.

That is, for a 5% drop in advertising, the editor needs at least a

10% cut in his non-salary costs. When ads are off 10%, non-salary editorial costs would be dropped 20%.

Staff travel and photography are rarely susceptible to cuts deeper than the ad sales drop. That is, it's hard to cut them more than 5% when ad pages are down 5%. This is because some editorial travel is public relations or image building. And, if staff photography can be cut heavily, perhaps too much of it is done anyway.

Cut Has To Be In Manuscripts. So the editor obviously has to make his heavy cut among purchased manuscripts! But, on this staff-written magazine, the news clipping service and the three technical writers' "columns" are staple items. Clippings provide "breaking news," as well as minutiae about the industry—openings, closings, new facilities, hirings, firings, promotions and obituaries.

Technical columns, such as those by the three experts, are in a magazine for appeal to special groups of readers. The editor omits a technical column with trepidation, if only to avoid having to answer complaints about the omission.

Which leaves our staff-supported editor with $150 worth of manuscripts to leave out, plus a like amount shaved from travel and photography. In other words, he can struggle to hold his ratio of 13.1% against a 4% drop in advertising. Below that, he's lost, so far as earning any cost control bonus is concerned.

The picture changes when this permanent staff is reduced by one person. With a manuscript budget increased by over $1,100 the editor obtains cost control sufficient for almost any ad sales fluctuation.

This amount includes more than the direct salary reduction of $960 per month. There is another $100 for those fringe benefits charged directly to the editorial department. This is included in the General Editorial Expense item on the chart.

Also $160 a month photography expense incurred by the former field man, including depreciation and insurance. These are now included in cost of manuscripts purchased.

Off-setting these gains is an increase of $110 a month in editorial travel. Remaining staff personnel must now cover some more far-flung conventions formerly attended by the field man.

But overall this editor now has a real "cushion!" His $1,240 for purchase of uncommitted manuscripts (i.e., above the cost of news clippings and technical columns) is truly a variable cost. He can now hold his 13.1% ratio against even that 10% drop in advertising we alluded to earlier.

What If Advertising Jumps? Ah—but suppose advertising pages suddenly jump *up* 10% instead? This can sometimes wreak more havoc in the editorial department than a drop of the same proportion!

Cost of manuscripts purchased jumps to $3,000 or more, since the staff should normally be producing close to its capacity. Moreover, the staff's elasticity is stretched merely to process this extra material into the magazine.

All uncommitted freelance manuscripts on hand get sucked into this suddenly fatter issue. This is why a bewildered writer sometimes, after a prolonged drouth, unexpectedly gets paid for two or three ancient manuscripts at one time.

Also the "boneyard" of staff-written material, already rejected as below standard, is hastily reviewed and pruned for possibly printable copy. This explains why staff-written material sometimes is so patently inferior to freelance contributions!

Of course another reason for inferior staff articles appearing in print is the fact they are "paid for in advance," in salaries, overhead and travel expenses. Once it's paid for an editor is reluctant to circular-file any manuscript!

Explains Why The Problem Persists. However, this detailed account of an editor's chief problem has purpose. It explains the stubborn refusal by many editors to pay on acceptance of a manuscript (often referred to as POA). "Acceptance" means within a reasonable time after receipt. It allows an editor time to return from a trip, meet a deadline, then read accumulated correspondence and manuscripts.

As can be seen from the discussion above, the only means for many editors to control fluctuating costs is POP, or pay-on-publication. We don't condone this practice—merely acknowledge its existence!

We explain why in the chapter on writers' pay. Briefly, if most of a writer's working capital is tied up in POP manuscripts being stored on editorial desks, it can cripple him or her.

Moreover, many editors place little value on a manuscript until they have accepted it. More POP editors lose manuscripts than their POA counterparts. More misunderstandings arise between POP editors and writers. Only POP editors hold a manuscript until it's obsolete, then eventually return it, possibly with regrets.

There Is A Practical Solution. A reasonable means of solving the problem does exist! Some publications use it as a matter of course. We commend it, or a suitable alternative, to publishers who desire to be fair to their own editors, as well as to writers.

This is to establish a permanent "manuscript bank" of $1,500 to

$3,000 worth of deferred manuscripts. These articles could even be "worked up" while in the bank, ready for prompt use when the occasion arises.

All *accepted* manuscripts are paid for within six weeks of receipt. If scheduled for immediate use, the payment is charged normally against the current issue of the magazine.

Otherwise it is debited against the manuscript bank as a deferred charge. This then does not become a current editorial expense affecting the editor's cost ratio. When the manuscript *is* used, the manuscript bank is credited, and the charge then made against the issue in which the story appears.

A top limit must be set on this manuscript bank. The editor should review his or her deferred inventory monthly, *tentatively* assigning each manuscript therein to some future issue.

The editor should not consign to this bank those manuscripts about which he or she has any doubts, as an excuse for not making a final decision. Otherwise the editor winds up with a bankful of "dogs." Then he's worse off, due to publisher pressure to use up stuff already paid for.

There *is* incentive for an editor to pay on acceptance. Writers favor POA magazines over POP firms at the same pay scales. Many will even favor a POA editor over a POP editor paying a higher scale!

In fact, when the writer gets low on working capital, he hasn't much choice! He then *has* to favor POA editors exclusively.

Editor Is Market-Sensitive. A different problem for an editor is keeping his publication focused on the exact "market" it professes to serve. Even the best writers, if they do not sense the market served by a magazine, are likely to invite frequent rejections because they miss that market.

Few business magazines are entirely without competition. Competing magazines all disseminate much the same basic information. Therefore each publication strives to create its own different aura, its unique image.

Each magazine's advertising salesmen strive to convince prospective advertisers that theirs is the only medium for reaching certain important groups of readers.

Suppose there are four major magazines in a field (which is not at all unusual). All present roughly the same basic information. But one stresses technical aspects. Another details production methods. The third reports sales and marketing factors. The fourth focuses on management techniques.

One editor speaks as an equal to an industry's sophisticates. Another educates and coddles the newcomers to this same business. Emphasis may be on specialty firms or on the multi-product outfits, on small operators or on mass-producers, the quality shops or the discount merchants, or chiefly on manufacturers, on merchandisers, on installers or on service people.

Furthermore, the format and style of a magazine is shaped to its readers' presumed habits. It may be designed for fast reading and discard, or for careful study and filing for reference. It may be worded for scholars, or for a lip-moving readership. Dependence on photos and drawings may be great or little.

Publishers spend tens of thousands of dollars with readership survey firms, to learn the reading needs and habits in their industries. Most major business magazines therefore have very definite, frequently-tested reasons for their editorial policies.

So, when an editor claims freelances "don't know" his industry, he often really means the writers ignore his paper's unique slant or posture toward that industry. This forces the editor to decide whether facts in a particular article warrant the editing effort necessary to fit it to the magazine's style and format.

For an editor to complain "freelances don't know the industry" really begs the question! There always are *some* people knowledgeable about an industry that will write about it for pay. As a matter of fact, that's where editors in the same field often come from!

The editor's problem is to *find* those writers who know his industry. This is why the ABWA directory includes areas of special and general knowledge in each member's profile, plus separate listings by industry knowledge.

Chapter 23

The Organization Chart

An "editor" produces a magazine or newspaper, we said, while a "writer" or "reporter" provides the copy that goes into the magazine. Generally a business paper editor also does some or much of the writing for his or her publication.

The editor reports to a "publisher." This latter person may alternatively be titled publications manager, business manager, general manager, or something else. But in any case, the editor reports to either the owner, or to an executive who represents the owner. And that worthy's functional title is "publisher."

To a reader, as well as many writers, the editor is lord and master of the magazine. Sometimes he may actually be so. Often he is also the publisher.

In practice, the editor is regarded by the publisher and/or owners simply as another oblong the organization chart. Here's a simple organization chart, such as might be drawn for the magazine described previously.

What the organization chart illustrates most graphically is the number of functions that must be performed by somebody on or for *every* publication. On the tiniest every slot could be filled by one and the same individual. On the largest each slot represents a separate department with an executive or supervisor and supporting staff.

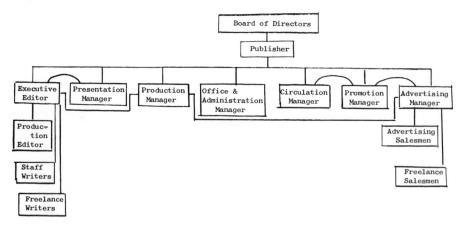

This chart only sets forth the major functions in publishing a magazine. "Chain of command" differs widely, even between publications in the same company. Much depends on stature, experience and capabilities of the individuals involved.

Production managers often report either to an editor or to the advertising manager. A presentation manager (art director) may be under the editor. Or the promotion manager could report to the ad manager. Yet sometimes the editor *is* also the promotion manager, especially if he's a noted personage in the industry.

Some "Editors" Don't Edit. In fact, the "editor" sometimes isn't even literary! He or she may be a person of recognized stature and experience in the industry, and have a considerable personal following. Thus his or her true function is public relations and image building for the publication. He or she speaks at conventions, consults with industry leaders, serves on industry committees, chairs or sponsors industry functions.

Such an industry-notable usually has a subordinate do the actual editing. But, he's not necessarily an editorial figurehead. Publication policy and procedures are greatly influenced by his expertise in the industry.

Many "working" editors, just through tenure and good common sense, acquire this same kind of stature in their industries. Such worthies usually retain working direction of their departments, whereas PR types who come from industry ranks do rarely acquire real editing capability.

Hence the freelance writer doesn't always deal with the "executive" editor. Moreover larger publications have sizeable editorial staffs. Here one member of the staff is assigned to screen incoming manuscripts for final consideration by the executive editor.

For good writers this is rarely a hardship. The "first reader" usually eliminates only "junk" or "slush"—whatever is patently unsuitable. Any manuscript with a germ of merit is passed along for at least a quick scanning by the executive editor.

Some papers place more authority with departmental editors. Here the first reader feeds the manuscripts to those department editors most likely to be interested. (One *very* good reason for confining each article to a single theme!)

Production Editor Puts It Together. The "production editor" has the most truly descriptive title. He or she prepares manuscripts for the printer, marks pictures for the engraver or for offset, then makes up the final page "dummies" for the printer.

This editor does the proof-reading, and keeps meticulous records showing where each bit of copy is at any given time. In larger publications, the production editor often does the actual editing of style and phrasing.

However, this individual is disguised under a variety of names on the masthead. Most frequent is "managing editor," which is confusing because this term on other publications may apply to the chief executive editor! "Assistant editor" or "associate editor" are other titles given this job slot.

The latter two titles may also apply to staff writers and reporters. "Field editors" are usually located geographically, alone or in branch offices of publications. Then there are special editors of all kinds, often labelled with descriptive titles such as "technical editor," "marketing editor," "engineering editor," "Washington editor," etc.

Very often the field editors and specialty editors are freelances. They hold such titles to swell the magazine's masthead. A "masthead" is where a publication's staff is listed.

Some Edit Several Publications. At the other end of the scale, some publishing houses have a single editor producing three or four smaller magazines, sometimes with the aid of a single secretary-assistant. Such an editor usually would make the proverbial paperhanger look like a chronic goof-off!

But this type editor also often depends almost entirely on freelance writers, for both news and feature material. Therefore many multi-paper editors can be quite demanding about quality of writing as well as content. They just don't have time to do a lot of manuscript re-writing and editing!

Others, of course, are just plain sloppy!

The "presentation manager" is often called "presentation editor." Actually he or she is the artist who designs and often illustrates the editorial pages.

"Editorial" here refers to *all* non-advertising pages. The traditional editorial page or column where the editor expresses personal opinion, often over his byline, is usually referred to around the shop as the "editor's page," the "opinion page" or by its special whimsy, such as "From the Rolltop," "Carney's Corner" or other personalized titles.

On larger magazines, or groups of publications, the presentation manager heads up an art department that also sometimes prepares ads for a publication's advertisers. This latter is done on a job basis.

With many small magazines, the editor may also be responsible for design of the pages, and the artwork, if any.

"Layout" Has Several Meanings. Use of the term "layout" in publishing can be very confusing to an outsider. Designing a page, or a "spread" of two facing pages, can be called "layout." This applies to either editorial or advertising pages.

Or the cut-and-fit pasting down of picture and text proofs onto "dummy" pages can be called either "layout" or "dummying." But if the pasting is according to layout already provided by the art department, then the term "dummying" is definitely used.

However, the "production manager" also "lays out the book." This process is arranging the entire sequence of advertising and editorial pages to achieve the most economical printing costs possible, without sacrificing good readability or appearance.

"Book layout" is a highly skilled craft! It's complexity is rarely appreciated until one has tried it personally.

Book layout deals with "forms." These are groups of 4, 8, 16, 32 or 64 pages, to be printed in blocks on sheets of paper of suitable size. The trick is to get the right colors to the right pages, while resorting to as few expensive printer's devices as possible. The resulting layout must then allow a sheet of paper to fold so as to bring pages in proper numerical order.

Also the more pages are concentrated in the largest possible forms, the lower the printing cost per page. The cheapest magazine to print, in cost per page, is made of a single 64-page form.

For instance, suppose one month's issue comes up with 40 pages of advertising. On a 2:1 ratio this calls for 20 editorial pages, for a total of 60 pages.

But to print exactly 60 pages calls for one 32-page form. plus one each 16-page, 8-page and 4-page forms. This would be four separate expensive set-ups and runs by the printer.

By adding four more pages of editorial for a total of 64 pages, you run this issue in a single form, with one set-up and one run.

The resultant saving in printer's charges will be many times the cost of buying an extra manuscript or two for the extra pages. And quite often a "house ad," promoting the magazine, can occupy one or two of those pages.

Advertising copy, illustrations and engravings are received by the production department, and forwarded by them to the printer with suitable instructions.

On the smallest magazines an editor may even do the book layout, including ad production.

The function of an "office and accounting manager" is sufficiently explained by the title. This is one department common to all types of business!

Finding and keeping track of readers is the task of the "circulation manager." For paying subscribers, this includes renewal billing and follow-up. For free subscriptions regular verification is necessary.

Most ghostly of all the organization slots is the "promotion manager." Promotion chores are most often assigned as a second duty to one of the other positions. Or, surprisingly, real planned and programmed promotion, as a separate and distinct publication function, is often simply ignored by business publications!

Circulation promotion and advertising promotion may be handled by one individual, or they may be done separately within each of those two departments. And sometimes promotion, as a form of creative writing, is assigned to an editor, even on well-staffed publications.

Advertising Department Larger Than Editorial. The cost of soliciting and obtaining advertising in business magazines ranges from equal to editorial costs to a ratio twice as high as editorial costs. (Editors like to think an inverse ratio should apply. That is, the higher investment made in editorial procurement and editorial quality, the lower the advertising budget likely to be needed. However, such an assertion is explosive in any publication office!)

Ad salesmen either have geographical territories, or else concentrate on special accounts. For instance, one might cover those accounts where engineering knowledge is needed. Another's accounts may require a background in education, electronics, textiles, etc.

There are freelance ad salesmen even as there are freelance writers. Publications based in the East or Midwest often have too few advertising accounts or prospects in the Far West, Southwest or Southeast to justify travel expense from headquarters necessary to call on them.

So they retain independent advertising solicitors. These concentrate in Los Angeles, San Francisco, Portland or Seattle, Dallas and Atlanta. Western and Southern publications, on the other hand are more likely to have staff salesmen in Eastern centers.

On magazine mastheads such freelances are usually titled "Western Manager," "Southeastern Advertising Manager," etc. They usually represent several unrelated and non-competing publications. This is because sales commissions from a single publication are rarely enough to support one good sales person.

There are a few freelances who successfully combine reporting and ad selling. But usually those who start in a dual role eventually slide over to concentration on one side or the other.

Chapter 24

A Word About Advertising

We must not confuse the *function* of advertising with advertising *practices*. For advertising is necessary to most publications. Nor is this only because it is the major source of revenue. It is also a vital means of communication that many readers need and look for. It tells what products and services are currently available and where to get them.

The "product news" section of a magazine usually makes only an initial announcement when a product or service is introduced, or is significantly modified in some way. Thereafter advertising in some form is necessary to keep the public or an industry apprised of the current availability of that product or service.

Suppose the Green Widgit breaks in the news in March. So we first read about it in March. But we don't need a widgit right now. Over the next six months, other firms announce *their* new model widgits. That news is published one time also.

Come November, our faithful old widgit finally gives up the ghost. We must have a new one at once. So we hastily review what we know about varieties of widgits and where to obtain them.

The Green Widgit actually would serve our needs best. But that initial notice appeared six months ago. By now the details are hazy. And anyway the retail or jobber salesman says his Brown Widgit is just as good. So we order one.

Advertising is assurance that facts about Green Widgits are fresh in our minds at the very time we need a widgit.

Businessmen Want Ads To Read. Eastman Editorial Research, after interviewing approximately 10,000 readers of business magazines, commented:

"96% of the active readers interviewed said they 'read' the advertising in the publications we surveyed, (either) on purpose initially (68%), or as they encountered ads in the course of reading or leafing through the surveyed issues (28%).

"44% (of active readers) said they gave advertising either more (13%) or about the same (31%) amount of attention as they gave to the editorial content."

Moreover, say the Eastman people, their readership surveys in external house organs and religious periodicals reveal very similar data. In other words, interest in advertising is not confined to business readers!

The fact is, advertising is a stabilizer in the market place! It expedites data communications.

Sources of Product Information. Four major sources of information about products and services are readily available to the average business man. In practice he uses them all, if he is a careful shopper. They are:

The *product salesman*—whose information is subjective, carefully designed to promote sale of only his own product or service;

Experience of others in the business—means a delayed feedback on new products, as well as information about one or two models only from each businessman contacted;

Industry exhibits—are excellent for comparing many models and quizzing their sponsors closely in a short period of time, but they are infrequent and costly;

Advertising in all its forms—is constant and readily available for all products in any given line. When a salesman pushes hard, competitive ads give the prospect pertinent questions to ask and solid comparisons to make.

Advertising Is Educational. For instance, the Green Widgit is said to be transistorized, lighter in weight due to an aluminum block. Armed with this information, the prospective buyer forces the Brown Widgit salesman to at least discuss the practicality of transistors and aluminum blocks, or their alternatives.

Without benefit of competitive advertising, it's possible the subject of transistors and aluminum blocks wouldn't even come up. That is, unless the salesman felt he could show his own product's superiority by discussing them!

This value of advertising to the reader is exemplified by the number of publications that devote all or the bulk, of their pages to advertising. In years gone by the Sears, Roebuck catalog was said to be second in reading popularity only to the Bible!

Many business magazines produce "directory" or "buyers' guide" issues, annually or biannually. These are packed with advertising! They may have little editorial matter, yet be kept by readers for buying-reference until the next year's version is issued. And even their "editorial" matter may simply be solid pages of product specifications, tabulated for comparison between brands.

Business Freelances Better Copywriters. Freelance business journalists find work in business ad copy writing if they so desire, especially for small firms without their own advertising departments. The business-oriented writer is called on because he or she can empathize with the intended reader of such ads, as well as with their sponsors.

So business magazine advertising is just as much two-way communication as the feature article! That is, the advertiser must fully understand the real needs of the reader. The reader must be helped to believe advertised products will fill his or her needs. Otherwise there is no communication—and no sale.

The psychology and techniques of writing ad copy are outside the province of this book. There are many good texts on the subject.

Our point here is that the experienced business writer has an advantage in writing copy for ads to business people, due to genuine understanding and empathy for their needs and wants.

Perspective On Ad/Ed Tensions. Another purpose in writing this chapter is to give perspective to the eternal tension between editorial and advertising departments on business publications.

It is not for a freelance to judge ad/ed policies of the publication for which he or she writes! If its editorial policies are ethically or morally incompatible, the writer had best not write at all for the publication. That's the strongest leverage a writer can exert!

Sometimes writers are pressured by publication ad salesmen to do articles because they involve pet accounts or prospective advertisers.

But the writer must realize it's still the editors who accept and pay for articles! So—clear all assignments with the editor first, before you turn a wheel or click the shutter. This applies any time an assignment or lead originates with someone other than the editor, unless you are sufficiently familiar with both the industry and the publication's policies to judge for yourself.

Once, at a trade show, an important business paper publisher himself gave the author a substantial "guaranteed" assignment to report on a certain product installation.

Checking with the editor, the writer learned a two-part story on a similar installation was already in process. They had no need for another. Shortly after, the publisher in some embarrassment rescinded his assignment.

Tread Carefully in Gray Areas. Every publication always has that "gray area" wherein the editor must decide whether a story has too strong an advertiser influence. It doesn't matter what a publication's standard policies are. Each still has its own gray zones.

Some publications are so blatantly "commercial" as to even charge advertisers by the page for printing stories involving their products.

Other magazines are so determinedly "neutral," as to blank out any trade names or other product identification in all story photos or other illustrations.

To the freelance writer, we suggest the facts in your story be written as objectively as *you* see them. Leave gray areas for the editor to deal with. But, beware of getting your by-line tagged with "hyped-up" articles, lest you earn the reputation of not writing objectively. (We'll discuss this further in the chapter on Ethics).

Good Faith Vs Hypocrisy. To the editor and publisher, we suggest the key to dealing with gray areas is really the question of good faith vs hypocrisy.

It's our observation that those magazines which most carefully level with their readers prosper best. This applies whether they are either honestly and sincerely objective, or are frankly and openly advertiser-supportive.

The magazines most often in hassles with advertisers seem to be those which try to appear objective, while pandering under their breath to the advertisers.

Readers are not fooled by hypocritical publishing! Moreover, they soon come to mistrust even the truly objective writing in such magazines (if there be any).

Chapter 25

Cost of Doing Business

"Can freelance business writing be profitable? Is it possible to make a good living at it? Could a freelance buy a house, put kids through school?"

Proper response begins with a freelance writer's cost of doing business. Pay methods make sense only in relation to a writer's actual costs.

Much of today's "logic" in compensating freelance writers stems from the Great Depression of 1931-1938! For example—

At that time the late Vince Rabuffo lost his job as cub reporter for a Rochester, New York newspaper. Much later he became the very successful editor/publisher of *Ice Cream Trade Journal*. But all through the Depression young Vince supported a growing family entirely by freelance business writing.

During the Thirties Rabuffo never received a check for more than $25. Many were for one and two dollars. Most were $5 to $15. He never was able to save any money. But neither did he ever join his neighbors in breadlines.

"Name Made News." Until World War II, most "trade journals" derived copy largely from freelances. Moreover it was the dogged aim of most editors to include in each magazine issue, under whatever pretext, as many names of people as possible. Even the longest convention registration lists were herded down the pages of many industry publications.

Any item that mentioned a business or its owner was saleable. A freelance's most valuable talent was in detecting or devising pegs, however ephemeral and shaky, on which to hang these business mentions.

Business management, as a well-organized discipline, was in its infancy. It was non-existent in most small businesses. Philosophy of business management, expressed by any merchant or manufacturer, was a saleable story, regardless how odd-ball or impractical such a business method might seem today. Some smart editors simply ran contradictory opinions in parallel columns for readers to judge for themselves.

On the other hand "thinkpieces" were also marketable. These were a creative grouping of points around a single subject or technique. They were usually drawn from a writer's accumulated observations after many interviews (or cribbed from other publications, a bit here, a bit there). They were not usually credited to sources.

Editors welcomed thinkpieces as guideposts to the "art of management."

Ernest Fair, for instance, developed thinkpiece writing in volume to a high art during the Depression. Even today Fair's thinkpieces, now spare, meaty and provocative, still show up quite often in business magazines. But that's another story.

Meanwhile, getting and selling trade journal copy was easy during the Depression. And pay was commensurate, like a half-cent to one cent per word.

You made a living. It was a simple question of how many calls you could make in a day or a week. Rabuffo was a wiry young man, and kept plugging steadily.

Depression Writer's Costs Minimal. Little photography was called for. (Vince often commented wryly that he turned to editing to avoid learning photography, when *Life* magazine pushed photo-engraving into a major business activity).

The typewriter was Rabuffo's capital investment. Total expenses involved pad, pencil, postage, rent, carfare and shoe leather.

Sometimes he hiked several miles a day to save carfare. Vince mapped calls so the last of them was farthest from home. If he'd had a good day, he'd blow a nickel on a trolley-ride home. All transportation was by trolley around the city, and even between cities.

Vince had no need to deal with CPA's, taxes, fees, licenses or insurance. For a long time he couldn't even afford a telephone, then finally managed a two-party line.

In that era a freelance writer's "take-home" pay was on a par with anyone who worked for a single employer. That is, every dollar received was available to the writer for immediate living expenses.

Job security for the average employee was far more fragile then. Workers took jobs where and when they could find them. They were laid off entirely at the convenience or whim of employers. Seniority rights, tenure, unemployment compensation were "socialist" concepts.

Compensation Logic Different. Today the picture is drastically different. (Remember our premise is that the logic of freelance remuneration today is still based on Depression thinking).

One fourth to one-third of a steady employee's income today comes as company-supplied fringe benefits—*tax-exempt,* or at discounted premiums.

But the freelance today must procure these same fringes on his own—out of taxable income, and at steeper individual premiums. Nor does he have the protection, if his revenue is cut off, of workman's compensation, unemployment insurance, etc.

Average Operating Cost is 60%. Average cost of operating a freelance writing business today is 60% of all revenues from that business. A 60% ratio has been confirmed repeatedly over recent years, by survey and by spot check of members of Associated Business Writers of America.

This 60% figure is *average.* It includes the *equivalent* of fringe benefits most generally provided, such as social security, workmen's compensation, unemployment insurance, two weeks vacation, etc.

Minus basic fringe benefit equivalents, the average cost of operation is 50% of total revenues. That is, only 50 cents of every dollar received by the average professional business writer is "eatin' money."

When we refer to "cost of operation," this covers only those expenses treated as deductible on Federal Internal Revenue Service returns. Some fringe benefits, such as health insurance, are also deductible, of course. But their deductions are made on our personal income tax returns.

In fact, tax returns do most clearly point out the distinction between John Doe as a writing business and John Doe as a person. It is John Doe as a writing business that must provide John Doe the person with that extra revenue needed for fringe benefits.

Three Typical Business Cost Ratios. Hence, in this discussion we deal entirely with John Doe as a writing business. The costs under consideration are those regarded deductible by IRS on John Doe's *business* tax return.

Now that 50% cost ratio, we repeat, *is* average. The actual range in operating costs among different writers is from 25% to 85% of total revenues. Moreover, in any survey of freelance business writing professionals, this range breaks down into three clusters or groups.

The group with the highest operating cost ratios might be called the *"executive type* writers." They maintain business offices and staffs, or use stenographic, phone answering and photographic services.

Their cost of doing business averages 75% of revenues, with a range of 65% to 85%. For a typical writer in this category to net a personal income of $15,000, a gross revenue of at least $60,000 must be generated.

Self-Contained Writers. A majority of professional business writers in ABWA fall into a second group who maintain offices in their homes. These are the "Self-contained" type. They range out 50 to 200 miles on interviews, occasionally make extensive trips that are expense-paid or promise solid returns.

The wife, if the writer is a man, often handles the phone, does the purchasing and much of the typing. Or a male spouse is often found contributing the necessary photography.

These writers farm out very little work. Yet they often overlook the labor of a spouse as a valid cost to be compensated for.

Writers in this group average 50% cost ratios, with a range from 40% to 65%. A $15,000 personal income for them requires $30,000 gross revenues.

Controlled-type Writers. The third group might be labelled the "controlled-type." Deliberately, or by force of circumstances, their work pattern minimizes operating costs.

For this cluster the key stricture is positive refusal to touch the typewriter without reasonable assurance of a substantial margin over costs. A large majority of business magazines, therefore, are automatically eliminated as markets for them.

Time (labor) is the major cost element in their work. They often pour out volumes of easily obtained and quickly written copy, often from phone interviews. Or they concentrate on long-term projects such as manuals, books, training texts and scripts, etc., where the client is willing to pay for the time requisite in mulling over and mature thought.

Many of today's thinkpiece writers are in this cluster, also. They usually are older persons, drawing on a lifetime's exposure to business and business people of all kinds.

Others are handicapped and house-bound, or have care of an invalid or children that restrict their freedom. Their operating costs are minimal, yet difficult to keep below 25% of revenues.

Accounts Receivable vs Working Capital. The controlled-type is most successful in minimizing two hidden costs that don't show up on IRS returns. One is cost of "captive" working capital. This is funds tied up in manuscripts held by editors or clients but not yet paid for. "My POW's" one writer terms his captive working capital.

Cost of producing a manuscript is money *already spent* by the writer. That money has become inaccessible and unproductive. Easiest way to measure this loss is to figure what the same amount of money could earn at the bank, say at 5%.

An active, prolific writer can have $2,000 to $5,000 expenses continually tied up in manuscripts out on editor's or client's desks. This is merely when they are paid for on a current basis. It's part of the "revolving fund" of working capital in which income and outgo need to be balanced. If the writer doesn't have this kind of "float" he or she probably isn't productive enough.

Receivables Must Not Build Up. But if the writer isn't watchful, the manuscript backlog, or accounts receivable, builds up rather quickly to two or even three times that much.

And $3,000 invested at 5% for just six months brings $75. That's working capital enough to fund writing of another good story!

In addition, when such captive working capital is substantial, a writer is forced to one of three alternatives. (1) He can temporarily refuse assignments that require large expense funding. Or (2) he can liquidate an investment, whereon its lost interest must be added to the cost of captive capital. Or (3) the writer can borrow funds, generating extra cost in interest.

In either of the latter cases, extra time is also wasted in procurement of the necessary funds, which is another hidden cost.

Stale Manuscripts No Longer Working Capital. Even more subtle, but just as real, is the cost of writing-off production expenses on lost, stale or otherwise unmarketable manuscripts. The most careful and competent writer inevitably loses a few. It may be a publisher goes broke after printing a writer's article. Or a departing editor left such a mess, the article can't be found. Or the circumstances of the story itself changed too drastically for modification, i.e., a fire, earthquake, flood, bankruptcy, embezzlement by the story's hero, etc.

Assuming the writer strives not to let unprofitable manuscripts accumulate, it is still realistic for bad debts to be included in operating costs.

Of course, it's understandable for a good-paying client to say, "Hey, wait a doggone minute! Why do I have to pay for your other client's goofs?"

The practical response is, "So I'll still be available here at Crabapple Corner or Industrial Row the *next* time *you* need a story from here."

If too many manuscript-mishaps occur, of course, the writer

won't be around long anyway. Yet "bad debts" are very much a cost factor in any business. Bad debts for auto manufacturers (dealers or fleet operators who defaulted) are in the price of *every* new car sold. Prices of hammers and chisels include losses due to bankrupt hardware merchants, etc.

The writer doesn't always see this in his own work because a figure for bad debts doesn't show in the operating part of the IRS return. The latter simply totals costs for 100 stories, say, but revenues for only 90 stories sold. Yet every nine stories sold subsidized the cost of a tenth that did not sell.

IRS Guide To "Reasonable" Costs. Business writers with whom we discuss income taxes report Internal Revenue Service quite reasonable in interpretation of costs—reasonable, but not liberal. The following discussion needs checking with your own tax people, for IRS practices change. We merely urge you to explore all factors in your operating cost.

The most controversial area seems to be the item of "Rent." IRS really scalds the part-time scribe who puffs mamma's sewing room into a full-time office in which no more than two or three hours' writing per week actually occurs.

But the full-time professional writer does get a fair break on space seriously used for work (or did at this writing). IRS judgments are largely influenced by hours-of-use and ratio of writing income to the expenses claimed.

With an office apart from home, a writer has a clear-cut case on rentals expense. But when, as is generally the case, part of a residence is used for business, there's always plenty of grounds for debate.

In the latter case, IRS allows a portion of residence cost to business expense. The exact portion is determined by the amount of space used for business in proportion to the total space in the residence.

Rooms or Square Footage. Suppose one room is used entirely as the office in a five-room house. This creates a business expense item equal to one-fifth, or 20% of total rent costs. Halls, entries and porches are not counted as rooms. However a weather-proof sun porch that is lived in generally would be counted as a room, especially since they sometimes are the office in question.

Alternately, if a large room is set aside for an office, it may be advisable to figure on square footage, rather than number of rooms. A re-modelled basement would be a typical example.

Suppose house and basement total 1,200 sq. ft. in area, and the basement office is 500 sq. ft. The writer would then deduct 40% of total rent as business expense. This is provided a reasonable amount of that basement room is actually used for business (and not half of it for ping pong).

It's much harder to validate rent costs where the business overflows a room designated as an office. Some typical examples might be:

Filing cabinets in a hall or closet.

Stationery or supplies stored in another room.

Film in the refrigerator freezing compartment.

Special table and lamp for note taking at a phone in another room.

Drawing board or easel in another room on which to sketch floor layouts or site plans.

Bookcase or magazine rack outside office used exclusively for business magazines, reference books, research data, etc.

Chair, table or lamp in connection with the above.

Bathroom or kitchen convertible to darkroom use.

Living room corner arranged exclusively for frequent interview of visitors.

Room set up for business meetings.

Snow tire storage for a business car.

Experimental film projection facilities for slides or video-tape.

Such auxiliary space usage is deductible *only* when the business function is *undebatably* its sole use. A major criterion would be whether its business usage *prevents* that space from being used for something else.

On review with IRS, it would also be necessary to show these auxiliary areas to be really necessary to their business functions. Can you prove they *need* to be outside the designated office? *Is* their use primarily for business, or only incidentally so?

As a practical matter, for IRS purposes, it is best to lump into one total the square footage of auxiliaries that are undebatably involved in business. This total may usually be added to the area of the designated office.

But also have a list available of *all* the marginal items, which you do *not* claim for deduction. Their existence emphasizes the inadequacy of the designated office, and the validity of the deductible auxiliaries.

IRS Aids Writer To Know Costs. Such a list is important also to remind the writer how much of a residence actually is a business cost, whether deductible or not. *Any* item used for business occupies space that *could* be used for something else.

The film is a case in point. Forty rolls of photographic film in the freezer draw as much current as equal volumes of hamburger and ice cream. When I sacrifice freezer space to preserve color film, this is for the ultimate benefit of clients who buy my transparencies. But in order to store the film, I must buy ice cream in quarts, rather than cheaper half-gallons.

What Is "Rent." But—what is "Rent" anyway? What if you own the office or residence?

A more understandable term might be "housing." This encompasses everything that protects the writer from the elements while at work (except when travelling).

But "rent" is an appropriate term. Even for the office in a residence, John Doe the writer rents space from John Doe the resident in the home.

Not everything applies to a given instance, from among the following elements of housing. They vary according to whether the property is rented or owned.

Rent paid a landlord

Depreciation on residence and/or furnishings

Property taxes, both real estate and personal

Fuel, power, water, sewage

Property insurance (fire, theft, damage, etc.)

Public liability insurance

Maintenance and repair

The item of "maintenance and repair" requires some careful distinctions. Where it affects the designated office space directly, it is an undebatable expense.

Office Shares Building Integrity. But a business office also shares in maintaining a building's integrity. Such expenses include: Painting the entire building; re-shingling the roof; repairing a foundation; replacing a furnace, central air conditioner, water heater, etc.

These are all expenses to be pro-rated, with the writer's business carrying its share.

On the other hand, repairs or maintenance to another room in the house, not involving the integrity of the business itself, is not a deductible business expense.

To establish "Rent" for the home office as deductible, all these housing expenses are lumped together. Then the ratio of business space to the whole residence is applied to that lump sum.

For instance, in the case of the basement office, depreciation, taxes, utilities, insurance, maintenance and repair on the whole residence total $3,000 for the year. The basement office occupies 40% of total floor space in the residence. Therefore 40% of the $3,000 comes to $1,200 or $100 monthly.

Does that seem a juicy deduction? It's also a reminder to the writer that he needs $100 a month income simply to cover his business rent. And usually this is money already spent before the $100 comes in.

It's also basis for comparison with cost of an office apart from the home. The writer can often afford a more desirable residence, if part of the cost is subsidized by business write-offs.

Employee Costs. Wages or salaries of business employees are obvious business expenses, whether part or full time.

Housekeeping or janitorial employee expenses are deductible only insofar as they care for business facilities.

A domestic's wages are pro-rated in the same way as housing costs. For the basement office cited, if a part-time domestic earned $2,000 for the year, $800 is deductible as a business expense.

If the domestic cooks, the writer must be able to show this permits more writing to be done.

Cost of a baby-sitter or day-care center *may* be deductible *if* proven necessary to free the writer for business activities.

Insurance for or bonding of all employees is also a legitimate expense item. It's also pro-rated for domestics.

Outside Service Costs. Akin to employee costs are services that lighten the writer's personal workload or provide expertise.

Heading the list are phone answering, typing, stenographic and mail forwarding services. Other are manuscript agents and analysts, technical consultants, newspaper clipping and readers' services, and messengers.

Special fees are proper expenses, such as royalties or commissions for quoting another author extensively. Other fees are bank and credit card charges.

Specialists Are Total Costs. Photo developing and enlarging is a major cost factor for many business writers. This subject is discussed in detail in another chapter. But however it is handled, the costs are a valid business expense.

Cost of lawyers or CPAs in connection with the business of writing is deductible. So are damages and court costs in certain instances.

Fees to ad or PR agencies would be proper business costs, where agencies are used. However the average writer does not think in terms of using outside advertising or public relations services.

Most writers' PR costs are self-generated. They get buried in other cost categories—and sometimes forgotten or overlooked. Included, besides special stationery, are press cards; direct mailings; brochures; directory listings (including yellow pages); ads in newspapers, journals or organizational programs; organization memberships, registration and meetings fees.

Business Information A Writers' Lifeblood. "Business information" services cover a wide spectrum of costs involved in communicating necessary information *to* the writer.

Chief among them is telephone and telegraph, including all taxes thereto. The basic costs are pro-rated according to average personal use by writer and family against business usage by the writer. Included with the latter are messages handled by the family in the writer's absence.

A writer soon learns how important it is to *log all toll calls* for several reasons: (1) To check phone bills for accuracy (Ma Bell does make an occasional error); (2) To pick out charges (calls plus proportionate taxes) that are to be billed to clients; (3) To have a record for future referral, in case a second call is necessary to the same person.

We ourselves enter all toll calls in our diaries, both inter-state and intra-state. We put down the name of the person called, area code and phone number. If a stranger to us, we enter name, title and company, plus a few words to explain the purpose of the call. The number is in red ink for easy finding.

One way to remember to do this religiously is to write the number in the diary first, then dial from the number as written.

We mentioned organization dues and assessments above as a hidden PR cost. How to get the PR values is discussed in another chapter. But there are organizations with limited PR value that still are useful to the writer. These are professional societies, clubs for specialists, quasi-educational groups, etc., by which the writer keeps on top of business trends and innovations. Cost of belonging is usually a deductible business expense.

Books, magazines, newsletters, treatises, manuals, tapes, courses, seminars, when pertinent to business, are all valid costs. So are library fees and expenses that give access to business information.

Entertainment For Developing Information. Another source of business information is people. Reasonable entertainment and gifts provided people while obtaining information, or as compensation for it, are also deductible. Emphasis is on the word "reasonable," however. IRS is well aware that business men frequently pick up the tab for meals with business writers. So be *most* reasonable when claiming entertainment. Document it carefully in your records (diary).

All *necessary* travel expenses are deductible. An unnecessary travel cost would be such an item as sightseeing, unless your story involved the sights seen. Leisure-time costs on combined business and pleasure trips ought to be separated and not claimed.

Also non-deductible are meals outside the home, if not away overnight. Exceptions are meals included in registration fees for meetings, or in connection with entertainment while gaining information.

Auto Expenses Can Be Substantial. One major benefit of freelance writing, when the individual is a truly active professional, is having a better car than personal use alone can justify costwise. Or else the family can justify the convenience and emergency protection of a second car.

This presumes, of course, that expenses charged to the car or cars are valid. If depreciation is not being conserved (banked) against car replacement, then auto expenses are not being correctly used. Depreciation ought never be mixed with working capital. Otherwise replacement funds won't be there when needed. "Living off depreciation" is a universal journalistic failing!

A writer working from home charges off more total auto expense, than office or factory workers, because commutation is not involved for the writer. On the other hand, the writer with a separate office, like employed workers, may not charge off travel between home and that office as business expense. Field trips are chargeable, whether they originate from home or a separate office.

Two Ways To Figure Mileage. There are two ways to estimate auto travel cost. One is to keep a log of all business-connected mileage, *including* trips to the post office, the stationer, the photo service, etc.

Next, on the year's total, figure 15¢ a mile for the first 20,000 miles, 13¢ a mile thereafter. This is what IRS *currently* allows (may allow more by time you read this). On this basis you do not take auto depreciation or auto insurance separately. They are included in this per mile rate.

If a writer spends substantial time at his typewriter and on interviews, he's unlikely to exceed 20,000 miles on business in a year.

Therefore the 15¢ rate should cover all his business driving.

The alternative is to lump *all* auto expenses for the year—depreciation, fuel, oil, maintenance, repairs, license, insurance, tolls, parking. Then estimate as closely as you can the proportion of car-use for business vs private activities.

A fraction is close enough, if it is realistic. Our business auto costs have varied from 3/4th to 9/10th of total car expense over the years. So you apply this fraction to the lump sum costs to get business auto costs.

The great variable in one's estimating is the one long vacation trip, or conversely one or two lengthy business trips. But the years in which we took only 3/4ths or 8/10ths of our auto expense for business all involved trips from New Jersey to a family home in eastern Kansas. (Even these involved numerous business calls, on occasion).

This second alternative is largely preferred by owners of standard-sized or larger cars, because IRS seems to lag behind the realities of auto operation costs. (It is said they apply mass fleet operation data to individual car owner operation.)

If the family has two cars, of course, one can be claimed as the business vehicle, and expenses kept on the cars separately.

While both cars are bound to be used for both business and personal activities, the cross-overs are likely to cancel out over a year. For instance, we have used a compact for errands around the city, whether personal or business, for ease of driving and parking. A heavier car made most road trips of both kinds in greater comfort, as well as accommodation of luggage and camera gear.

But since the fuel crisis, we've dispensed with the heavier car entirely.

Depreciation Is A Big Cost Item. "Depreciation" can be a substantial cost item for many business writers. The function of depreciation is to spread over several years the cost of long-lived equipment and tools. It makes operating costs bear a reasonable relationship to earnings derived from those costs.

Major depreciation costs for a writer are the residence, if owned, and the car, if not leased. These are depicted on a separate "depreciation schedule."

Depreciation deducted for business is in the same ratio as other costs in the same categories. That is, if the writer is claiming 40% of rent, he claims 40% of residence depreciation also. If 3/4th of car expenses are claimed, then 3/4ths of annual car depreciation is claimed.

An item is depreciated when it will have a *useful* life of three years or more.

As a practical matter, low-cost items are not depreciated but taken as direct expense, regardless of predictable life. This applies to small tools and minor pieces of furniture—scissors, wastebaskets, hand staplers, card files, postage scales, etc.

Taxpayers often use an arbitrary cost cut-off point, such as $25, $50 or $100, below which depreciation is not taken.

The following are normally depreciated by a writer:

Typewriter(s)
Adding machine or calculator
Copier
Duplicator and major accessories
Dictating and transcribing equipment
Tape recorders
Phone answering devices
Cameras and accessories
Darkroom equipment
Projectors
All necessary furniture
Room heater, air conditioners, humidifiers, fans
Cabinets, shelving
Furnishings specific to the office
Alterations to adapt an office
Encyclopaedias, business book sets

All equipment and tool maintenance, repairs and insurance are direct expenses, as are lease or rental of equipment or tools.

Depreciating Remodeled or Rebuilt Equipment. However, an item is sometimes re-built or altered. Its probable useful life then is likely to extend beyond the original depreciation period. In this case the writer adds the cost of re-building or altering to the depreciation still allowable. Then that total is depreciated for the new life period.

Suppose the writer has a metal storage shed in which supplies, files, records and paraphernalia are stored. The shed cost $300 new. It's being depreciated over ten years at $30 per year.

Starting the sixth year frost heaving has warped the shed, pulled rivets, created leaks. So another $120 is spent to put a concrete pad under it and correct the warpage.

The shed's predictable life is now once more at least ten years. Of the initial depreciation, $150 still remains to be taken. This added to the new expense totals $270. So now the writer charges off $27 yearly for ten years as depreciation on the shed, which extends the depreciation another five years.

Similarly, putting a new or re-built engine in a fully depreciated car gives it "new life." The replacement engine and installation cost can be depreciated over two or three years.

Miscellaneous Cost Items. All business-connected supplies are chargeable—stationery, postage, record books and forms, letter heads, business cards, manuscript envelopes, photo supplies, drawing supplies, etc., and etc.

Also direct expenses are items of special clothing—hard hats, safety glasses and goggles, safety shoes and specially treated apparel (flameproofed, water resistant, etc.) not otherwise worn in private life.

The cost of moving an office is usually taken as a direct expense. But cost of remodeling the new office is depreciated. This is true whether the move is within a building or to a different location entirely.

Business Taxes Increasing. Finally, the state, county and local tax men are closing in on freelance writers. They regard John Doe the writer as a genuine taxable business enterprise.

Hence, in many states and communities, writers are subject to licensing as businesses, as well as liable for business personal property taxes at higher than domestic rates, and for unincorporated business taxes.

If the preceding pages seem unduly obsessed with the Internal Revenue Service, it is because IRS influence has largely shaped the American business community's concept of costs of doing business. Therefore IRS definitions prove to be the most accessible and easily understood for the average person without an accounting background.

At the same time, the author, by no means whatsoever, claims to be expert on taxes. The reader is stringently warned *not to take our word for anything!* Check questionable points out with your local IRS people or with a competent tax expert. For one thing, we have found in our travel around the country that interpretations differ on the same points among local offices and individual tax people.

Therefore the real intent of this chapter is to: (1) Show that writers have far more operating expenses than the reader may have realized: (2) Provide a sort of checklist against which to compare your writing facilities; (3) Establish a realistic background against which to judge the value of payments and fees received for writing efforts.

The Irreducible Minimum. A 50% average cost ratio, as described earlier, may seem not to apply to certain writers hunched over lap-held portable typewriters in bedroom corners.

With two or three reference magazines and a sheaf of notes under the chair, one's "office" conceivably can be compressed to less than 10 sq. ft. (3 ft. by 3 ft.).

Such an irreducible minimum represents only 1% or 2% of a home's floor space. It involves $20 to $50 proportionate rent per year at most.

Yet John Doe, huddled in the corner, *is* a business. At least the tax authorities all say so! Correspondence, accounting, tax work, purchasing, phone, filing, maintenance and repair, scheduling—all the elements of big business impinge on that solitary chair. And how many can actually be confined to a 3 ft. by 3 ft. square.

If Mr. Doe will review his activities and inventory facilities, he'll find his real office is scattered all over the house. He may not be able to convince IRS! But he'd better believe it when evaluating his revenues against his cost of operation.

How About Unpaid Labor. Then too, John Doe is most likely to be guilty of our last and extremely touchy point under costs of operation for writers. This is the persistent blindness to how much unpaid labor is contributed to a writer's efforts by relatives, girl friends, boy friends, boarders, neighbors and acquaintances, and to what it really is worth.

A writer spends 12 hours on a manuscript and receives $144. He figures twelve bucks an hour is quite acceptable.

But he forgets Mom totaled two hours typing two separate drafts. Junior spent nearly two hours more rushing negatives to the photo shop, retrieving the pictures and taking the manuscript to the post office.

For a true total of 16 manhours, the family's return is $9 an hour, rather than $12. At the 50% cost ratio, that's net $4.50 an hour. Or hold Mom and Junior to $3 an hour. Then Pop still nets only $5.00 hourly.

Granted they had the time, were glad or even proud to help Pop. But if this writer farmed his typing out and paid a cabby to post the manuscript, those would have been legitimate costs. And Mom and Junior could earn *real* wages doing the same work for someone else.

Bald fact is that one-third to one-half the publications in this country who use freelance work are subsidized by writer's families working at hourly returns less than the Federal minimum wage.

That's their privilege! But the purpose of this book is to show how to make a living at freelance writing.

Chapter 26

The ABWA Pay Formula

There is *no infallible formula* for fairly compensating a freelance writer. Conscientious editors agonize over the problem. Scrupulous writers are numbed by efforts to present reasonable invoices.

In practice, invoicing by writers is rare simply due to its many uncertainties. It's easier to throw one's self on the mercy of the editor or client, then scream in pain if the check doesn't seem big enough.

A pay formula I devised is now used by many members of Associated Business Writers of America (ABWA). It provides a way to most easily estimate fair pay. Since either editor or writer can use it, the formula makes a starting point, a structure for negotiation, that is mutually understood.

Before examining this "ABWA Pay Formula," however, let's review its background.

Editors have paid by word-and-picture rates, by the printed page, by flat fee, by position in the book, and by "break-point" (i.e., send a second small check, if the writer squawks loud enough over the inadequate size of the first check).

The above methods are all arbitrary. Writers mostly accede to them on a take-it-or-leave-it basis. And for the most part these methods are too inflexible to adjust for many variables in writer costs or labor.

Therefore more editors now negotiate the manuscript prices after a fashion (Will $150 be all right?). More writers today send invoices along with their manuscripts, occasionally even with those submitted on speculation.

But the sorry crux of all negotiating and billing is they are generally done in the dark about many important factors.

Factors In Manuscript Pay. Six major elements influence pay for a manuscript.

Weightiest factor is the *time* involved. This includes unproductive but unavoidable "overhead" time not attributable to any specific manuscript.

The second factor is the *complexity* of the story, whether due to inaccessibility, nature of interview or details of composition. In a way this is a function of the time element.

The third factor is *cost* to the writer, including indirect or overhead expenses.

Fourth is technical *skill* shown in handling all phases of an article—the manner of interview and writing.

Fifth is *knowledge* of the industry, the technique or discipline under discussion, as well as business principles in general.

Finally, the sixth factor is *wisdom,* evidence of mature thought in presentation and conclusions.

The first three factors (time, complexity, cost) largely reflect the nature of the story itself.

The last three (skill, knowledge, wisdom) express the caliber of the writer. What is he or she worth in publishing's generals labor market? What pay scale could this writer command if on a publishing staff?

All six of these elements enter into the jigsaw puzzle of setting a fair price for a manuscript.

Many editors and other clients also trot out a seventh factor, with unflinching frequency. This is the magazine's or client's *capacity to pay.* Sometimes, of course, the client is right, in that the outfit is going broke, making it a risky market for writers anyway!

Generally, however, this a hypocritical defense in the face of reasoned negotiation.

For the average business magazine, the total freelance writer fees (sometimes called "correspondents' credits") represent 0.3% to 5.0% of gross revenues.

Therefore living-wage compensation to freelances is not likely to be *the* factor that sinks a magazine. Conversely, when good pay procures better copy, it can be instrumental in helping save a marginal publication.

Any useful pay formula must primarily ensure that a writer's *every* productive hour be profitable. This is why the time factor is weighiest. The other five factors simply condition the profitability of the productive hours.

The ABWA Pay Formula. So here's the ABWA Pay Formula, based on hourly return:

$$F = 2W \times (H + .25H)$$

"F" is the manuscript Fee or the total payment for the writer's work. It involves *all* forms of payment, including expense reimbursement, retainers, advances, bonuses, merchandise, gifts.

"W" is the *Net Hourly Wage.* This is what the writer must earn per productive hour to achieve a reasonable standard of living. It also is what a specific writer could earn on an editorial staff.

Net Hourly Wage is found by dividing 50 into the *annual* salary a writer would be capable of earning if a publication employee.

This figure of 50 omits two weeks' vacation out of total 52 weeks in the year. So a weekly wage is the result. This wage divided in turn by 40 (for a 40-hour week) establishes a Net Hourly Wage.

The same result is obtained if the *annual* salary is divided by 2,000. That is, 50 weeks times 40 hours equals 2,000.

This Net Hourly Wage, then, is the net income the writer should have to live on, *after* all business expenses are paid.

As explained earlier, survey of Associated Business Writers of America show average cost of doing business to be at least 50% of gross revenues.

Therefore the Net Hourly Wage must be *doubled,* in order to cover a writer's average hourly cost of operation. Thus "2W" in the formula expresses this doubling of the net hourly wage. The term for "2W" is *"Gross Hourly Rate."*

The "H" in the formula is the number of "Productive Hours." This is total hours directly involved in producing the manuscript—interviewing, research, writing, photography, travel. Generally speaking these hours are directly attributable to a given article. Where two or more interviews occur on the same day or trip, interview time is pro-rated.

Finally, the ".25H" adds another one-fourth of the total Productive Hours spent on a given manuscript. It represents indirect labor of "Overhead Work" not directly attributable to a given manuscript.

"Those who prefer fractions to decimals can substitute $\frac{"H"}{4}$ for the ".25H" in the formula).

Overhead Time To Be Paid For. The explanation for this ".25H" comes from another ABWA survey that showed this an average ratio of

Overhead Work. That is, for every four days of writing, interview and travel, one additional day (at least) is taken up with Overhead Work. Or, if you prefer, every four hours of Productive Work involve an added hour of Overhead Work.

This means one-fifth, or 20 percent, of an efficient writer's time goes into phoning for interviews, querying, scheduling, correspondence, bookkeeping, mailing, purchasing, maintenance, etc. This is a conservative figure indeed.

By contrast, in the average publishing house many of these chores are handled for editors and writers by secretarial and clerical staffs. The latter are usually on the editorial payroll, also.

Obviously a freelance must likewise get reasonable compensation for Overhead Work. Otherwise his bank account, if any, bleeds to death!

The most simple way to do this is pro-rate overhead time among all the productive hours. Add 15 minutes to every productive hour, or one hour to every four productive hours, or even one week to every four productive weeks. Which is exactly what the ".25H" does.

How Formula Works In Practice. Suppose an editor believes a writer capable of earning $10,000 a year at a staff job. Simple evaluation is "what caliber staff writer is needed to handle such a story."

This editor also has an assignment expected to take two days for travel, interview, photography and writing.

A $10,000 salary divided by 50 weeks gives $200 per week. Divided in turn by 40 hours this results in $5 as the *Net Hourly Wage.*

To cover average expenses this is doubled to $10 per hour. Now $10 is the "2W," or *Gross Hourly Rate,* in the equation.

Total productive hours are two days, or 16 hours, which is "H." Then 25% of 16 equals 4 hours. So total hours to be compensated for are 20. This is the "H+.25H."

Therefore the fair price for that article, by a writer of that caliber, is $10 x 20 = $200.

Any writer can figure a manuscript fee by this same formula, after deciding what he or she is reasonably capable of earning in a staff position dealing with similar material.

Writer Needs A "Billing Rate." But most important, a freelance writer must, and we repeat emphatically, *must* establish for himself or herself a *"Billing Rate."*

This is simply the ABWA formula applied to one productive hour's work, which means adding 25% to the Gross Hour Rate. In the example just quoted, the Gross Hour Rate is $10, the Billing Rate is $12.50.

Once a writer establishes a satisfactory permanent Billing Rate, the rest of the arithmetic may be set aside until a writer's targetted annual income is revised.

Meanwhile, for each job the writer does, this Billing Rate is simply multiplied by the number of productive hours put in on that job.

Whenever payment falls below the Billing Rate times productive hours, the writer has fallen behind in obtaining his or her desired annual income.

The Shorter Formula. The ABWA formula is susceptible to some short-cut arithmetic (now that we've explained its rationale). Note that the Gross Hourly Rate was $10 when the desired net annual income was $10,000. This is a constant ratio!

That is, by ABWA formula Gross Hourly Rate will always be 1/1000 of the desired net annual income. Move the decimal point three digits to the left on your desired net annual salary. The result will be the Gross Hourly Rate needed to acquire that personal income or salary for the year.

You must *gross* $7 per hour for a $7,000 net salary, $9.50 hourly to get a net $9,500 income, or $15 per hour gross to attain personal income of $15,000.

We now arrive at what, for some at least, may be an even simpler formula. We substitute ".001S" for "2W." We replace "H+.25H" by "1.25H." This formula now reads:

$$F = .001S \times 1.25H$$

In this equation, "F" is the Fee and "H" is the number of hours, as before. "S" is the annual net income (salary) to be earned by the writer. Thus ".001S" is the Gross Hourly Rate.

Perhaps the following table will clarify the distinctions between terms.

"Net Annual Income" is comparable to a staff salary. From it the writer expects to pay personal taxes, insurance, etc., that any salaried employee likewise pays on his own.

"Gross Hour Rates" include fringe benefits an employer generally pays for in the employee's behalf, averaging 25% to 30% of that employee's salary.

This is about as far as comparison can be pushed. No pay formula will ever provide neat, exact parallels between staff and freelance incomes.

Net Annual Income	Net Weekly Wage	Net Hourly Wage	Gross Hourly Rate	Hourly Billing Rate
$10,000	$200	$ 5.00	$10.00	$12.50
12,000	240	6.00	12.00	15.00
15,000	300	7.50	15.00	18.75
20,000	400	10.00	20.00	25.00
25,000	500	12.50	25.00	31.25
30,000	600	15.00	30.00	37.50
40,000	800	20.00	40.00	50.00

Several Billing Rates. Some individuals need several Billing Rates. Consider a writer who is a specialist in one particular area. He or she is also willing to work in other fields, about which less is known, at a lower Billing Rate.

Even three Billing Rates are conceivable. For on-the-job consulting work, a specialist might charge $50 per hour. For a manuscript on this specialty, the fee might come to $30 per hour. But for reporting in less-familiar areas (possibly as fill-in work) this same writer might charge only $15 per hour.

It's Relatively Simple. Hopefully by now the reader is muttering, "This is all so obvious! Why does the author carry on so?" If so, then we will have made ourselves understood.

It *is* all relatively simple. Yet editors and writers have failed for years to come to grips with any fair and reasonable formula.

One reason is that everyone worries about the variables in pay methods, rather than nailing down the constants.

"Suppose," an editor asks "we send a freelance to Rome or Israel for five days' work? Won't travel cost far outweigh net hourly wages?"

In most cases, surprisingly, the answer is "No."

No writer's client is likely to send a $7,000-a-year cub reporter 10,000 miles round-trip. Pay scales tend to rise with an editor's investment in travel. Also a writer's travel-time rises in proportion to travel expense.

Moreover the 25% overhead factor is keyed to productive hours, including travel-time, and not to travel expense. So the 25% factor rises with the pay scale. This is warranted on the writer's behalf because his overhead time arranging for a long trip is likely to be greater.

Another mental block for clients is paying a Billing Rate for what to them are unproductive hours spent in travel.

That, bluntly, is the client's problem. If the writer charges less for travel time, he must make it up elsewhere, perhaps in a higher Gross Hour Rate. Moreover, it's the writer's normally productive hours that are chewed up in travel. If he can't get his Billing Rate while travelling, he'd better forget the trip entirely and turn to something profitable.

Best solution is for the client to provide travel expenses and arrangements that ensure the quickest trip possible.

Type of Work Vs Quality. One other point about compensation is important to bear in mind. Type of work and quality of work must not be confused.

We described in our first chapter the "legman" who is a human tape recorder, indiscriminately scooping up all the information he or she can latch onto.

The "reporter," we said, supplies a structured story in the rough, or even semi-polished. And the "author" provides a polished article, usually coupled with mature judgment and sensitivity to special trends.

Quality for *each* type of journalism can range from superb to gosh-awful. Pay scales also range from highly rewarding to pitiful—for each type. But pay scales should reflect performance, as much as type of work.

Each type of journalism is a different "mix" of three separate functions—interviewing, writing and editing.

The legman leaves practically all structuring and polishing to editors. By contrast, an author does virtually all the editing, as well as the writing. In between, the reporter blends the functions according to circumstances.

Time Usually A Quality Function. *Editing is a time-consuming function.* Hence the author-type writer produces less total wordage in final print than does the reporter. And the latter generates half as much published copy as the average legman.

Therefore a business journalist needs to be judged for compensation in at least three separate areas—skill at interviewing, skill in writing and skill in editing.

Conceivably the legman who garners all the facts in depth, plus background and current opinions, justifies a higher pay scale than an author with a nicely polished story built on a spare skeleton of facts.

This doesn't mean a skilled legman deserves pay *per story* equal to an author. For the legman puts in fewer hours per story. But legmen, reporters or authors *of equal skill* do justify comparable net return *per hour.*

Perhaps, in this day of TV reportage, this is not too difficult to comprehend.

Cost of Background Study/Research. One more sore point in editor/writer relations needs to be touched on. This is hidden cost of background reading, so urgently needed to keep up with industries being reported.

Some writers, especially in fast-developing complex industries, claim to spend up to half their time in reading or study of industry source material—magazines, research reports, manuals, association bulletins, etc.

It has been this author's experience that this reading is always by far heaviest when exploring an industry new to me. It tapers down as we work more fully in familiar industries.

But for a full-time pro, reading can be expected to consume from four to ten hours a week. When I say, as I often do, that I have a 50-hour week, this allows for eight hours per week of reading or study.

Clients are not charged for general background reading per se. They *should* be charged when reading is "research" specific to an assignment in hand.

If an article would be incomplete or inaccurate without specific information obtained in reading, that time is a valid part of that job. It is "research," or as frequently termed, "literature search." It's chargeable at the writer's regular Billing Rate.

This is where the ABWA Pay Formula helps the novice business writer. One of the criteria for pay scale is knowledge of an industry. A low knowledge level can be counter-weighed only by greater application of time in reading or research.

That is, the novice devotes more time to reading or research for a given article, than a writer already well-informed on the subject. Hence the *Hourly Billing Rate* is lower for the novice in that particular area.

But, *if* the novice does careful research, more productive hours are involved, earning more hours of pay at the lower Billing Rate. Then the quality of the article could approach the quality of a similar article by the informed writer. At least the spread in quality between the articles would be less than original difference in knowledge or expertise between the writers themselves.

Thus similar total pay is often warranted for such a story, whether done by the expert or the novice, *if* the novice truly does his "homework."

Plea For Analysis. All this seems to have brought us full-cycle to flat-fee payment by editors or clients. Maybe so. But at least there would be a fair rationale for such flat fees, when based on the ABWA Formula. There can be realization that overhead time and overhead cost logically must be compensated. Otherwise the writer won't be there the next time he or she is needed.

Chapter 27

POP/POA And The Crystal Ball

"POP versus POA?" Payment-On-Publication versus Payment-On-Acceptance? Which is more reasonable, more fair to writer/or editor?

To a writer the problem seems so easily solved! Editors should treat manuscripts like perishable merchandise (which they certainly are), and pay for them in thirty days!

The "reasonable" attitude of editor or client is that freelances are independent businessmen, who have deliberately chosen a career that involves considerable risk.

The writer's rebuttal is that many businesses even offer discounts for cash-on-the-barrelhead. So there's nothing reprehensible about expecting (hoping for) payment in thirty days.

There's logic in this for sure. Even before a manuscript is mailed out, half the eventual payment has *already been spent* by the writer, for direct expenses and for overhead costs. Same is true of course for any merchandise. Plaint of writers is that editors don't seem to regard manuscripts as perishable merchandise.

Ten stories one-month-old might involve $750 or more in expenses. These, plus ten stories two-months-old, plus ten stories three-months-old add up to investment of $2,250 working capital.

Hence, on these 30 stories, a writer doesn't even get back his working capital until about 15 have been paid for!

Hopefully, all articles eventually do sell. Thereafter the writer continues operation with that same $2,250 level as a working capital revolving fund.

But it doesn't always work out that way. Even a slight "recession" can scoot the value of outstanding manuscripts up to $4,000 in just a few months. These are manuscripts that still are saleable, but are paid for more slowly.

Keeping Expenses Covered. Nor could 100% POA (payment on acceptance) ever work fast enough to keep a freelance entirely current on expenses. The only way a writer completely avoids committing working capital for lengthy periods is to:

(a) be on a permanent retainer;

(b) be on a drawing account for expenses, like an editor or salesman;

(c) receive expenses advanced against specific assignment;

(d) have manuscripts paid for C.O.D.;

(e) have expense vouchers paid on receipt by an editor, regardless of an article's eventual fate.

Some freelances do work in one of these ways with regular clients. This, however, is usually after first establishing good experience relationships.

Moreover, it is significant that those editors consider such writers as staff members. The editors may even deny they ever use freelances, even while we note ABWA members (known freelances) on their mastheads.

POP/POA Defined. Further clouding the POP/POA question are confused definitions!

"POA" (payment on acceptance) can be *any* time *before* the magazine's issue carrying your story is dumped at the Post Office.

"POP" (payment on publication) occurs any time *after* this date of mailing.

Let's talk about POP first. Advertisers in a magazine are not usually billed until after an issue is in the mail. This is to make certain there are no slip-ups in preparation or printing, and that the advertiser is getting exactly what was contracted for.

Therefore a magazine's revenue for a specific issue comes during the month after it was mailed (or later—sometimes much later).

Some publishers strive or even have to pay the cost of a specific issue (including manuscripts) from the revenues for that issue, insofar as possible. Thus writers on POP are actually treated like "services." They are paid like printers, photo processors, ad agencies and commission salesmen.

On the other hand, for a writer to be POA is to get paid like editors, artists and other staff members—in advance of publication of the particular issue being worked on.

Worked-on Is The Crux. ". . . issue being worked on!" That's the crux of the POP/POA problem!

For an issue *can* literally be put together editorially the night before it goes to press! Very many small magazines have part-time editors who completely edit and make up the "book" in the week before printing.

When editors of such publications assure us they pay on acceptance, they are technically correct. They simply don't accept manuscripts until just ready to use them.

Moreover, due to limited staffs, these smaller magazines tend to be heavy buyers of freelance work. So they are at a focal point of the POA/POP controversy.

By contrast, editorial content on some papers is laid out as much as six months ahead. Special issues or departments may begin to shape up as far as a year ahead, though this also is rare.

But because of this long-range programming, there actually are very few editors who pay on acceptance for *uncommitted* manuscripts to be held indefinitely in a "manuscript bank." This applies especially to business magazines.

Editors who *appear* to do this are more likely to be planning issues far ahead. Actually they are assigning manuscripts to specific issues at time of acceptance. That is, they accept the manuscript for an issue now being worked on—which won't be published for five or six months yet.

Editors are rarely moved to pay C.O.D., any more than an equal number of tavern operators, township high schools, or TBA dealers. Credit managers in other kinds of supply businesses make full careers of whittling accounts down from 120 and 90 days past due to 60 and 30 days past due. So hoping for 30 to 60 days settlements is more realistic for a freelance writer.

And since a C.O.D. arrangement is not likely, it is generally more practical for a writer to ignore POP/POA, as such, as being too nebulous.

Instead, work toward editor agreements to accept or reject within 45 days, and to pay at least half in 60 days, to cover the writer's costs (alternative "e"). Six weeks is usually ample time for a busy editor to finish a field trip, tidy his desk, and turn to manuscript selection.

Perishability The Real Problem. The writer's most serious problem is manuscript perishability. After initial "filling the pipeline," once a writer gets producing regularly, income comes in fairly regularly (or at least "steady by jumps").

But Palmer's Law of Manuscript Vulnerability states "a manuscript three months old increases 10% in perishability every month thereafter."

I cite a study of my own experience during a recession in the Fifties, in support of this law.

My average level of committed working capital reached $3,500 (when a buck bought a lot more, too). Over two-thirds of my sales were POP. Average age of manuscripts outstanding was more than six months. And 15% of the manuscripts were perishing on the vine.

First step was to drop two major POP accounts. I sure hated to do so, because I enjoyed these fields tremendously. But, as one editor flatly stated, he wasn't "about to be dictated to by any hack writer!"

To three good-guy editors we explained my working capital problem, and said that thereafter we'd be unable to send more manuscripts, until those in hand were paid for. These fellows didn't exactly go POA, but there was a decided stepping up in the speed with which stories were used, and paid for.

By next year's end, over two-thirds of my output was paying out in 90 to 120 days. Average age of outstanding manuscript dropped to four months. Mortality rate slid under 5% of all manuscripts. *Net* income doubled.

It's significant that while the change in mortality dropped from 15% to 5%, almost all that 10% difference lay in manuscripts *over* six months old. From the prior year, there was 20% mortality among manuscripts six months old, 50% among those nine months old, and 85% among those a year old.

Handicap From Capital Attrition. When a writer's working capital thins out, meagre income results for several reasons.

You spend too much extra time following up old manuscripts, prodding editors for action.

You take fewer field trips into fresh areas, further exhausting the nearby fields.

You gamble less on promising new areas.

Worst of all, you plow more into markets that already are surfeited.

You tighten up on the number of negatives exposed or printed.

And you do all this even to good-pay accounts, although the problem is not of their making!

In the final analysis, simple refusal to work for low pay, slow pay or foul play is the ultimate weapon.

A writer's great booby trap is his or her own eagerness to do a story, just because "it's there," then hope the economics will work out alright. A writer must ask more questions before *starting* a project rather than afterwards.

So we lean from our ivory tower to admit we've too often been guilty ourselves. It's really awfully hard to resolutely walk away from the makings of a darn good story! But it's pretty difficult to go without eating, too!

Chapter 28

Who IS Your Competition?

Struggling to make a living at their trade, freelance business writers often complain about "unfair competition." In fact they sound very much like many of the business people they write about? This "competition" includes "housewives," journalism students, senior citizens, or any others who write for free or for a pittance, often just to see their bylines in print.

These writers also castigate all magazines that chiefly use PR stories or glorified press releases donated by businesses.

The irony about these latter objects of wrath is that many of those same PR pieces or press releases are written by freelance business writers, at prices better than these same magazines would pay for them direct to the writer.

Moreover, one *professional* business-writing freelance will produce more *good* saleable copy in a year than a hundred housewives, journalism students, et al. For 99% of the latter are dabblers and talkers. They spend most of their time daydreaming about writing.

The other one percent are starting on their way to professionalism. And within their first six months they, too, will begin wanting to know "how the hell do you make a buck in this business!"

Real competition is always that factor which actually determines price levels in a given market. Therefore the tough competition for a freelance is actually the staff writer. This includes not only those on magazines, but salaried writers in company PR offices, in PR and ad agencies, or holding governmental and institutional press jobs.

Editors "Empire-Builders" By Nature. Editors tend to collect subordinates on every possible pretext. Once assembled, an editorial staff is fiercely defended against every alternative. To avoid reducing staff, many editors don't hesitate to paint as grim a picture as possible of freelance faults and foibles.

Associated Business Writers of America has conducted a low-key campaign for years to convince editors and publishers that editorial staffs are costly enough to warrant good pay to freelances as a practical alternative.

Typical Case History. Here is analysis of one year's performance by an individual personally known to us. Eddie was a very competent reporter on a magazine termed "the bible of the industry." He's a careful writer. His work requires virtually no editing. Usually every finished article gets printed.

Over twelve months span, Ed produced 147½ pages that appeared in the "book," or 12-plus per monthly issue. This does not include "wash-outs" scrapped for one reason or another. ("Wash-outs" are interviews that didn't jell into stories.)

Of the published work, 21 pages were developed from research at his desk and in the publisher's library. Material for the remaining 126½ pages were obtained on frequent field trips. Working out of New York, he ranged from New Haven, CT to Washington, DC, and west to Milwaukee, Dayton and Louisville.

Ed attended eight conventions. These took a lot of time and energy, produced less good copy in proportion to time consumed than is popularly supposed. But conventions were important to Ed's publisher for their personal contacts, for fresh leads, or for background and sensing new trends. Therefore single-page convention reports are included in the page-count just given. But Eddie also contributed input for editorial policy from his convention contacts.

This reporter traveled by car, bus, rail and air, as proved most convenient. He stayed at decent hotels and motels, ate well, but worked long hours "on the road." He usually made several story calls in intermediate cities between New York and the point farthest out on a trip.

Using a popular press camera (2¼-sq. negatives), Ed also took his own photographs. Selected shots were enlarged to 8x8 or 8x10 size. All photo processing was done outside by a quality commercial photo shop. That year 192 of his pictures were published in the magazine.

In addition, Eddie supplied a dozen sketches (floor plans). To do these drawings carefully in the rough took more time and effort than a photograph. Thus Ed supplied a total 204 illustrations (pix plus sketches).

Cost of A Good Staffer. At the time (1975) Eddie was getting $200 per week or $10,400 for the year.

Fringe benefits in publishing, says U.S. Chamber of Commerce, average 20.8% of payroll—and these *are* true labor costs. So 20% of Eddie's paycheck was $2,080. Overhead support amounted to 10%, by his publisher's estimates. This was for desk space, typewriter, supplies, phone, secretarial and clerical back-up, bookkeeping, personnel work, etc. That's another $1,040. So salary, plus fringes, plus overhead totaled $13,520 for the year.

For the 21 pages of research work, this was the only editorial expense that applied. These pages were 14% of total pages. So 14% of $13,520 equals $1,893. Divided by 21, the cost per research page comes close to $90.

Pages of solid type in this business paper ran to 1,000 words per page. The average, of course, was less because of headings, subheads and artistic white space. A conservative figure is 900 words. On this basis Eddie's research articles, done in the office, cost the publisher 10¢ per word.

The balance of salary, fringes and overhead was $11,627, which applies to copy obtained on Ed's field trips. Also his travel expenses for one year amounted to $3,267. Together these equal $14,894.

Dividing this by the remaining 126½ pages reveals it cost $118 per page to keep Eddie on the road (in 1975).

His pictures cost an average $5 each. This covers film, as well as maintenance, depreciation and insurance on camera and strobe light, plus outside processing. It is based on a ratio of two negatives exposed for every enlargement made which is very conservative.

Pictures, as printed with their captions and surrounding white space, would fill full pages at the rate of four to six per page, if lumped together. It depended on how expansive the editor and publisher felt, and how much they splashed with big pictures.

On a space-occupied basis, Eddie's magazine averaged five pictures to the full page. This was virtually 41 pages out of those remaining 126½. Actual photo cost per page, five times $5, equals $25. This added to wage and travel cost per page of $118 made the publisher's photo cost per page run $143. This was over $28 procurement cost per picture as printed.

Now the remaining pages (85½) include all the body text derived from Eddie's field work. At the $118 page cost, they run the publisher in excess of 13¢ per word.

All this calculation gave the editor of this particular magazine in-house cost standards against which to compare freelance costs:

Cost per field-trip page—$118, or per word—13¢

Cost per research page—$90, or per word—10¢

Cost per photograph as printed—$28

Staffer's "Gross-Hour Rate." To carry this one step further, in comparison with freelance costs, let's work out Eddie's "gross-hour" rate.

Eddie worked 240 days in the year under study. This equals 48 five-day weeks. Part of his overtime and his convention weekends were offset by extra week days off. He also had two weeks vacation, six paid holidays and a four-day illness.

However, not all of Eddie's working hours were directly productive of copy and photographs. He has overhead work, the same as freelances do. There are correspondence, scheduling, setting up appointments, filling out expense reports, office meetings and conferences, business visitors, coffee breaks and maybe a little politicking.

Altogether one-sixth of his time was not devoted directly to producing copy. One-sixth of 240 days is 40 "over-head" days. Subtracted from 240, this gives 200 "productive" days in the whole year for Eddie.

Now add the total cost of his photographs, $960 to salary, fringes and overhead of $13,520 plus travel costs of $2,267. The total is $17,747. Dividing by 200 results in a cost-per-productive day of $88.74. This divided by an eight-hour workday comes down to about $11.09 per hour.

So $11.09 is Eddie's gross-hour rate. And if Eddie kept regular 9-to-5 office hours, his gross-hour rate would work out to about $12.68.

These compare with the $10.40 gross-hour rate needed by freelances to earn Eddie's official salary.

Staffer's Pluses and Minuses. Now—why are many publishers willing to pay more for staff written work, than to use more freelance material.

The staff person is likely to have increasingly better industry knowledge. His or her exposure to the industry is more intensive and more constant than for most freelances.

The staff writer is easier to control and therefore more dependable, having fewer scheduling conflicts.

Identity with the paper is genuine. Behaviour and performance are more easily supervised. Policy and style are better ingrained, show up in first drafts that require less editing.

Finally the staffer is always in training, preparatory for better editorial positions within the organization.

There are negatives, also. When the staff writer goes off the beam, there's tendency to use his or her work anyway, because it's already paid for.

Staff costs tend to raise faster than productivity.

Advancement opportunities are limited, hence turnover tends to be high, and replacement training frequent.

Older staff people settle into biased ruts, lose initiative and alertness.

Freelance Pluses and Minuses. The credit side for freelance use starts with flexibility. Reporters are on the spot already, or near it, a saving of both time and travel cost. They can make callbacks and follow-ups quickly, when necessary (if adequately compensated).

Freelances don't need to be tightly scheduled by editors for cost control, as is generally advisable for staff field trips.

The writer on the spot can arrange interviews to convenience the persons interviewed.

There is wider, better-balanced geographic coverage. Even a casual reader can often identify wholly staff-written magazines by their limited geographic coverage. At least two-thirds of the case histories will concern businesses within 50 to 100 miles of the publication's home offices.

Names of writers on mastheads are not a reliable guide to staff size. Some editors will use one or two stories a year each from six freelances, then list all their names as "associate editors" or "field editors." This supplies geographic coverage as well as an inflated staff image.

But the real pro editor who masters the technique of using freelances operates with a minimal staff. He or she manipulates freelances like an army already stationed in the field, moving them forthrightly to wherever the action is.

To get adequately paid, the freelance writer must produce. But if an assignment proves a genuine washout, cost to the editor is minimal. It is only cost of the nearby freelance's time and expense for exploratory contact, versus the greater cost of sending a staffer to the spot, then having the story blow up in his or her face.

Pro business freelances have better understanding of business per se than do many homegrown staffs subject to the mental incest of a tight little editorial group. The varieties of industries contacted by a freelance provide a perspective much less distorted by one industry's bias, taboos and emotion.

Freelances have no company ambitions. They don't, or they shouldn't ever, get involved in company politics. Company politics are the most costly, time-wasting practice *any* independent journalist can indulge in, unless actually paid for that purpose. To put it bluntly, this is simply involvement with no payback—at least for the writing function.

Flexible Use of Freelances. Finally, independent writers cushion editorial costs. In recessions an editor can cut manuscripts buying proportionally, whereas laying off a staffer must usually be a whole-hog-or-none decision.

Many a shrewd editor *prefers* to work through freelances even when the volume of freelance copy used might seem to warrant putting on another staffer. Such an editor deliberately maintains a *pool* of freelance contributors. Then depending on the depth of a recession, freelance material is pared to fit the exact economics of the moment.

On the other hand, when a staffer is no longer fully utilized during recession, there is continuing question of whether or when to let him or her go. How long will the recession last, and how deep will it slump?

Lay-off is postponed as long as possible, because of loyalty to the individual, because the editor's investment of time and money in that person, and due to increasing levels of severance costs.

To avoid the problem, such an editor doesn't maintain merely a shallow pool of freelances, at one or two stories annually from each. For, if even a brief recession dries up the pool, the freelances scatter quickly to other sources of immediate income. Then the editor as economics improve, has the tedious process of weaning them back, or finding new ones.

But when the editor customarily works in depth with a pool of writers, its level can be lowered substantially without cutting off any key freelance completely. Then, with pipelines still open, though under lowered pressure, it is easy to raise the pressure gradually as economics improve.

Obstacles To Freelance Use. The debit side to freelance use, as editors see it, primarily involves four areas: (a) limited industry knowledge; (b) limited control; (c) unsuitable copy; (d) "haggling."

Industry knowledge is the biggest factor in discrimination between freelance and staff writers. It's also hardest to define!

The specific knowledge required of either staffers or freelances is a middle-ground. It lies north of those good management techniques applying to all business. These techniques are familar to any good pro business writer.

And it lies south of those highly technical aspects about which the editor himself defers to professors, scientists, engineers or highly-trained specialists.

So, however presented, this middle area is basically news. It's detection and proclamation of changes coming or already here. It's analysis of ground swells, with occasional whitecaps that may even belie the force below the surface, until breakers crash on the beach for all to see.

A staffer absorbs industry information by osmosis every hour of the work day. The publication office is a constantly-fed stewpot of information from the industry it serves. Nomenclature, data, power centers and trends settle into the staffer's subconscious, ready to surface on demand.

To compete, the freelance must learn deliberately much of what the staffer absorbs through the skin. Chapter XX deals with this problem of a freelance's self-education.

ABWA A Market-Place. The second problem, limited control, has three elements; (a) locating freelances; (b) contacting them; (c) scheduling.

Associated Business Writers of America came into being partly to serve as a "marketplace" where business editors and business writers could meet. It provides free geographically-arranged membership lists for anyone desirous of locating proven professional *business* writers.

Or ABWA will sell at modest price a membership directory, geographically arranged, with profiles of writers, including their areas of industry knowledge. Unlike many association directories, this is revised annually.

Alternative ways to locate writers are: by referral of other users; by contacting other writer organizations; by compiling a list from ads in various media; by use of various writers' agencies; and by contacting newspaper reporters located in the story areas.

Historically, editors sometimes find even the best-known writers difficult to track down. As with the rest of our population, 20% of all writers move each year. Others change business mail addresses or phone numbers as they re-arrange their working setups.

Moreover freelance writers as a group are more "volatile" than regularly-employed persons. In personal crises, they may drop out of the freelance market, latching onto steady jobs at least until they recoup.

Or a writer gets involved with producing a book or other long-term project that effectively limits availability for extended periods.

Some writers are much more volatile than others, of course. That is, a larger percentage of turnovers involves a smaller number of writers than 20% of the total group.

Yet any list of freelance writers, if not updated regularly, is bound to be at least 50% inaccurate and non-current three years after compilation.

This is why ABWA goes to the added expense of regularly updating its membership list and directory.

Problems of scheduling freelances are, in our opinion, much exaggerated. True, editors do control movements of full-time staffers, whereas assignments must fit into the other commitments of a freelance.

But editors in many multi-publication houses share staffers with seeming equanimity. All it takes is a little advance planning and prompt communication!

Know Editor's Foibles, And Adapt. Third complaint by editors against freelances is unsuitability of copy, as presented.

The standard advice of experts to writing novices, of course, is to study the style of a magazine—then copy that style as faithfully as possible.

Yet I vividly recall my bewilderment over one editor of a well-written magazine. This editor complained, almost bitterly, that certain manuscripts were *so* tightly written that he couldn't blue-pencil *anything* in them without ripping the fabric of the story.

Certain editors do have compulsive need to stamp part of themselves on every bit of copy that sees print, however well and tightly written in the first place.

By contrast, one client using newspaper format printed everything just as it came in. If your copy was rough due to crash deadlines, you braced for shock on opening each new issue. Whole sections of copy would be dropped, or articles even split, for space reasons, without the slightest restructuring or editing for sense and continuity.

Style *is* important to good writing. But far above and beyond style is the need for logical structure and clarity. Make sure the manuscript says what you meant it to say. Be clear about why you said it.

If the story is clear, sound and relevant, you'll sell it regardless of niceties of style.

More on this matter of style was covered in Chapter XI.

Communication Requires Standards And Data. Editors' final complaint about "haggling" with freelances is quite justified, on the surface. They refer to an excessive amount of accusations, recriminations, name-calling, even threats of legal suit.

An editor/writer rhubarb can become bitterly emotional on both sides, to the point of paranoia in editors and writers alike.

But a very large part of the hassling is entirely unnecessary!

The problem is lack of real communication. This in turn stems from almost complete lack of understanding by either side, of the other's needs and working circumstances.

Most editors have never freelanced to the point of being completely dependent on their own productivity for a living. And fewer publishers have been freelance writers in that same sense.

Likewise few freelance business writers have served in full-time editorial capacities, as dependent "organization" men and women, subject to direction by a publisher or department manager.

By-and-large most writers *and* editors want to be fair and honorable. Problem is that few on either side really know "what's par for the course."

Very often ABWA has served as informal arbiter between an editor and a writer deadlocked over some issue. Almost invariably a lack of communication is exposed. And this lack most often stems from neither party's knowing what to communicate about, or the basis for such communication.

Therefore another major reason for the existence of Associated Business Writers of America is trying to establish a "par for the course."

ABWA strives to arrive at acceptable standards of dealing— standards understood and accepted as reasonable and practical by writers and editors alike.

Then, as these standards are arrived at, ABWA attempts to communicate them as quickly, widely and clearly as possible.

A major purpose in writing this book has been to set forth the opportunities and strictures of freelance writing *and* of business paper editing vis-a-vis freelances. Hopefully the book will become a basis for sound communication between them.

Even though a given writer or editor does not agree with the author's conclusions, either will be able to assert more clearly any point or principle about which they disagree. They can describe that with which they disagree.

That alone is real progress!

Chapter 29

Retainers, Sustainers and Sidelines

Business papers are a common source of retainers. Many so-called "editors" or "columnists" on business papers are actually freelances on contract, retainer or guarantee. This is true also of the many specialty editors by-lined in newspapers, consumer house organs or consumer magazines.

The more successful freelance *business* writers I'm in touch with, the more I realize most have sustainers of some kind. "Sustainers" are steady clients or continuing projects that provide the writer a dependable financial base. Sustainers usually cover at least the writer's "nut" or fixed overhead expenses.

Sustainers Pro And Con. The most comfortable and compatible sustainer, of course, is several editors or clients who buy predictable amounts of your wordage each month at profitable rates.

Several times I've achieved this idyllic equilibrium for shorter or longer periods. Whenever economics got tough, these clients may have clamped down a lot in their buying, but they rarely shut me off entirely.

This is "comfortable" because your eggs are in several baskets. Inevitably one editor quits, gets transferred or promoted, or becomes involved with a drastically new editorial policy (often imposed by the publisher). But when his "Dear John" letter comes, the writer who serves a cluster of clients is not left staring into an empty basket. He or she still has sufficient cash flow to remain solvent while scrabbling to replace the defecting editor.

When The "Plug Is Pulled." A fellow writer, who edited a prestigious house organ, had it snatched away through a sudden major policy reversal by his client's management. He was actually doing an excellent job. But the client wanted that money for a different new project. (Incidentally, after demise of that house organ, the organization went steadily downhill!)

Meanwhile over half this writer's income disappeared overnight. And one rarely finds a replacement overnight.

Three different times I myself have fallen into this trap (you'd think I'd learn) of letting one account pre-empt my time. I didn't actively cultivate these three particular sustainers. But each gradually enveloped me, because the work was so challenging and different. Each time in my enthusiasm I came to the point of doing little else.

In *each* instance I failed to assess whether I was getting involved in a program of potential durability or a short-term one-shot project.

Each time, when the plug was pulled, I suddenly found myself entirely out of touch with former markets and editors. I had to start my random article writing from scratch all over again. When a writer abandons regular clients, they rarely await his or her return! After any writer's desertion it's inevitably a new ballgame.

So, though not *a* sustainer strictly speaking, the cluster of magazine editors or clients is mentioned first because it's well worth cultivating. There's safety in numbers. The deterrent usually is need to inform oneself on more industries and disciplines, and deal with conflicts in scheduling.

It is a big mistake, moreover, to feel a particular cluster is permanent. They *never* are. Yet many writers tend to feel hurt or affronted when a cluster goes sour. Change *is* the biggest factor in *our* way of life. We might just as well accept it, get used to it first as last, and learn to cope profitably.

What's A Good Balance. Most writers who lean on a single big account for a sustainer never develop the cluster. There is neither the time nor the imperative to do so. This is not bad, but has its drawbacks, as our friend learned with the prestigious house organ.

The late Donley Lukens always insisted *no* client should represent more than a third of a writer's income, but that it's smart to try to build two accounts to a total of 40% of income. This is to assure coverage of the nut.

Of course, a writer is never likely to reject a major client's assignments simply because they dominate his or her time. But it's important to retain awareness of one's vulnerability and to not entirely lose touch with other markets.

To build a cluster, the writer develops a semblance of expertise in each field. Then, to keep the material flowing steadily, he or she probably has to cover a sizable geographic area, or else find disciplines latent with plenty of new raw material. A small or local work area usually calls for a mix of magazine editors and businesses as clients.

Frankly, I myself have been able to maintain fully-editorial clusters only when ranging widely from home base, or even barnstorming a sizable section of the country. I find that after a few months of intensive dredging, the quality/quantity of material from one type of business in a given locale always peters out.

Retainers A Mixed Blessing. A "retainer" is a flat fee paid monthly regardless of activity or wordage produced per month. It may or may not include extra pay for wordage over an agreed-on quota.

The primary purpose of retainers is to eliminate constant accounting between editor and writer. Another function is to assure an editor priority or exclusive use of the writer's service.

Hence the writer on retainer is somewhat restricted in time and movement, though little more than he or she would be if on a tight self-imposed schedule of random writing.

But there is more pressure when, in the midst of producing a hot article for someone else, an urgent phone call requires you to drop everything and handle a retainer job at once.

When thus firmly committed, a stringer or retained-writer sometimes has to push through a weak story for the client, while watching a juicy story in another field slip by untouched for lack of time.

Moreover, the *writer* is never really freed of accounting work by being on retainer! Un-monitored and uncontrolled retainer-work follows Parkinson's law. No matter how much time is contracted for, retainer-work tends to fill all the time a writer has available.

Take the one matter of background reading. If you have an account that averages one week's work per month, say, you read most of every issue of that magazine, and you at least scan its major competitors. Your background reading tends to be just as great as though you were a full-time employee, because you are expected to be immersed in that industry. You must be ready to cover every assignment knowledgeably.

If working in several industries by random writing, however, your background reading may be spread thinner, but the time investment isn't so vulnerable if you lose the account. You just don't take non-retainer assignments in areas beyond your ken. I have spent two days researching background on a retainer-assigned story that should have taken half-a-day if I had already had expertise in the area!

If I hadn't been on retainer, I would have passed up the assignment as unprofitable.

Once that research is done, of course, you do have broader knowledge on which to base future writing.

Keep A Log On Retainer. But if the writer doesn't keep a log of time spent earning his retainer, he or she is likely to wind up wondering why there's never time enough for other work. A log measures the effect of Parkinson's Law.

From a writer's viewpoint, if the editor has work enough for you to warrant a retainer, there's no real need for one. Hourly compensation, space rates or per-article rates will generate more revenue in the long run for the same work, with less concern about when to blow the whistle on the editor for overtime.

Above all, the retainer must reflect the writer's expenses. I once did an easy monthly "column" at modest pay for a small magazine, apparently to their complete satisfaction. But when local material ran dry, they would not underwrite even a little travel expense (50-mile radius instead of 25 miles). So the column had to be terminated.

Sometimes, however, wordage is of less importance than your presence in a geographic area. A New York paper, for instance, may desire a Chicago or Kansas City editor, because a major competitor is published there. In such a case a log serves to keep tabs on actual hours spent at meetings, advertiser functions, etc., that actually generate little wordage.

Getting To Edit Small Publications. Probably the sustainer most common to business writers is editing or producing house organs, newsletters, bulletins or information services. Their clients are business firms (large or small); trade associations; consulting firms; foundations; professional, fraternal and special organizations; civic units; unions; schools; libraries; churches; etc. A new, rapidly-growing category of clients is the managements of shopping centers, building complexes and "new cities."

Most such jobs come through personal contacts, reference by people who already know your ability, background and availability.

Make Availability Known. However, *making your availability known is critically important.* Even your *closest* business acquaintances *do not know or understand what you do,* anywhere near as much as you think they do. Or just as likely they assume all your time is already spoken for. That's another axiom.

Never, when you have some time to fill, be too shy or too proud to circularize or to phone former business associates and contacts. Tell them you're available, that you are looking for solid clients. You might be surprised how often they know of a part-time slot begging to be filled by someone of your caliber.

I myself am much more quick than formerly to hand my

business card to anyone who'll take it, describing briefly what I do.

Moreover, I've gotten over the novice writer's tendency to cloak myself as reporter for whatever client I represent at the time (inferring I'm on the staff). Now I declare myself a freelance at the earliest reasonable opportunity.

That is, if on retainer, I say, "I'm the reporter from *Goober News*." If on assignment I say "The editor of *Goober News* asked me to see you. If a story is on speculation "I'm seeking a story (or some information) for a goober publication." Then at the first logical opportunity, I clarify my status.

Advertising in newspapers for sustainer or for random writing work has been a "sometime thing" for me! It draws mostly requests in the month of May to do college theme papers and theses at minimal rates. (Perhaps I haven't written the right kinds of ads). Incidentally, it's illegal in many states to ghost-write themes and theses.

Small display ads in a newspaper's business section, in Chamber of Commerce bulletins, or regional business magazines may be more fruitful. In any case, the more choices of potential assignments one generates, the better one's chance is to upgrade accounts and total income over the long run.

This is in contrast to simply waiting for assignments to float in over the transom. It is easy to be complacent just because one is busy, without regard to *real* hourly earnings or potential for increasing them.

Research And Feasibility Studies. A by-product of much article writing and association bulletin writing has been, for me at least, an occasional interesting and profitable research project. These are usually on the order of "feasibility studies."

Usually such an assignment comes because a busy executive is confronted with a project, a problem, or a new discipline, about which he knows little, but which he must learn a lot in a great hurry. Maybe his organization or company has proposed moving in a new direction. So the executive wants *some* inkling of the kind of booby traps they might encounter.

If he's been exposed to a good pro freelance writer, this executive realizes here's a guy or gal who by training and experience is already an investigator, researcher and report writer all rolled up in one. (Sometimes, of course, this executive may need nudging to realize the fact.)

For instance, a firm acquired the rights (in a merger) to a machine completely outside the scope of its traditional field. I was asked to nose around and see what possible uses this machine might have, what its market potential might be.

A first broad study led to optimistic findings. It prompted a second more exhaustive study in answer to specific questions pinpointed by the executive. The answers I then dug up convinced him the firm would be justified in assigning scientists and engineers to the project. At that point I gracefully bowed out.

For a trade association I did extensive research in quality control by the aerospace and defense industries. Purpose was to extract basic techniques that small businesses could use. Then I prepared bulletins and finally a seminar on the subject.

A large trucking company found its bill-of-landing grown so complex and involved in usage, that half its employees were ignorant of its full function. I was retained simply to follow its multiple copies every step of the way, then describe all steps in detail. This was for their internal use only, 72 pages of double-space typing. A resulting brochure was used in training new employees who would be involved in any way with the bill-of-lading.

Another firm had me line up all points of common interest and those areas of conflict between its field and another industry. This in response to a suddenly proposed merger with a firm in the other industry.

A trade association had me explore what was involved in setting up a "data utility"—a computer-based library expected to receive and store the total input from a complex industry.

When the new marketing department in another trade association appeared to be non-productive after two years operation, I was asked simply to observe what was actually happening and make a report. There proved to be no effective means of communication to the top executive. So the marketing director was virtually in limbo. Here is a case where my major qualification was being an outsider not pre-conditioned by routine and politics within the organization, yet reasonably knowledgeable about good business management.

For a state association, I wrote a presentation to the state sales tax commission on possible industry exemptions. This was after careful study of the law and after conference with industry leaders. Their legislative committee made the actual verbal presentation without me. My work was for the record with the sales tax commission.

During a long Northeast drouth in the mid-Sixties, I did crash research on water conservation for a state association, wrote a lengthy series of reports, helped stave off severe state regulation of water use by that industry.

A recent assignment was exploring the potential for solar energy in one industry. Speeches on the topic at state conventions led to the chore of arranging a workshop at that industry's national convention.

"Expertise" developed in that research has subsequently welled up in articles and assignments involving solar energy for other associations and magazines.

Who Needs Feasibility Studies? Okay, all these examples are enumerated to show they have several things in common. Recognizing these factors, the writer may sometimes be able to sell his or her services on similar projects. Note the following:

(1) Each incident represented a very urgent need.

(2) Each situation had been thrust on an overburdened executive, usually with an overburdened staff.

(3) Each was too temporary in nature to warrant adding another person to the staff.

(4) Yet each situation was complex enough to call for professional ability to research, analyse and report in concise, orderly fashion.

I might add that in every instance, only moderate knowledge of the client's basic industry was necessary, beyond good general knowledge of business practices. None of the reports required excessive technical sophistication. They simply helped clients decide whether to dig deeper, and if so, in what direction.

As one executive put it, "Just give me a good toehold—I can take it from there."

Help With Excess Workloads. In similar vein, I've collaborated with four technical men and women in writing, editing and producing "how to" books under their by-lines.

For a monthly magazine, I've prepared extensive editorial copy and photos for a "13th issue," an annual directory. This was part original researched copy, part editing of contributed material.

Several ABWA members help magazine editors produce "convention-daily" newspapers. (I've never happened to get involved with one.) But I do know they require a pro who can get copy fast and accurately under pressure.

These convention-daily assignments come from prior contact with an editor, through the ABWA directory, or from careful cultivation of the convention bureau in your city. Or the printer in your city who processes these convention dailies may give your name to his clients.

For a local association, I collected and arranged material on basic management principles for seminars suited to small mom-n-pop shops—twelve sessions in all. This stemmed from having served for a couple years as "secretary and moderator" of two small management groups of non-competing business men in a particular industry. That in turn had come from preparing monthly management bulletins for another association.

Many Other Sidelines. Two manufacturers, in different industries, had me prepare case-history-type articles. These they or their PR agencies placed in business papers too small to pay the freight themselves.

Mostly through association connections, I have ghosted articles and speeches—sometimes as many as six speeches for one convention. On one occasion I prepared only the outline notes—so the speakers could more comfortably deliver them in their own style.

Formal presentations have been prepared of entries in special contests, for individuals as well as businesses and associations. For example, a small association entered a contest for the best new program in the past year (which happened to be a pension program for member firms). I prepared the copy and exhibits that made up their presentation. It was a winner, on strength of the program, not necessarily because of my presentation. But *somebody* had to perform this chore; and the association executive just didn't have time to do it.

Skits, roleplays and videotape scripts have been developed for employee training, consumer education and convention programs. In most of these I didn't need to know the technical information, I simply did the verbalizing, in collaboration with experts.

Syndication Is An Art In Itself. One time, too, I laid a real fat egg! I tried to syndicate a series on quality control for a variety of small businesses. Despite rampant consumerism, my brand of quality control info apparently didn't go over with editors. Or else I didn't persist long enough.

"Syndication" is selling an identical article to non-competing magazines in different fields. It *is* a valid sustainer. Several business writers are quite successful at it.

You must have, or develop, a special knowledge that can be applied in many industries. You also need to go through a long, patient, unprofitable period of assembling a group of consistent users of your column or series of articles. Once assembled, they usually stay with you reasonably faithfully. Their turnover's moderate.

They will, that is, so long as you supply fresh or useful material every month, week, or whatever period promised or contracted for.

You don't try to make a killing at syndication, but give editors solid meat at moderate cost. You price it out realistically to return you the hourly billing rate set for yourself, to cover all necessary hours put into the syndication.

As an additional sideline, I've done straight photography: for legal evidence; for sales brochure on a hotel; for a training manual already written by a technician; for 280 ID cards; for several educational seminars; for illustration of those four technical books referred to earlier; and to accompany convention speeches made by others.

All of these involved little or no original writing on my part. Most were black-and-white. Some were color. Several jobs involved color slides. On one occasion I did research on conveyorization in one industry, prepared some 60 color slides, and made a full report at its annual convention.

When Is An Employee A Freelance? Of course, most orthodox sustainers really are, or verge on, part-time jobs: Editing and reporting; PR; Advertising copy; Training or teaching; Book reviews; Manuscript screening; Phone and door-to-door surveys, etc.

The line between freelance and employee blurs easily. Technically you're an employee if the payor deducts taxes, social security or fringe benefits. A freelance is paid a flat fee, plus expenses on occasion, but assumes all responsibility for personal taxes and fringes.

Yet one association always insisted on deducting taxes, etc., from my fees, though I worked for them very irregularly, was paid by the hour, and invoiced them for time and expenses. I was also issued a W-2 for IRS purposes.

Multiple Sales Don't Just Happen. Multiple sales from a single interview are not exactly a sideline or sustainer. But they do add revenue. Yet most business writers have "tunnel vision" in respect to opportunities to do this effectively, including this author!

One-track-minded writers like me miss many chances to convert material obtained for business stories into articles for consumer magazines, and vice versa. They overlook ways to convert parts of a major article to shorticles for other markets, etc.

The most fruitful fields in which to do this are sports, recreation, travel and hobbies. The latter include anything that lends itself to a "do-it-yourself" project.

When the writer of a business column in our regional newspaper died suddenly, I briefly and unsuccessfully negotiated to handle this freelance. The modest retainer I proposed was "shockingly high." (The column has since disappeared entirely).

But this struck me as one good way to underwrite some expenses while running down story leads around Middlesex and Somerset Counties. I still think such an arrangement would be a sound sustainer.

Summing Up. To sum up, sustainers are helpful or necessary under several conditions:

1. When one's logical territory is too small to support a full-time random-article writing career, say less than 100,000 population within a 25-mile radius;
2. When one's background, knowledge or experience is too limited to readily handle a wide range of topics in a diverse array of industries;
3. When one's health or physical limitations prescribe limited "field" activity;
4. When a sense of relative security bolsters one's overall effectiveness. This factor definitely must not be discounted. Worry over finances does affect your attitude on interviews. It nibbles at your concentration when writing. It is senseless to weaken one's efficiency with such mental drain, if it can be honorably avoided.

Sustainer And Sideline Promoting. To ferret out such sustainers or jobs, one can advertise in local papers and file with temporary help agencies. But be specific as to type of work desired. Otherwise you get all kinds of "junk" proposals, such as the themes and theses at penny rates and questionable ethical values, as described earlier.

Much more effective in the long run, though more laborious, is to make up a mailing list to be repeatedly circularized. You can get most of the names from the classified phone directory. Select only those firms or prospects' names and addresses that appear to be in reasonable driving distance (25 or 35 miles?).

Include newspaper editors, advertising agencies, PR counsellors, sales managers of business firms, consulting outfits, the convention bureau, chamber of commerce, trade associations, fraternal organizations.

Circularize these places with a form letter. List briefly what you can do or wish to do. State specific functions, rather than say you'll "do anything." Give the briefest biography, enough to show you're a pro. Invite queries for more information.

Make it simple but neat. Don't shoot your wad making it elaborate. You will want to repeat the mailing, sometimes with revised material.

Best of all, try to distribute these pieces personally the first time around. Sometimes you get a trial assignment on an initial personal contact. The client might not have thought to initiate a contact. But suddenly, since you're there, he or she will decide to give you a try. For almost everyone has *some* nagging writing chore he or she wants to get out of the way, having procrastinated for a long time.

In any case, once personal contact is made, you have a name to address for future mailings, or even a person to phone.

Make Talks, Use Slide Shows. Another way to get your name and talents known is to prepare a talk on some phase of business which has fairly broad appeal. Offer to make this presentation at all organizational meetings that directly or indirectly involve business people (chamber of commerce, rotary, junior executives, sales management groups, etc.) Their program chairmen are *always* desperate for new topics.

For example, on your rounds in the area you cover, take color slides of striking new or remodeled store fronts. From the owner of each get basic details of construction, reasons for particular design, comments on effectiveness, costs if possible. Then organize these into a talk that seems to develop specific points.

Other talks could involve landscaping, show rooms, loading docks, stock control, conveyor or pallet management, employee benefits and facilities, uniforms, etc.

Don't hesitate to include conflicting philosophies. *You* don't have to judge or to be authority. You simply show them a slice of business life that truly interests them. Let *them* criticize and evaluate. I'll guarantee the discussion afterwards will be lively, especially if conflict was developed clearly.

A by-product of such talks will be spin-off articles and plentiful local leads, both from discussion and from business people who approach you after each talk.

Don't forget to hand out business cards liberally, and circulars if you have them. Conclude your talk with a brief "commercial."

Book Is Ultimate Sustainer. Finally, the ultimate sustainer is to write a book. As our society gets more and more complex, there is steadily increasing need for simple "how to" manuals and booklets of all kinds. Every year a new crop of beginners in every industry and discipline needs help in learning their trades.

So look for an area without useful beginner's information. Or note those with instruction material that is obsolete, or too abstruse and complicated for beginners. If you think 5,000 copies might sell there—go to it. A small simple book may break even at 2,000 or 3,000 copies.

Remember, the technical experts are usually expected to write basic texts. Most experts, however, have forgotten what it's like to be a beginner. Freelance business writers can often fill the gap!

Of course, books really aren't true sustainers until you have a couple out and already trickling back some royalties. You'll need capital to live on while writing the first ones. Or you produce them in tag-ends of time and by midnight oil, while making a living otherwise.

On the other hand, books can be written when there's a lull in article writing, or for a change of pace, or to glean further revenue from information already gathered, or when the highway is drifted in snow—if you can but discipline yourself to do it.

For making books your sustainers is the most demanding in their need of "seat-of-pants-to-seat-of-chair" self-discipline. Like a farmer's span from spring-planting to fall-harvest. It's usually a long, long time to the final pay-off!

Chapter 30

Travel or Stay Put?

"May I respectfully inquire," wrote Bart Rawson, then editor of *Commercial Car Journal,* "Where the Hell are you?"

It didn't help much to report we were in Miami on a rush assignment. For earlier we'd written Bart from Biloxi that our next stop would be Houston! And he wanted us to swing up later to Dallas and Tulsa ("since we were in the area!")

Which points up one fallacy about this being the "carefree gypsy life" for which wandering journalists are so envied. You either keep in *very* close contact with your editors, or you miss good assignments. It can be tedious detail work. But not doing the work can be fatal.

If a writer-on-the-go depends on assignments, then any itinerary and timetable announced to editors or clients usually ought to be followed reasonably closely. When revision is necessary, advise your editors promptly, whether it's timing *or* destination that's affected.

Otherwise your frequent unpredictability can cause editors to ignore in toto all your professed itineraries. One cross an editor won't bear too long is spending time and effort to line up leads or assignments for a writer, then have that worthy give them the brush or ignore them entirely.

Editors do not have inexhaustible reservoirs of good leads. Each assignment handed out must be weighed as to its promise of suitable material in the hands of the particular writer to whom that lead is given. Therefore it's real easy to ignore writers whom experience has proven will abandon itineraries at a whim without warning.

"Barnstorming" vs "Stringing." Should one travel widely, "barnstorming" for material, or is it better to stick close to home base, building up a "stringer" business? A "Stringer" is a freelance regularly providing editors with part-time local coverage, usually on agreement to "represent" them news-wise in his or her area.

Business writers who *can* choose often find it hard to decide. And somehow, after the choice is made, the other side of the fence always beckons.

So one must first recognize that barnstorming is entirely different from local coverage. The economics aren't the same. Editor/writer relationships differ. Work methods are dissimilar, even reversed in many cases. Marketing and cost control in barnstorming have little relationship to the same in stringer operation.

Even as a way of life, barnstorming and local coverage appeal to different temperaments. Their values also vary according to a writer's economic and family circumstances.

Five Years Barnstorming. For instance, over a 5½-year span in the Fifties (*now* recalled with nostalgia) we lived in a 28-foot travel trailer. Except for four permanently-stored cartons, all our material possessions were in or attached to our mini-home-on-wheels.

During those 273 weeks, we stopped at 27 different cities and major towns. Lengths of stay ranged from one night to ten months, averaging six weeks. We did return to several places more than once.

From our various temporary "homes" we worked an additional 35 nearby cities and towns. At almost every stop our stay stretched out longer than planned, as we kept turning up fresh story material.

We roamed below the 40th parallel, roughly from the Mason-Dixon Line to eastern Kansas, and south to the Gulf of Mexico. Our concentration on this South-eastern quadrant was for three practical reasons.

First, there are many Southern sectional magazines. These increased our potential market for manuscripts, in each industry about which we were knowledgeable at the time. They provided secondary markets for material not suitable to, or rejected by, primary national publications.

This was important. For we could not depend on assignment, except from key editors whose assignments generally determined our itinerary. Otherwise we were moving too fast for the somewhat time-consuming process of generating solid assignments.

So we "bird-dogged" much of our own material as we went, submitting our articles on speculation for the most part.

Only 15% of our work, therefore, was on assignment. Yet we sold over 90% of our manuscripts. This was possible because we were thoroughly familiar with our regular markets.

Most of the unsold 10% of articles were from probes into fields with which we were less familiar.

Secondly, all the South at that time (late Fifties) was in the throes of rapid modernizing and industrializing. Yet freelance business writers were still sparse throughout the old Confederacy. Therefore several national editors were receptive to at least token

Southern coverage, simply to widen their geographical representation.

Thirdly, living costs at that time were still modest across most of the South. Yet national business papers were largely in the North. So writing income paid at the higher Northern scale stretched much farther in the South than in the North.

Moving With The Seasons. We moved with the seasons. Our program was to "summer" in an upper tier state (Tennessee, Virginia, Kansas), then "winter" in some deep-South city (New Orleans, Biloxi, Orlando). Spring and fall we worked north and south in easy stages.

But not consistently! Leisurely-paced Biloxi proved so delightful, we overstayed beyond all practicality for ten months in a trailer park directly overlooking the Gulf. (Always a breeze, even when it was oven-like 200-yards inland).

Local story sources were soon exhausted. So we expensively "commuted" from Biloxi to New Orleans, Mobile, Montgomery and Pensacola for fresh copy.

On another occasion, a long sojourn in Topeka near Hazel's relatives forced me to commute to Kansas City, Omaha and Wichita for story material.

Later Nashville became our medical center, after a couple of operations necessitating frequent check-ups. So, as we repeatedly worked back toward Nashville, we would load up enroute with notes and negatives from several cities.

Then we'd settle down to two or three months writing and photo enlarging in the Tennessee capital. While we were out "on the road," Dickerson Trailer Park faithfully held our favorite "pad" open for us, by parking only transients on it in our absence.

We didn't always write on location. And sometimes we made a jump of several hundred miles. Therefore we had to be sure of our material. Before leaving each city, all negatives had to be developed, and all interview notes expanded and checked out. A deficiency in either would delay take-off long enough to retake pictures or fill out the notes.

Thus there was often that tense time, on the final night in each city, when the last roll of film came out of the developing tank. Not until it was inspected could we say positively that an early-morning start was "go" or "no go."

Such was our idylic gypsy life!

Caution About Trailering. However, a word of caution before the reader closes the deal on that travel trailer. This way of life was practical for us *only* because we had no house, no apartment, to support or worry about.

When we bought the trailer, we relinquished a comfortable but expensive Westchester apartment. We sold practically all our furniture accumulated over several years. There was real trauma and tears over parting with favorite pieces, the piano, a considerable library, etc.

But we had found ourselves spending less and less time in the apartment, more and more time in motels on the road. Too often we felt constrained to return several hundred miles, simply to write at home because of the rent we were paying there.

Why Roam Anyway? The great advantage in roaming, for the business writer, is the capability of selling more manuscripts to fewer markets, due to the wider geographic spread. This in turn requires knowledge of fewer different fields. As a writer you also gain much broader perspective and deeper knowledge of each field.

We found familiarity with at least six markets (kinds of business), in which editors consume articles rather omniverously, is required. Either a single editor takes most of your output in his field, or several editors in one field collectively sop up this output. That was twelve markets for the two of us.

The writer needs to be skillful at "bird-dogging," i.e., rapidly and methodically nosing out leads or prospective stories in a strange territory.

A knack for organizing small work-spaces, or of adapting and adjusting to motel rooms, tourist homes, etc., is quite important.

A vital personality requirement is the ability to withstand or cope with "anomie." This is that very lonesome feeling of total unrelatedness to one's surroundings. There are times when one feels that "Gee, I could run off this mountain curve and *nobody* would ever miss me!"

The flow of material has to be steady, regardless of working conditions. Nor can the writer succumb, so frequently as tempted, to diversion with sight-seeing and tourism (unless able to convert these to articles for travel magazines). Sight-seeing hours usually coincide with work hours. If too many of the latter are unproductive, a writer's cashflow dwindles dangerously.

This way of life is not for a family with school-age children. A temporary exception is barnstorming during a lengthy vacation, mixing business with pleasure. But even this tends to be too strenuous for a writer who really *needs* the vacation.

We ourselves have found that in the long run the mixed vacations just don't pay off. The only exceptions are when a business trip takes you to an area where you haven't been before. Then it pays to get the business out of the way, before turning with a free mind to your sight-seeing.

Chain Stores and Shopping Centers. Roving without assignments depends on scooping up, almost on the run, a lot of quickly-detected story material.

Up through the Fifties this was not too difficult to do. The majority of businesses were small. Many businessmen were uninhibited and highly innovative. You saw the boss immediately, got down to business in a very few minutes.

But chain operations and massive shopping centers have changed all this. Every non-routine act by an outlet manager must be cleared with each chain's home office. So first the writer declares his purpose to the outlet manager. Then the latter repeats the story over the phone to a district manager, who may have to check with three vice-presidents—and even the board of directors, on occasion.

Moreover chain operations are so stereotyped that innovations, whether good or bad, are more and more difficult to find. This means that in any given shopping area, the ratio of potential new ideas or concepts is much lower than prevailed 25 years ago.

So today, even the Palmers, with their past successful experience in barnstorming, would be cautious about roaming at large without at least a solid core of assignments.

The Planned Trip. Barnstorming has largely given way to extended organized trips out from one's permanent home base. For instance, the late Howard Fogel, a New York bachelor with an itchy foot, regularly criss-crossed the country in a series of field trips. And many business writers make sectional tours, often so regularly that their editors get to depend on them.

In setting up such a trip, the general procedure is to write, phone or visit a few editors who know your work, or whom you possibly can impress with your credentials. You supply these editors with a tentative itinerary and timetable.

You ask for: (1) firm assignments that can be fitted into the itinerary like stepping stones; and (2) leads for possible stories. You make clear the leads may be bypassed if you fall behind on your solid assignments.

An itinerary is usually built in two stages. You start with two or three major assignments as "bench marks." That is, these will determine the key stops on your trip.

You then contact those editors whom past experience has proven most fruitful with assignments and leads. The idea is to try to cover time and expenses for each leg of the trip as though that leg were a trip by itself.

A Sample Itinerary. For instance, assume a home base in Philadelphia. You nail down solid assignments in Detroit, Tulsa and New Orleans. Anticipated payment for these assignments will pay at least your travel expenses via these three cities.

Now you approach favorite editors for assignments or leads enroute. These often are not directly between your key cities, but involve wide swings. So you might fill in stops for an itinerary that reads: Detroit, Milwaukee, Cincinnati, St. Louis, Kansas City, Tulsa, Shreveport, New Orleans, Memphis, Knoxville and Roanoke.

Now payment for your assignment in St. Louis should cover time and expenses between Cincinnati and St. Louis, as well as time in the latter city, plus writing time on that assignment wherever the writing is done.

The Memphis assignment likewise ought to absorb travel cost from New Orleans plus time in Memphis. And so on.

Of course it never works out that neatly! But by concentration on filling the gaps in planning your itinerary, it is possible to better control the expense/revenue ratios, than if the writer simply takes off after receiving two or three farflung assignments.

Leave Some "Cushions." Good economics require the time-table be as tight as possible. Yet time cushions are needed, for delayed flights, for icy driving, or whatever. Best places for these time cushions are just in advance of each assignment.

If you are good at bird-dogging, you may want to allow an extra day or two in each city for scrounging up whatever stories come to hand. While always a gamble, if it does pay off, you wind up with a better ratio of sales to travel expenses. But schedules must be maintained. Assignments *must* be fulfilled, even though it means leaving behind a really juicy story, in order to honor your agreement with an editor.

Howard Fogel told of his bus being immobilized for an hour by street construction. He noticed an unusual drug store window, hopped off, got a story, and was back on the bus in time to resume his journey.

Yet even with the tightest schedule, you must add one day in seven for contingencies or for a "sabbath." On extended trips, such breaks are necessary to wipe out cumulative fatigue, even though no emergencies arise. If you travel on a weekend, you need a day off during the week, or you go stale and make increasingly serious mistakes.

Most Writers Stay Put. The greatest asset of the writer who stays close to home is dependability. Editors know that at any given time the stay-home writer's locality can be covered quickly and competently.

Scheduling is much less arduous for local writers than for the wanderer. If a story hasn't matured when first contact is made, the interview can be postponed, several times if necessary. Or the writer can do follow-up stories as a project progresses.

Local contacts are built up year by year, until the writer has a wide web of individuals whom he feels free to call on for background information, and for technical guidance too, if need be. Moreover these contacts often feed the writer leads that might be missed otherwise.

In addition, it is from these contacts that all kinds of sideline writing and/or editing assignments come. These are aside from business paper writing.

The ratio of travel time to interview and writing time is less for local reporters than for roamers. Hence lower total fees are acceptable as adequate compensation for the writer with modest travel expense.

The opportunity for local writers to query editors in advance of in-depth interviews assures a higher level of acceptability for stories. However, I have often phoned editors about story possibilities uncovered while enroute between stops. Avoidance of a single major reject can compensate for a lot of phone calls.

Retainers are not exclusive to local stringers. *Some* roaming writers are able to arrange retainers or permanent travel advances, *after* they establish a relationship of mutual confidence with an editor.

Such retainers are most often supplied to travelling writers who serve as sectional or regional correspondents or "editors." They are "local" in the sense they cover the same territory repeatedly and frequently. For several years, for instance I maintained an almost-monthly circuit from Washington, D.C., to Boston, from a Central Jersey base.

Local Business Writers Need More Markets. Major drawback to local operation is necessity to be familiar with many more industries, than when "on the road." This is because the local story material in one industry in rapidly exhausted. Only exception is when something spectacular and ongoing springs up in a locality. And that, my friend, is a true serendipity for a writer!

If a local freelance writer is shrewd in marketing, a reasonable living can be made by one such writer out of an area population of 35,000. Such skill would be rare, of course, and probably more profitably employed in a larger market.

However, a reasonable rule-of-thumb is that every 50,000 population will support a full-time pro freelance business writer. That is, a metropolitan area of 300,000 will support six full-time freelance pros.

This allows for nibbling in the market by housewives, senior citizens and journalism students, plus occasional forays into the area by roaming journalists.

At the time we ourselves were barnstorming, we could quickly tell which communities were being adequately mined by a professional freelance. One of the first comments we'd make to a prospective interviewee would be that we hadn't seen his story angle featured anywhere, and thought it should be (which was true, of course).

So, after the third or fourth prospect in a row said, "Oh, yeah, sure, we were in the National Weekly," or whatever, we knew we were in for tough digging.

But all local writers find some industries more compatible to them than others. We always were able to plow enough ground to pay our way. There would be four or five of the twelve industries we knew best between us that weren't sufficiently covered by local writers.

In seven years of barnstorming we were never completely blanked out of any city. That is, we always found enough to pay for our time there. Hence we feel safe in declaring no local writer, however professional, ever really plumbs a local business writing market to its fullest depths.

Finally, as the local writer gets more solid in his locality, the area of his coverage can be steadily shrunk, unless he *likes* to run around. Or as usually happens, the writer on a solid base can become more selective about clients and more demanding about even the local travel expenses.

Chapter 31

Tools of the Trade

Literary classics have been scribbled on scratch paper in dusky tavern corners. Live battlefield accounts blurt from battered typewriters teetered on upended cartridge cases. Vivid biography slips from lonely prison cells on toilet tissue.

Successful writing is not dependent on fancy tools of the trade. Yet many a "literally" career is vainly spent re-arranging barely-used furniture about sterile workspaces, in desperate hope a germ of creativity will somehow be miraculously born.

Poor workmen blame their tools! Good workmen acquire and maintain only those tools best suited to their needs. Whatever is unnecessary is ignored, or better yet disposed of, lest it get in the way.

Human Robots Have Problems. Engineers have made a fetish of the perfect workspace that requires the fewest possible unproductive moves by a worker. With stop-watch and tape-measure, they figure the fewest steps, the shortest reaches, the least body twists and turns.

Then the bosses fume over constant employee visits to restrooms, unnecessary trips to the tool room or stock shelf, frequent smoke and coffee breaks.

Immobility is contrary to human nature. The heart pumps our blood, but physical movement also helps to circulate it. Even in our sleep, physiologists tell us, we change position repeatedly throughout the night, partly to stir sluggish blood.

Hence, if you engineer a job-site *so* compactly that most of the body becomes semi-immobilized, an almost-explosive need results to get away from the job. It is *vitally* necessary to periodically flex the muscles and to twist the body, until sluggish blood is pumping around a bit faster.

This physical phenomenon, therefore, deserves consideration along with efficiency when a writer equips and arranges an office or workspace.

As a simple example, I now keep my stationery cabinet on a shelf *behind* my typist chair. It had been snugged under an end of the typing table. Fresh sheets of paper could be twitched from it without un-hunching shoulders or turning the head.

Now I must turn at least half-around, lean slightly, and reach above my head. Shoulder muscles flatten and stretch as the torso twists. Eyes are briefly re-focused at a different distance and angle. Thus I'm forced every few minutes to become unimmobilized.

Telephone Location Best-Engineered. The only tightly-engineered workspace in my office is at the telephone. Every minute on the phone is ticking off cash money like a taxi-meter, for me or for someone else. So I can well afford to be immobilized during most periods of telephoning. Even so, I have a longish cord to permit standing and stretching, or a step or two from the desk.

The phone is on a corner of the desk. Except that a window prevents, it could be on the wall. A desk pullout shelf under the phone provides layspace, should the desk be covered with other work. Half-sheets of mimeo paper secured with a spring clip are ready for notes.

On a shelf immediately above the phone are: my daily schedule calendar; a regular monthly calendar; address book; diary; telephone book; forms for phone messages to others; forms for noting assignment details; a road atlas.

Nearby on the desk are a can full of pens and pencils standing upright for ready grasping, and a small electric clock.

In a drawer under the phone are active files that include: Current projects; Leads; Carbons of manuscripts out; Recent correspondence; Pending correspondence; Pending business; Receipts; Accounts receivable; Bills payable; background material on disciplines currently worked; information for chores or shopping; some active personal files.

The Tall And The Short Of It. Procrustes was the mythical Greek host who shaped guests to fit the beds. Short ones were stretched on a rack. Tall ones got their feet chopped off. How users of tables and chairs were dealt with has not been reported! Yet there must be a strong Procrustean mind-set in the office furniture business!

Some day a market-oriented office equipment maker will design low-cost desks with three or four inches height adjustment. I envision modular designs, perhaps with pedestal bases of differing heights.

Hazel was five feet tall. I'm nearly six feet. With a twelve-inch difference in standing height, there was an approximate six-inch difference in seated height. For her, footrests or platforms have always been necessary office equipment not always made available by various employers.

224

Hazel in earlier years spent many months at various office desks with feet dangling and the chair edge cutting circulation in her legs. Or with feet comfortably on the floor, she has had to work with arms akimbo on a desk nearly at chin height.

I, on the other hand, have sat at desks where my knees scarcely fit under the center drawer. On one in particular I used to get slivers in my knees, if I left it too abruptly. (Today I'd cover the underside of the drawer with Contact paper!)

We solved our separate problems by making our own desks. I buy two-drawer steel file cabinets for mine, then lay a ¾-inch sheet of plywood over the top. Cleats on the underside of the plywood keep it from skating around on the smooth cabinet tops. There is no center drawer.

Hazel found a couple of unpainted wooden night stands with lower drawers large enough for file folders. These were just the right height for her when spanned with a similar plywood top.

My desk top is 29 inches from the floor; hers was 25 inches.

Our "modular" desks have other advantages. The tops are larger than the depth of the file cabinets. Thus we have the expanse of executive-sized desk tops at much less cost than commercially-made desks.

Both desks are easy to move. Section by section, Hazel has moved hers single-handedly. Nor is there any problem at all going through doors or around corners.

These plywood tops are clear-grained on one side only. We mopped on warm boiled-linseed-oil. Then we rubbed them smooth, after they soak up all the oil they can. The result is a soft, non-glare finish, easy to clean, simple to restore. (The desk tops, we grant you *are* combustible!)

Typing tables pose similar problems. Fortunately the standard 26" height is comfortable for me. But I had to make a stand 23 inches high for Hazel's machine.

She needed something her heavy electric standard couldn't kick around. I took another unpainted nightstand with large and small drawers in it. A shelf was screwed on to one side at the 23" height she required for the machine.

For support, the space under the shelf is enclosed at the back and on the outer end with solid panels of ½" plywood. Each corner in the space underneath is braced with three 2-inch angle straps. It looks a bit primitive, but it's rock-solid.

Service Most Important In Typewriter Choice. Bull sessions inevitably get around to which brand typewriter is best for writers. But I believe that's the wrong question!

Most important to us has been which model can be most quickly and efficiently serviced or repaired in our community?

Typewriter down-time can be frustrating and costly at critical points in your production. You can lose more in revenue, than you pay out in repair costs.

We now buy service contracts the minute warranty periods expire. They provide periodic cleaning of the machines' deep internals as well as repairs. And on breakdowns, the serviceman appears within 24 hours and makes most repairs on the spot.

The cost is little more than before, when you count the cost and time of two or more 25-mile round trips plus a minimum wait of one week that prevailed before we signed the contracts. The more-regular cleanings also reduce breakdowns, as servicemen make careful inspections, in hopes of forestalling added trips.

Which Model Typewriter. Today's touch and pressure controls on most typewriters minimize the basic distinctions between brands. Writers can usually soon be at home with almost any modern machine.

We suspect individuals usually favor new machines most similar to the ones they learned to type on (allowing for modern improvements). So try out a few. Type at least a full page of copy on each machine. Then choose the one that *feels* most comfortable.

Electrics *are* preferable. I speak as one grudgingly convinced, and still badly subject to disconcerting extra letters and a jumping carriage when too fully engrossed in my writing.

One advantage of the electric I've never heard mentioned. But perhaps my failing is unique. I *always* seem to have a cut, slice, prick or nick on one or more finger tips. On manual machines, these can be distracting torture. On the electric, I can often ignore them. Arthritics, of course, *must* use electrics.

Electrics produce uniform typing, a real sales asset for a manuscript. And they're much less fatiguing when you have one of those solid days of typing, often into the wee hours.

Their disadvantages: they're more expensive; they take getting used to (you learn to arch your fingers like a pianist and tap directly down); they cut up ribbons faster; they're useless in a power failure.

Most modern machines do give years of relatively trouble-free service, once they're past that seemingly inevitable adjustment period of loose screws, dangling springs and floppy levers. Most serious troubles we've had were with models of entirely new design. When the look-alikes to IBM's Selectric came out, we had plenty grief with two machines of one brand in particular (bought because our regular office supplier handled them).

Typewriter Life About Same As Car. Typewriters *do* wear out, if a writer is truly productive. Hazel's big electric standards lasted about ten years. My heavy electric portables were five or six years. The type on both becomes notably blunted about the same time parts begin to break frequently. Then, like a car, it's best to trade for new, rather than repair any more.

If repair service is not quick in your area, it pays to have or pick up a second-hand manual machine at low cost, to have in reserve as production insurance. A manual is suggested as reserve if power failures are frequent.

In our case we always keep each supplanted portable as a spare, and trade in its predecessor that was previously serving as spare. These spares are usable enough for short emergency periods, though no longer dependable for heavy duty.

While I was on the road much of the time, I used an electric portable similar to an older unit at home, kept for a spare. Their similarity in operation resulted in ready changeability with minimum frustration. If one uses a standard at home and a portable on the road, it is wise to have the same make, so that margin releases, tab and back-up keys are in the same location on both.

Some repair shops will loan or rent a machine while your typewriter is serviced. It never hurts to ask! But it takes valuable time to get and return it.

The 12-inch carriage on my portable takes an 8½" x 11" sheet longways. This is useful in making up charts, tables and forms of various kinds. It also takes 12" manila envelopes, if light-weight and claspless.

The wide carriage is also easier to keep free of erasure crumbs. With the standard 8½" x 11" sheet centered on the platen, you can move each half of the sheet beyond one side or the other of the machine, while erasing.

Softly Does It In A Motel. I keep the portable machine also to take with me on extended trips. It provides the quickest way to expand notes at night, while they are still fresh.

Yes, you can type in a motel after midnight without getting thrown out. If you type on the bed, it will muffle the sound, becoming much quieter certainly than the TV in the room next to you.

I set the typewriter on a corner of the bed that is farthest from any wall. My legs straddle the corner. If the top of the typewriter case doesn't remove, take out the machine and set it on a stiff brief-case on the bed, or even a firm suitcase. Even telephone books on the bed will provide an adequate base.

I have also utilized: a coffee table, a straight chair, a vanity bench, a luggage rack. Each had a pillow on it, plus my briefcase. The pillow not only muffles the sound but also absorbs the recoil of the electric carriage.

I carry a 12' extension cord that will reach almost any wall socket from a motel room bed.

Some day our market-oriented office furniture designer will come out with a sturdy but light collapsible typing table for characters like me. It'll have a cushioned top and coil-spring feet. It also may have a hood lined with foam rubber, with a bracket for copy, and a fluorescent light.

Is anybody listening?

Crucial Piece Is Typist Chair. When we toured five years in the travel trailer, our two typist chairs went along. In social hours, guests lounged on the sofa bed; we each sat in our own typist chairs. In terms of best practical quality available, our typist chairs are always the most luxurious office equipment in the house, even today.

With feet flat on the floor, the typing surface should just comfortably clear the knees by an inch or two. Thus, as the typist sits erect, the upper arms hang loose. Only the forearms are raised for typing.

Still with feet on the floor, the back of the thighs rest *lightly* on the edge of the chair. If the chair is too high, which is often the case, even with taller people, blood circulation is cut off. The legs get vaguely uncomfortable and the typist becomes less vaguely restless and irritable.

The back-pad should be set so the person is squarely on the chair, balanced well for every typing motion, and sitting straight, rather than hunched forward.

Thus because of its three-way adjustability this makes a good commercial typist chair the best investment a writer can make in office furniture.

But stick to your cartridge box or tavern table if you wish. It's a free country!

If the size of the room permits, indulge yourself with a reading chair, for change of both position and pressure surfaces against your back and bottom. If you can't go for a rocker or Morris chair, a sturdy folding lawn chair with a pair of thin pillows will do nicely. The latter has the merit of disposal when you need the space.

I edit rough copy in my rocker. A secondary supply of pens, pencils, ruler, paper and clips is permanently at hand by the rocker.

The extra chair serves for visitors also. A TV table is supplied when a writing surface is needed.

Copy Stand Should Not Vibrate. A copy stand or easel should *never* be on the typing table. Standard electric typewriters especially will vibrate even a heavy table. And vibration conveyed to material being copied, or to notes being read, results in continuous eyestrain. (So does watching a page being typed. Learn to touch-type and save your eyes!)

The vibration can be so slight as to be almost sublimnal. But it is very real and very fatiguing.

I put the copy stand on the desk next to my typing table. I have used a TV table and also a music rack. Another time a two-drawer file served. Hazel had an extra cheap typing table acquired with Green Stamps. It overhung her lowered typing stand, so her copy was up close.

If you don't wear bifocals, a shelf right above the typewriter permits the copy to be shifted there for change in neck tensions. It is always restful if you can move the copy one side to the other at intervals, to change your head and neck angles.

The copy stand or easel should be strong and flexible, capable of holding notebooks, pads, drawings or photographs. (You'll study the latter while typing captions). I've taped a clip-board upright on a small easel designed for holding heavy books while reading. This gives me a clip at the top for loose sheets, plus a ledge at bottom on which to rest pads, photos, etc.

Impedimenta—Meaning Gadgets. We're all tempted by the myriad of desk-top gadgets in the impulse-item displays of stationery and variety stores. Somehow, once on our desks, they rarely serve as expected, yet we're reluctant to discard them. So they continue to clutter without purpose.

I do have a 10-inch turntable. For it, Hazel painted four cans with white enamel, trimmed top and bottom with gold-braid-like tape. These vary from a low flat salmon can to a tall fruit juice can, and circle the back perimeter of the turntable.

In them stand many of those small tools that usually cram a desk's middle drawer: scissors, letter-opener, pens, pencils, erasers, staple-puller, small plastic slide rule.

Front of the turntable holds a stamp pad, stapler, postage stamp dispenser, small envelope moistener. A small squirt bottle of baby oil is for dry fingers that get slippery handling much paper.

Next to the turntable is a couple of Sears' 10"x5"x6" nine-drawer plastic cabinets. Drawers of clear plastic reveal their contents. This holds all the other items usually jumbled in a desk's middle drawer—and in much more orderly fashion.

One cabinet drawer contains stamps, in folded strips from sheets of 50 or 100. These are in several less-used denominations.

Another drawer has refills for pens, leads for pencils, and a supply of staples. Paper clips in four sizes fill another drawer. Red and black grease pencils (china Markers) and soft lead pencils, for cropping or labeling photographs are in a fourth drawer.

Fifth drawer has a razor-blade-knife. This is chiefly for cutting corrugated cardboards into protective stiffeners mailed with photographs. The drawer also has: a paper punch; a mileage guage for estimating trip distances on maps; and a pair of tweezers.

Sixth drawer has rubber bands in three sizes. Seventh has all our spare keys—car, house and luggage. Each key has a properly labelled tag (we learned the hard way).

Eighth drawer has small name and address labels, pencil sharpeners in two sizes and art gum erasers.

Finally the ninth is full of my obsolete business cards. We use the backs of these cards for small notes (a phone number, street address, individual's or product's name). They fit in pockets or purses during errands, don't crumple, and are stiff enough to be readily found among several pieces of paper. Also they're stiff enough to hold in your palm while scribbling.

On top of the little cabinet is a two-pound-capacity postage scale, which spares us trips to the post office for weighing manuscripts.

There Must Be Lay Space. As few items as possible are permanently on my desk. For when a big story in progress it can really take up a lot of "lay space."

Other broad lay space should be available for temporary use (I've even used the floor at times). Be prepared to spread out photographs or half-sheets of story paragraphs on the kitchen or dining room table, to re-arrange them in logical order. Even a bed may serve the purpose.

On real big stories I have spread out over the large dining room table, one metal folding table and six folding TV tables. The latter are always useful to have in a corner of the office, if a single large table is not at hand. I keep four TV tables readily available.

If space for tables is lacking, but you do have a tier of shelves, try the following. In normal use, concentrate storage of light bulky items on that shelf nearest chest height. These items may then be quickly removed, freeing this particular shelf for sorting purposes.

Mechanized Arithmetic Is No Luxury. Across the desk from the phone is the adding machine, which records calculations on tape. For many, many years I stubbornly did without, and survived unscathed. But now we couldn't be without it.

For one thing, tax reports alone have become both more complicated and more numerous for even the smallest businessman. Moreover the personal and business accounting necessary to validate one's tax accounting has become extremely time-consuming for small businessmen.

In addition, business reporting deals more solidly every year with numbers in all sorts of combinations—dollars, weights, measures, times, quotas, etc., etc. Since calculating became less a chore for me, I now find myself double-checking interview data much more conscientiously.

In my check book, after every ten checks are issued, I run my check stub computations through the machine. Sorry (or glad) to say, I catch five or six errors a year before they get me into trouble.

The electronic calculator came late to our home, because I used a slide rule fairly deftly for multiplying and dividing, in rough computation. The slide rule, of course, is limited in accuracy for extended digits.

However it's a dramatic sign of the times that a major section on simple slide rule use has been cropped from this manuscript. The pocket calculator has replaced my slide rule completely.

Reference Books Readily Available. To keep the desk top clear, there are reference shelves directly above. The lowest can be reached while seated.

On this shelf is the stationery cabinet mentioned elsewhere. With an open front, this cabinet was subject to breezes fluttering sheets out onto the floor. But heavy 5" x 8" cardboards, tossed to the back of each shelf on top of its contents, weighted them down effectively. Lifting each sheet of paper or carbon on removal keeps the cardboards sliding back where they belong.

Reference books must be easy to snatch or toss back in place. To keep books from slumping or leaning on each other, I put in a dividing partition like a bookend.

But then Hazel came up with the better idea. She placed several cardboard boxes of varying sizes on her shelf, and later on mine, with the open side outward. These are covered with gay adhesive papers, such as Contact.

Books are grouped loosely in each box, so we can grasp them easily. Yet with only five or six to the box, there is no room for them to slump or topple.

That takes care of the small dictionary, thesaurus, directories, technical handbooks, etc. But the big dictionary is a problem. Things keep getting stacked on it, detering its use except in desperation. A solution probably is to make a special easel for this dictionary, then install it on a shelf at chest height (to Hazel, not me). By sloping it we can keep gadgets from roosting on it.

Current reference material goes stale rapidly as you move from one project to another. Therefore this shelf needs weeding and re-organizing every three to six months. Which is another reason Hazel's divider boxes are so handy. You just shift them and their contents back and forth to fit your current reference needs.

Maps Can Be Decorative. Yes, I have a compulsive weakness for maps of any kind. Can't pass one by without studying it. Hence I'm admittedly biased in saying three big maps should be posted on the office wall, if at all possible. One is of your city or community, another of the state or geographic area you cover, and the third of the United States.

If your room arrangements permit, the local and area maps should be accessible to the phone. Make it easy for yourself to discuss travel distances with editors or clients. A long cord on the phone may help provide this accessibility.

A United States map may seem unnecessary to a local correspondent. Yet I refer to mine frequently, even when a trip is not in prospect.

For instance, I've just done a story on an express company that brags about *two* round trips daily between New York and Philadelphia. Then I read another firm makes three *round* trips between Chicago and Milwaukee. I know another guy is knocking out *four* RTs daily between Dallas and Fort Worth!

Was I just plain gullible? Or is the first trucker truly doing an impressive job? That's when I really study the map. I find New York/Philadelphia is 90 miles, Chicago/Milwaukee is 75 miles, and Dallas/Ft. Worth is 45 miles. These figures are only approximate from the big map, (measured by ruler) but they do salve my conscience.

(PS—there should also be a U.S. map over the desk of *every* editor or client who uses freelances.)

Posted maps develop your perspective of both distances and directions. Map details are stamped subliminally on your mind, even when you don't study them.

232

Wall maps should not be subject to direct sunlight, lest they discolor and fade. In smoggy areas, maps could well be covered with clear plastic. The handy man can also enhance a map's decorativeness with a nice frame.

Where Are You Keeping It? Outdated files and magazines are the bane of freelancing! How much value, space or time, can one ascribe to correspondence, background material or magazines six months old, a year old, two or five years old?

Most of us simply avoid decisions. We stack outdated stuff indiscriminately. When the office gets too crowded, we just throw it *all* out. Or an attic or basement may postpone that ultimate heave-ho until fate in some other form intervenes, like fire, or moving to a new address.

Few writers can afford to maintain "archives." To be of any real value, they require meticulous indexing and cross-referencing. This could become a full-time occupation in itself, and of questionable profitability to a busy writer.

As a rule-of-thumb, one two-pedestal desk, plus one four-drawer file (or equivalent), plus a total 15 feet of shelving should contain *all* current data, plus outdated material the average business writer *should* keep. At least this has been *my* experience.

An expensive file cabinet just isn't needed for outdated material. You won't use it that much. Used cabinets in good condition at modest cost can be obtained in any city and in most towns. Also "transfer cases" have become quite sturdy. They serve just as well, if not overloaded.

Active files belong in the desk, or perhaps in a two-drawer file right adjacent your workspace.

Should you not have sufficient closet or shelf space, an excellent alternative I have used is a row of three-drawer files, or of transfer cases stacked three deep. Their tops provide a work surface or lay space at a height of 38 to 40 inches. They can be topped with a sheet of plywood to cover the cracks, or even formica if you go first-class.

When you are really "saddle-sore," but have to keep typing or working, you can move your work or portable typewriter to this file-top surface and work awhile standing up. It's a wonderful relief! While using my standard electric usually now, I have kept my portable on the counter sometimes for that purpose. This also keeps the portable available for a quick memo, without pulling a manuscript page from the big typewriter.

The big problem, of course, is to keep from stacking junk on this layspace.

What Do We Use? Our offices are bedrooms of a large mobile home. Each has a shallow closet 6½ feet wide, in which we installed shelving. File folders fit neatly in cartons that brought us mimeograph paper. The carton ends are labelled with felt pens.

The closets came with metal folding doors. These were neat, but made closet corners inaccessible. Hazel replaced them with pairs of gay terry drapes that open for access at any point desired.

Occasionally we run the vacuum cleaner extension hose over top of the cartons to inhale the fine dust.

Details on filing and storage are covered in other chapters, about Organization and the Hot File.

Looseleaf Binders Over The Transom. Rarely have we bought looseleaf binders for storing information. In our freelance writing, binders trickle in steadily from all sources—product information, parts lists, routing guides, training manuals, reference data, etc., etc. Almost any sizeable business dispenses information in varieties of looseleaf binders. And just in process of gathering story material many fall into our hands.

They may be gaudy with advertising, but they usually are good quality, sturdy and tough-covered. So we simply put two and three strips of embossed tape over the original titles, to indicate their current contents. The original material, if obsolete, is discarded.

If a cover is *too* garish, we may cover it, or at least the binder's back, with colored adhesive paper, before putting on our own labels.

Need Copier Easy To Use. The copier, like the adding machine, we did very well without, until we had one. But you should select a unit easy to use! We got an inexpensive portable model when it was first marketed. It requires some assembly before use, or else it takes up too much space when left open. We'd use it more, if it were easier to get at.

But now no original expense receipt gets out of my hands. When a client requires receipts with expense statements, copies are provided. Thus I'm always fortified against IRS without further recourse to my client.

One outfit used to demand copy of my phone toll bill, even if I claimed a single toll call. I made copies at the local library, until we got the copier. (Always thought it was a ploy to cause me to overlook smaller charges.)

All drawings I make are copied for protection against loss or damage, before the original is mailed with a manuscript. I used to take photographs of drawings, then file the negatives (developed but not printed) with carbons of stories to which they belong.

Advertisements, brochures, or any one-of-a-kind exhibit, are also copied. On speculative articles, the copy may be submitted, with an offer to send the original if the manuscript is accepted. This is when I feel it would be difficult to replace the original.

A newspaper clipping having story-lead potential may be copied. The copy is sent to the editor with the query, keeping the more fragile original in my file.

Duplicate invoices for delinquent accounts are from the copier. Also repeated follow-up requests for manuscript action, with "reminder" added in red ink.

Whenever I borrow forms, bulletins, or magazines for reference, I copy the data needed and return the borrowed items promptly. This reduces my responsibility, especially if production of the article itself is delayed.

Multi-copy questionnaries are more easily prepared on a copier. In fact, any typing job requiring more than three carbon copies is better done through the copier.

Odd Copier Uses. Odd uses for the copier pop up unexpectedly. After a hectic meeting one night, I whacked out ten double-spaced pages of expanded notes in my motel room. Early next morning, I hit the 200-mile road home.

Awaiting me there was a frantic message. A story had blown up on the editor. Could mine get in soon enough to replace it?

After a hasty phone conference I quickly edited the expanded notes, ran them through the copier, dashed to the Post Office, and air-specialed the notes to this editor. He hurriedly organized them and sped on to his printer to make the deadline. Then he paid me finished copy rates for the job!

Without copier protection, however, those notes would have been too valuable to be floating around loose, and almost impossible to replace.

Photo releases also go through the copier for protection. Editors have misplaced releases and the time and expense of garnering releases over again could really eat a hole in a writer's profits.

Best Is Cheapest In Some Tools. For some smaller pieces of equipment "best is cheapest" in the long run. If a tool doesn't do its job adequately, you bought too cheap. The criterion is the amount of labor involved or saved.

First on the list are scissors. Of good steel, they should hold their edge for a long time. At least a four-inch blade is advisable to deal adequately with *cardboard,* whether or not it's corrugated.

At the same time they should be slim enough so you can see what you're cutting on critical work. For the flexible writer gets into situations where trimming and piecing together is part of the task.

Handle and test a pair of scissors before buying. They will differ greatly in design and handle. Be sure they are comfortable when applying pressure.

A ruler should have a bearing strip or overhang its full length. If it has a square, flush side, ink or lead crumbs creep under the ruler and smear the paper. Be sure ruler markings are legible, preferably slightly grooved so they won't wear off.

Generally a wastebasket should be deep, rather than wide. Writers generate a lot of waste paper. Few resist cumpling each discarded sheet.

So, when you press down in a wide basket, crumpled papers ooze back up like a spongy cushion. But jam down in a taller, narrow basket, and the trash is likely to stay put. Of course, it may require more shaking to empty the basket, too.

During periods of hectic deadline stress, dispense with trash baskets. Weight the bottom of a paper supermarket bag with a discarded magazine or section of newspaper, to make it stay upright. Then just throw the bag away when it's full.

Typing Ribbons Are Like Cereal! Price comparisons are as futile with ribbons as with cereal, until you know the ounces of cereal in the box, or yards of ribbon on a spool, as well as the quality.

Good nylon ribbons do pay. I was convinced of this against my earlier judgement. We first tested nylon ribbons under hot dry conditions, then had moved to more humid country by the time we tested cotton ribbons. Hence the latter showed up best on a price-versus-performance basis. But our testing was invalid!

All ribbons perform better at relative humidities comfortable to humans. Hot arid air, whether due to an Oklahoma summer or room heat in winter, makes any ribbon more brittle and its ink less fluid.

Our recent tests, at comparable humidities, show some nylon ribbons have double the life of the cotton we were using, without the smearing, cutting and piling up that often occurs with cotton.

Today's carbon ribbons undeniably do superior work that looks like good printing. But we question how much they're needed on manuscripts. Nylon ribbons produce very legible copy at less cost. *We* ourselves now use dual-ribbon machines. Carbon ribbons are for formal correspondence. Nylon ribbons handle all else, manuscripts as well as memos and most personal correspondence.

With carbon papers, however, we ourselves haven't found a parallel. Many expensive lines don't exhibit sufficient superiority over variety store brands to justify their prices. You have to make your own tests on whatever is available locally.

When we receive snap-out carbons on invoices and memos, we re-use them for copies of our own invoices and memos. Snip off their paper strips and they match a 5"x8½" memo sheet. You get four or five uses from such carbons, saving your full-size carbons for longer copy.

Envelopes, Labels And Cardboards. It's rarely practical for a writer to have manuscript envelopes printed. For one thing two to four different sizes of envelopes are usually needed to assure snug fits of manuscripts. So you're always running out of the wrong size of envelopes.

Better alternative is to have pressure-sensitive labels printed. Then the identical label can be used on any size or style envelope or carton.

The writer's name and address goes in the "From" portion. The blank space for the "To" portion should be deep enough to hold, without crowding, at least five single-spaced lines from *your* typewriter.

These gummed labels range upward in size from 2½" x 3½". Printed copy on them may be simple or elaborate. They can have insignia or bits of promotion if desired, or warnings such as "fragile," or "photos enclosed," or "first class."

I prefer the simple small size which fits #10 envelopes as well as larger ones. It also fits on a packet of 4"x5" film, with space for stamps.

You buy 1,000 or 2,000 printed labels at a time. But since they are used on everything, there's reasonable expectation they'll be used up before you void them by moving to a new address.

Rubber stamps vary greatly in quality. Price isn't always the measure of quality. Test the stationer's samples before you order your own. Good rubber stamps leave a clean sharp imprint that resembles printing. This is provided you come straight down on the paper and lift straight up, without rocking when you apply pressure.

Make Cardboard Stiffeners. Commercial photo-mailers are another item that seems over-priced, at least for the writer's needs. A regular strong manila envelope with one or two corrugated cardboards are equally protective.

Cardboards serve two functions. They discourage folding by postal workers, mail room clerks or others. And they protect photographs from sharp jabs, as from the corner of a heavy package or some piece of furniture or equipment.

If you have no other source of cardboard boxes, ask at your supermarket. They have plenty. Since the advent of supermarket bags, the stores have to dispose of their cartons instead of pack groceries in them.

I use a yardstick to measure out 8½ x 11" and 5½" x 8½" pieces, then slice them with a razorblade knife. A slice the length of one side of corrugated board won't quite go through. But after the slice, fold along it and the knife practically glides down the crease the other side.

If a manuscript is six pages or more, you can safely sandwich photographs between the manuscript and a single cardboard. With fewer pages, it's advisable to use cardboards front and back.

When return envelopes with clasps are enclosed, the clasp-side must be away from the photographs, preferably with the manuscript intervening also.

No-clasp envelopes are best to use, but they aren't so readily available as the other.

Cardboard should fill the envelope, even if manuscript and photos do not. Otherwise, with cardboard slipped to one side, and photos slipped to the other, a blow on the edge of the cardboard can put a crease in the photo.

Though this chapter is devoted to equipment and supplies, we allotted discussion of cameras to the photography section and tape recorders to the next chapter.

Cars Are Tools, Too. Some random comments are pertinent about cars as tools for writers.

If yours is a station wagon, you are advised to camouflage the camera case, tape recorder and quality luggage.

One station-wagon-owner friend of ours taped false bottoms six inches from the top of three grocery cartons. The real bottoms were cut out except for a one-inch lip as stiffener. In the open tops of the three cartons he respectively dumped mason jars, some old clothes and bundled yellowed newspapers. Then, whenever on a working trip, he'd drop these dummies over his gear and luggage.

Another freelance used to trade in his Cadillac every two years. He didn't have a Cadillac income, but said once he got the first one paid for, it didn't cost all that much to make the trades.

He claimed it gave him instant status whenever he walked in for an interview, assuring him of quick and cooperative action.

I've discounted this claim for three reasons: (1) One is rarely able these days to park in sight of the person to be interviewed, unless you confine yourself to drive-ins; (2) Some businessmen do think you're crazy to drive a Caddy around a traprock quarry or swamp road construction; (3) A publisher once saw this Caddy and refused to let the editor (me) raise the writer's word and photo rates, as requested and deserved.

Of all the several cars we've used or rented, the most practical all around was a 1962 Buick Special V-8 sedan. It was well-powered compact with excellent visibility in every direction. It was just big enough to be comfortable; it was nimble and inexpensive to drive, whether in traprock, New England blizzards, New York's taxi jungle, or limitless freeways and turnpikes.

Many business writers get into all manner of hard-hat-and-safety-shoe situations. Their cars must be able to rough it as readily as the writers.

For this reason I've always used over-size tires in premium grades, heavy-duty batteries and generators, twice-a-year tune-ups and plug changes, and premium lubricants. This car was still fairly nimble around town and as a back-up, after thirteen years and 145,000 miles.

Freelance Writer In The Middle. Much of this chapter has suggested a tightwad string-saver and Yankee do-it-yourselfer. In truth, the freelance writer is a misfit in the American economy, along with many small mom-n-pop businesses.

We often need more sturdiness or productivity in our tools than is provided by popular domestic models. Yet real mechanization is still beyond the writer's capacity for effective utilization.

So a writer is forced into constant improvisation, if he or she is to make every minute and every dollar count. (Do you remember when we used to say "make every penny count," and then "every nickel," and then "every dime?")

Freelance writers fight for small savings the same as any small businessman. Big dramatic savings are scarce and not too readily achieved, except for major changes in an entire operation.

For the writer, the gross hourly wage is still always the key factor. If something is built or bought, how many hours per week, month or year can it save? That is, what is its "cost-effectiveness?" Can the cost be regained reasonably quickly by increased production in those hours saved?

The "X" in this equation, of course, is the individual writer's hobby quotient. Does he or she *like* to make things in spare time? Does the challenge of improvising have a recreational value?

If so, indulging this hobby might have real additional value in keeping the writer from going crazy! It's a pleasant change from banging the typewriter.

Chapter 32

Offices for Freelance

Greatest mistake the new freelance often makes is to begin by renting a business office! The reasons for doing so are quite laudable: Lack of disturbance or interruption; conveniently arranged furniture and equipment; space for layout of work; an impressive "business" address; proximity to a business center (if you live in the suburbs); easier to forget work during nights and weekends.

But this office incurs duplicate rent, phone, utilities (air conditioning to keep you awake in many climates), and possibly steno service. *Every month* the bills roll in, even if you're sick, travelling or on vacation.

To support these added facilities you must produce at least two extra stories per month over what you'd otherwise produce from your home. That's 24 additional stories per year, averaging $100 to $150 each, depending on the cost of living in your area. (We speak in 1978 terms.)

Another consideration for caution in setting up a separate downtown office is the amount of time you will be away from it. This may average up to half your total working hours, when you'll be either interviewing, researching, or running business errands.

This means either having someone to cover the phone while you're out, or using an answering service, or having a recording device connected to the phone.

If you see your way to making this added "nut," that's fine! The separate office has many advantages. Otherwise, forget it! Work at home, lest you create your own private "rat race" just for the status of a downtown office!

Office at Home. At home, however, you *should* have a room to escape to. This is not indulgence of artistic temperament. It's a long-term practicality. Unless you live alone, or the family is out of the house during most working hours, you need isolation for *their* sake as well as yours!

Sooner or later, the most charitable relative gets ominously edgy under subconscious strain of tip-toeing around you six or seven hours per day! This includes loving wife or husband, or doting mother, or the most unusually considerate youngsters. It involves other kids, pets, TV, radio, family phone calls, piano lessons, sudden conversation, singing—and visiting neighbors.

The very *minimum* practical size for continuous office use is a room 6' x 8', or at least 50 sq. ft. in area. It helps if you can use most of two walls for shelving or files. I *know*, because that was the size of my combined office, bedroom, darkroom in our travel trailer.

If you don't have an available room, make one—remodel, add to or convert something!

At one time or another we've seen all the following converted into practical offices: Sun porch; Side porch; Extension of porches, front or back; Dead end of a hallway; Large closet; Former pantry; Dinette; Ell of a living room; Attic; Basement; Garage; Breezeway; Toolshed; Woodshed; even an abandoned greenhouse.

Partitions Are Flexible. Insulated partitions can be installed at modest cost, often with door built in, for the equivalent perhaps of two months rent for a downtown office.

We suggest *insulated* partitions because they usually face family living space. Insulation will muffle sounds, even when the door remains open.

For rented quarters, freestanding partitions can be made by fitting a rigid frame around walls, floor, and ceiling. The partition is then constructed inside this frame. If shelving or bookcases are incorporated with the partition they can provide supporting structure.

Partitioning often presents less of a problem than providing heat, cooling and electricity! This is because the space to be converted is often outside the normal living area, and therefore not properly supplied with these utilities.

Utilities Shouldn't Be Makeshift. The best lighting comes from an office-type ceiling luminaire. This has egg-crating or other devices for even light distribution that eliminates shadows.

Uniform lighting is preferable to the spot lighting of separate work places. A brightly-lit work space surrounded by dusky background creates excessive eye-strain over extended work periods. This is because the eyes are constantly trying to adjust to both light levels. (For the same reason TV-watching is easier on the eyes in a moderately-lit room, than in a dark room.)

If you do use spot-lighting, the whole area in your direct field of vision should be lighted. That is, make every effort to eliminate strong contrasts of dark and light.

Best alternative to the luminaire is the kind of desk or torch lamp that throws much of its light on the ceiling, to be reflected around the room.

242

If auxiliary heat is used, add some means of humidification, even if only setting shallow pans of water on top of or near the heater. Your office is likely to be out of mainstream air currents in the house. So it may not even share moisture normally evaporated from cooking, bathing or house plants.

Therefore dryness of nose, throat and skin, besides being unhealthy, can become very distracting (and writers do distract so easily at times).

Moreover, humidification makes paper, carbons and stamps much easier to handle (even reduces those nasty paper cuts). Typewriter ribbons, carbon paper and stamp pads last longer, especially in their darker phases. They also print more cleanly at proper relative humidities (40%-60%).

The home office should have a telephone extension. This is true whether or not there normally is someone else around the house to answer the phone. When you are alone, time is wasted trotting the length of house or apartment to answer and hang up on the latest phone-advertising atrocity.

Moreover the writer needs a phone close to calendars, appointment pads, current files, notes and workspace. Otherwise difficulty in using the phone can actually be a mental block to getting certain work done!

A shoulder-rest should be attached to the phone. A writer often needs both hands for note-taking, poking through files or handling a reference book.

If lengthy phone interviewing is frequent, it will pay to get a phone operator's head-piece. This can be provided with a switch between it and the usual hand-piece. (Then see if you can keep the teenage daughter away from it!)

Trailer, Motor Home or Camper. So far, we haven't discussed trailers, motor homes or campers as offices. Where their use is permitted by local zoning restrictions, they are ideal—in size, in their self-contained utilities (including bathroom, if possible) and in their isolation.

Phone connections to a trailer or camper body can be through a disconnectible "phone jack" on the side of the house.

Trailers and camper bodies, even though they already have many built-in units, do lend themselves to many minor modifications. This includes extra shelves, cabinets, stands, brackets, etc., for placing everything in the handiest locations.

The trailer kitchen can be readily partitioned off and remodeled as a darkroom. Sink, cupboard, layspace and power outlets are all already at hand. 243

Should the vehicle be used for family vacations, as well as an office, it must be organized for easy transfer of contents to the house and back. This calls for portable files, supply cases and equipment.

If the vehicle is for business travel, then the office arrangements must not conflict with living requirements. All equipment must be easily secured, "ready for the road."

Above all, don't remodel the vehicle irremediably! You may want to trade it in sometime! (We removed a large closet from one mobile home to gain space. But we stored the parts. It was simple to replace them when we traded-in the home on a new one.)

How About Part-Timers? What we've recommended is for the fulltime freelance truly making a business of writing. Obviously the part-timer or moon-lighter cannot always economically justify all these special facilities.

Writing mothers meet deadlines in the living room or kitchen, with eye and ear attuned to playpen or crib. Dads peck away while the kids squirm over homework.

Such writing is dedicated, even heroic at times! But it's rarely efficient! It requires intense concentration, sometimes in oblivion to riots in the playroom or crisis in the kitchen.

Moreover, the living room or bedroom office makes it almost impossible to get away from your work. It's always there, staring you in the face, chiding you to get at it and get something done.

The old rolltop desk has definite advantages. Close it, and you more easily forget what's inside. Also the kids keep sticky fingers off your freshly-typed manuscript.

The rolltop's successor is the new compact "home office" now marketed by several furniture companies. It looks like a deep chest-high cabinet, until you swing out the front and raise the top. These reveal typewriter, adding machine, files, supplies, books, notes, already for you to draw up a chair and go right to work.

If You Must Be Downtown. But sometimes things just aren't compatible around the house! Then separate office space is not only warranted but even advised. It's hard for a writer, or anyone else, to be productive amid perpetual non-cooperation, criticism or conflict.

But the private office is not our only option. For a New York editor neither knows nor cares what sort of place you forget your umbrella in.

Look in the classified phone directory under "Office & Desk Space Rental Service." There are firms that make a business of renting to solitary business people parts of a big office, or small private offices. They also provide business office services on a per-job or piece-rate basis.

Typical ad for such a service reads: "Private furnished offices or attractive desk space; parking; air conditioning; carpeting; receptionist; 24-hour answering service; complete secretarial service available."

If this doesn't produce suitable space, or if the offices too much resemble Grand Central Station, try running a want ad in the newspaper. Many small firms are eager to cut office overhead where they can. They will share surplus desk space, as well as phone, receptionist and typing or steno expenses. And often they don't think of the possibility until they see your ad.

Minimum space in such a rental set-up should cost no more than the rent on a bare office of normal size. For that you get use of furniture and business services that would be extra in the independent office. Or you may supply your own furniture and equipment. And perhaps you can even buy supplies cooperatively.

Consider Shared Offices. An alternative is to share an office with another individual, who presumably may also be out half the time. Then arrange to stagger your hours so that one of you is always in the office. The other person needn't be a writer, though probably a professional of some kind.

Obviously we lay great stress on having the phone covered constantly during working hours. One objection to use of freelances, many editors say, is that "you can never get hold of them." Once an editor is able to contact a writer reasonably quickly when needed, the editor begins to find more use for that particular writer.

It isn't always necessary to pay cash rent. Walt Donop, California freelance, trades his services for office space in an advertising or PR agency. He has his own phone, hooked up so the switchboard girl answers it in his absence. A rough log of his work performed each month for the landlord is matched against stenographic, typing or other services used by Walt.

The independent phone is more costly than sharing a landlord's phone service. But there's a bit of protection, if the sharing doesn't work out, in that the writer doesn't necessarily lose a phone number familiar to clients. Aside from incompatibility, there is always the possibility a landlord's growing business will squeeze the freelance writer out, regardless how satisfactory an arrangement may have been.

To sum up, there really is a reasonable sequence that can be followed by a writer as he or she prospers: the home office; the office bartered for services; the leased desk space and services; shared offices and services; the independent office; and, not too illogically, the writer becoming a landlord of sorts, leasing some of his or her own office to other professionals.

Chapter 33

Getting Organized

There is perpetual need to organize our time! Fresh appointments keep chewing into production time on current assignments. Too often we sweat under midnight oil to meet deadlines, because we let production time slip away.

We're grateful to Harold Schmidhauser, management consultant, for a simple but effective method of time control. Harold conducts many management training sessions of varying lengths on a freelance basis. Therefore juggling both dates and time to prepare for them is a routine chore for him.

Schmidhauser uses a pad of ruled paper. He marks the month at the top of a sheet. Then he enters days of the month on each line consecutively down the left margin.

On the proper lines he enters his fixed obligations, to show which are not "free" days. That is, he's not available on those days. For instance, a speech is noted for March 7, a seminar for March 13 with two days personal consultation on the two days following. A half-day workshop is to be on March 21, and so on.

Flexibility The Key. But the key to Schmidhauser's system is scheduling preparation well in advance of every assignment, rather than assigning preparation to days just before the event itself.

When Schmidhauser contracts for a new speech, seminar or training session, he marks the dates on his pads. Next he estimates conservatively how much time for preparation will be needed.

Assume it's a group new to him. He needs to do a little research on the industry involved. So he estimates three days of preparation will be needed for this particular event.

On his chart he picks three days about a week or ten days prior to this engagement. He marks them as reserved for preparation for that particular assignment.

But these three days are not rigid. One reason for scheduling so far ahead is to leave his schedule flexible. If a second assignment is offered that falls on one of those preparation days, he moves the preparation days to other open days. This gives room for the newer assignment *and its preparation time.*

In the sample just cited, Harold has March 16-17 down to prepare for the March 21 date. If he gets a March 18 assignment, those two days are switched to preparation for that. March 19-20 becomes preparation for March 21, instead of for some assignment after March.

When his schedule shows *all* days marked, either for jobs *or* for preparation time, he flatly refuses any further jobs for that month.

Schmidhauser recommends lined paper over desk calendars as being less expensive. When a sheet of paper gets smudged from frequent erasures, he simply makes out a fresh sheet.

We compromise by mimeographing sheets with 1½" squares, seven across and five down, as on standard calendars. They are blank, except for the square lines, plus days of the week across the top. We then fill each sheet with dates in the proper squares for each month.

Assignments and production plans are noted in the squares the same as Schmidhauser fills in his lines. While costing a bit more, we prefer calendar blanks because they show what day of the week is involved.

At the same time, if our sheet gets too messy, it too is cheap enough to discard and start fresh.

Phone Check List. Not so many assignments come over the phone. But it is good to be prepared for them. A permanent check list of all pertinent questions should be handy to the phone. Or even better, the writer should design an assignment form. Then keep a supply of forms at the phone ready for each assignment.

Questions on the form would include at least the following:

Name of person making assignment, with title, magazine or firm represented, address and phone number;

Name and address of the firm to be approached for the story, with phone number, if known;

Person to be interviewed, if known, with title and function;

Theme or slant of article desired, and precautions or taboos, if any;

Approximate wordage and pictures desired;

Deadline, if any;

Rate of pay for article, for pictures or drawings, and for expenses (if included);

Time of payment, whether POA or POP;

Compensation ("kill-fee") if article fails to jell through no fault of the writer (not often a consideration, but should be on a list as a mind-jogger).

This Is A Business Transaction. The editor is giving you, the writer, an order for merchandise. It is best for you both to have *all* terms and details ironed out in advance.

Writers tend to confuse their business dealings with social amenities wherein one does not ask embarrassing questions. *In business, there are no embarrassing questions!* That's an axiom.

Moreover, it is easiest to be firm about terms *before* one has time and expenses invested in a job. It doesn't cost a thing to quit before you start!

So keep that check list handy, or use the special forms.

In fact, some writers who work mostly from phoned assignments make a practice of filling out their own assignment forms in duplicate. They then send the copy to the editor or client as acknowledgement of both the assignment and its terms.

Having separate special forms for each assignment makes for relaxed discussion of details. Information can go onto the form haphazardly, just as the editor gives it, without interruption. Then with just a few questions the gaps on the form are filled in at the close of the discussion.

Form Goes With Folder. This assignment form is then clipped to an empty file folder. Into this folder goes everything that pertains to that particular job—correspondence, news clippings, notes, illustrations, ads and mailing pieces, samples small enough to file, pictures, references, etc.

A busy writer usually has several jobs or articles in process at once. Some may even be complete except for pictures to come from the developer, or waiting for approval by an interviewee, or pending an additional interview or research. The manuscript carbon goes into the folder also, at least until payment is received.

These folders can be accumulated in a portable metal file box, in the front of a suspension file, or even a grocery carton of suitable size. The main point is to keep them handy for quick reference and review.

Follow-Up Is Good Business. Writers *should* be *most* businesslike at that very point where many go timid! This is in the matter of follow-up on manuscripts, or delayed payments, or when taking exception to payments or proffered payments.

It does help for a writer to remember he himself, or she herself, is not perfect! Then the fact editors are also human can be treated with restraint.

Most editors should be allowed six weeks to read and accept or reject a manuscript, unless a different time is expressly agreed on. Deadlines, travel, special projects, vacations, illness, can all defer action on manuscripts. And this above all is an action none of us care to have taken *too* hastily at any time!

We ourselves try to follow-up on an *assigned* story, if we don't hear from the editor in a month. For an *unsolicited* manuscript, we make the first follow-up at two months. We then repeat all follow-ups necessary at three-month intervals thereafter.

Control Thyself! We indulge in no sarcasm, no dirty cracks, however justified! Just short, polite notes, with only enough information to make clear what manuscript we're talking about.

Editors move about in the business writing field. Feisty, vitroilic letters in the files, read out of context with the circumstances, can prejudice a new editor against a writer. And editors, moving from jobs hamstrung by harsh house policies, often carry their scars with them to more lenient environments.

Temperamental outbursts, by a *business* writer especially, must be regarded in perspective. The writing game is loaded with neurotic would-be writers. They're constantly popping-off at imaginery persecutions based generally on impossible expectations. (As editor I once was bitterly castigated for months for not including one man's unsolicited flowery poetry in a business magazine for drycleaners.)

Hence it is natural for editors to relate a writer's more passionate outbursts, however well justified, to such immature amateur yowling.

It's axiomatic that a *business* writer gets farthest who best keeps his emotions in check, and who confines himself to the pertinent facts of the case. Give the editor the benefit of the doubt.

Publisher Is The Boss. We previously noted that editors are subject to directions and whims of publishers. When a publisher says "Run *this* story," and your article has to make way for it—the editor makes way, because his or her boss says so!

Writers rarely deal directly with publishers, unless the latter also do the editing. So correspondence directed to a publisher from writers is likely to be shunted back to editors with instructions to "take care of this."

However, there *is* a time for writing the publisher. This is when a writer has really gotten a raw deal from an editor. Calm, polite, this letter should lay out the facts in clear, concise order, and then state what the writer feels should be done about them.

Quite often this results in a check, or whatever adjustment is called for—if the "beef" is truly warranted. It's also likely to close out that editor as a market, which might be no loss. But on occasion such a letter has resulted in healthy revision of policy toward freelances.

In any case, however, a "letter to the publisher" is to be used sparingly and judiciously by a writer.

No Special Follow-up Forms. Special forms, such as recommended for phoned assignments, are handy for speeding up many paperwork chores. However, we do not recommend them for follow-up of slow-moving manuscripts. Use of forms in this case suggests the writer has many such slow-movers out to editors. The implication is that this writer's work doesn't sell too readily anywhere!

Out of a year's production, a professional writer just does not have that many slow-movers, that he needs to mass-produce follow-ups. (Or else his work *doesn't* sell too readily, and he'd better do something about his marketing procedure!)

It *is* practical to devise a model letter, to use as a guide in composing follow-ups. This simply ensures all pertinent details are included in each actual follow-up letter. Then variations will suit circumstances.

Good Letterhead Is Important. A nice-looking letterhead has value beyond making a writer feel important! It suggests the writer is in business to stay. He or she isn't simply freelancing between jobs. This is an important consideration for editors plagued by the here-today-gone-tomorrow nature of most freelances. Presumably any writer who invests in a nice letterhead expects to be around awhile.

The letterhead also personalizes the writer. It removes some of his or her anonymity. Therefore it's good to devote extra care to a letterhead's design and content.

Just asking a printshop to "run off something suitable" is a mistake. We ourselves have regretted it a couple times we've done so. The printing, the craftsmanship, have always been good, but the letterheads did not represent or appeal to us as expressing our personalities.

So take your time. Study every letterhead that crosses your path. Compare type styles and sizes, arrangement, balance, color of paper and ink. Then design a letterhead that *truly* pleases you. You're going to be looking at it 500 times per ream! So 500 times you're going to feel good or blah about it.

At the same time, consider the recipient. What impression of you, as a professional writer, will this letterhead give the editor, or the person you wish to interview or obtain data from?

Now, if laying out the letterhead does come too hard, don't hesitate to show the printer the examples that you like. Then work it out with him from there.

Printing a ream or two of letterheads is peanuts to most printers. Many will try to rush you. But this page is to be *you!* It's worth a premium in time as well as money to have it just right.

So do your homework. Be ready to give the printer an idea right at the start of what you need and want.

What Goes On Letterheads. Three bits of information should virtually jump off the letterhead at its recipient: Your name, your address, your phone number. Never be tricky, cute or arty at the expense of clarity. Don't be overly modest, either. Your letter is a business document, to be handled briskly and efficiently by the recipient. It should be designed to that end.

Add information only if useful. Beware of information that limits rather than "sells." For instance, to say you "specialize in all types of insurance" might infer you write about nothing else.

Important information is your proximity to a large city, if this is not clear from your mail address. Many editors have little knowledge of metropolitan area geography.

When we lived in North Bergen, New Jersey, near the Lincoln Tunnel, our letterhead noted "Thirty minutes or local call to Times Square." It let Western and Southern editors know we could cover metropolitan New York as readily as any Manhattanite.

We also carry the seal of Associated Business Writers of America on our letterhead, to assure editors we are responsible and competent *business* writers.

There's always that fine line of propriety in listing organization affiliations, degrees, honors, etc. They are appropriate, but be discreet, for your business letterhead *is* a sales piece.

How Much Is Enough? It used to be quite the vogue to list on your letterhead all magazines that have bought one's output. Something like a man-killer notching his gun butt. This may awe one's relatives and neighbors, but editors are rarely impressed. Any name on such a list could represent a single four-line news bit, a one-time lucky shot, or a new product release.

With each new letterhead ordered, we ourselves have claimed less in the way of functions. We used to list several types of writing, for fear of being overlooked in some capacity.

But really, it's enough to list one's self as a "photo-journalist" or "business photo-journalist." This covers the two basics of business and journalism. However we do use the ABWA seal of course to certify our competence.

Some writers go in for bright-colored envelopes with names in giant type. The idea is that rush-manuscripts can be snatched by editors from stacks of incoming mail. But to us this seems more a psychological prop for the writer, than a necessity. It's useful only where deadlines are truly critical, for daily papers or weekly publications.

We used to use the erasable bonds for our letterheads. They make a crisp-looking page on a quality-grade paper (20-lb bond). But now the error-correcting tapes permit use of regular bonds and we avoid the nasty paper cuts characteristic of erasables.

Letter-perfect typing is important. It's part of the professional image. Only a Samuel Clemens can send in a page of commas and periods and tell the editor to insert them where necessary.

We keep typewriter keys clean, to always have sharp characters on the typed pages. As editor, I always had a negative reaction to manuscripts freckled with ink-clogged o's, d's, b's and a's. Often the story material was good and was bought anyway. Yet—messy type is subconsciously associated with illiteracy. So why handicap oneself unnecessarily?

Learn To Read A Map. Our next suggestion may sound insultingly obvious. Yet it's surprising how people, writers included, live for years in a city without learning their way around.

Day-in, day-out, we go to a job, to stores, to church, maybe to a club, or visit friends. We can almost follow blindfolded the few routes to familiar places.

But which is the shortest route to that factory on the northeast corner of town? How do you negotiate those one-way streets to the River Road pier? When is it just as quick to push on through city center, as to go roundabout?

A business writer, in contrast to writers in general, could well do for his own city what I do for any new city where I expect to work for a while. On arrival I promptly get a street map of that city and study it.

Some motels sell (or hand out) street maps, especially those with newsstands. Gas stations in major cities often have good street maps, free or for a small charge. Stationery stores, book stores, news stands are good map sources. Chain drug stores, variety stores and discount stores often carry them. The local chamber of commerce also often has maps.

I pore over the map, not once but several times. An hour on the night of arrival is not too much time to study a map. It can easily save a matching hour or more of critical working time on the next day alone.

For one thing, you never can fully trust the directions of even the most articulate motel clerks! They pronounce street names so as to be unrecognizable on street signs. They remember three red lights, but forget the red blinker in between. "About a mile" varies from 1,000 yards to three miles. The Sunoco gas station turns out to be Exxon, and the old brewery at the corner where you turn was torn down six months ago.

Study Maps Methodically. On your map, first find the street on which your home or motel is located. Mark the exact location by a small circle in red or green ink. Checking the cross-streets that bracket your location will help pinpoint it.

Next, determine the orientation of the street where you reside. How does it run according to the compass? Every good map has a little cross on it to point out north, south, east and west. It's usually in an upper corner, or else right by the name of the city. Sometimes it's fancied-up to look like a compass. Other times it may simply be a single arrow pointing north.

Now, through that little circle that shows where you live or stay, make a cross. Its arms should point the same as the compass cross on the map. This shows how the street is oriented at that site. Put a little arrow point at the end of the north arm.

Find Reference Points. If you're lucky, your street runs exactly north-south or east-west. This is most likely to happen in the Mid-West. If not so lucky, then determine just what direction the street runs. Unless a former Boy Scout or Navy gob, don't worry about subtler compass directions. Just say your street runs a little north of east and a little south of west, or whatever.

Next pick out a few major streets that *do* run north-south or east-west (if any). Even though they are not *the* main streets in town, try to fix them in your mind. They become your compass in full scale, an enlargement of that little compass cross on the map. (Oh yes, that's Battle Ave., which goes east-west. It must cross Myrtle St. to the right here somewhere.)

Now observe the relationship of your home street to these north-south and east-west "compass" streets. If your street wiggles, note which *sections* parallel the "compass" streets.

It's also good to identify the obstacles that distort the street patterns. Besides rivers and lakes, these include parks, cemeteries, campuses, big institutions and factories, railroad yards, golf links, dumps, cliffs, etc. Often a street is cut in two by such physical obstacles.

Get Positively Oriented. The purpose of all this is to *positively* orient yourself to the compass! This is very important. For people tend to orient themselves to the center of a city, or to a route they travel often. In a new city, we usually orient to the route by which we enter it.

Hence people often have a distorted picture of how outlying sections relate to each other. This is especially true if a river or craggy hill winds through a city.

We recall three extreme examples of dis-orientation. Nashville Tennessee, curls around East Nashville like a crescent moon. In frontier days the latter was truly east of the center city. But the major business growth has been southeastward along the Cumberland River. So today East Nashville lies due north of at least half of Nashville.

From Kentucky three main north/south highways enter the area through East Nashville. Hence "north" to the visitor is toward East Nashville.

In Colorado, *downtown* Denver's street grid runs northeast-southwest and northwest-southeast. But the surrounding city is squared to the cardinal points of the compass.

Hence one drives in due west from the airport. Circling to approach a hotel, the 45° bend in the street is easily overlooked. Then, as one leaves the hotel again on a downtown street, the odds are 50/50 whether you wind up east or south of your hotel.

Of course, in Denver one soon learns that the hulking mountain range always broods over that city from the west!

In Trenton, New Jersey, West State Street runs quite logically east-west. So does East State Street, until it curves 90° to run north-south over half its length. The shortest way from 1800 East to 1800 West, therefore, is not via State Street.

Many cities, large and small, have "beltways" or circumferential boulevards. If one comes on them unprepared and disoriented, it's often hard to know whether to turn right or left.

All of these anomalies disconcert the stranger in town. But thoughtful study of the map beforehand, can usually prevent a lot of wrong-way driving.

The above all applies directly to autoists. But even if the writer is dependent on public transportation or cabs, it's still helpful to know your way around. Also street maps usually show the bus or subway routes.

Very often knowledge of distance to the next assignment determines whether you try to make it today, or before lunch, or before your 3 p.m. appointment.

Handy Map Storage. How and where to file maps is something of a problem. I use accordion-type folders designed for valuable documents, cancelled checks, etc. Most are just the right size for folded maps.

One holds a dozen county maps and three or four city maps for the New York-Philadelphia metro area. Another folder contains state road maps and the city maps most used on longer trips. These stay handy by the desk, yet either folder is always ready to be snatched up for a field trip.

In each folder are two big paper clips. Just before starting a trip into unfamiliar territory, the proper map is refolded to expose only the route to be covered. The map is then secured that way with the paper clips and laid on the car seat for reference.

On return, the map is restored to its original fold and restored to the folder. (As to folding a map, you're on your own! Each seems to fold differently.)

I also keep the latest road atlas at home as ready reference for areas I don't usually invade. This goes with me only on vacation trips.

The Right Clothing Helps, Too. One economic "benefit" from freelancing is greatly reduced cost of clothes and clothing maintenance. Of course, if you're a compulsive clotheshorse, this has psychic drawbacks—or else you buy clothes anyway!

"Dress-up" business clothes are needed only one-half to one-fifth as much as when one "goes to office" every workday. The amount depends on the frequency and extent of interviewing done.

This in turn greatly affects one's buying habits. Suits, shirts, ties, topcoats wear for years! It's advisable to buy conservative styles least subject to fashion cycles and fads. Or else be prepared to give away practically new garments every two or three years.

Even so, it pays to get well-tailored garments in the few clothes one does buy. First, because well-fitting clothes are always in better style than the latest ill-fitting fads. Second, a well-tailored scribe feels more at ease in any company. And third, perhaps, weight control can be an important by-product of the low-inventory wardrobe.

Since wardrobes are limited, especially in travel, they should have mix-and-match flexibility. At times, business writers scramble around rather dusty, sooty or greasy places. It isn't always practical to wear the same slacks, skirt, jacket or sweater a second time, as may have been planned.

For the same reason, I stick to fabrics or styles that clean or launder repeatedly without trouble.

Styles ought to suit the writer's personality, of course. But it should be possible to forget clothes during an interview. One must have both hands free, without need to hang onto hats, scarves, or whatever. Shoes ought to be plain and sturdy enough to walk on crushed stone, sand, mud or ice.

For similar reasons, it's advisable to avoid embellishments that flap, flutter, swirl or stick out. Dangling neckties and necklaces are dangerous in many industrial situations. Zippers are more practical than buttons, especially the big ornamental buttons. Jackets should be securable with belts, buttons or zippers.

Scheduling Time Carefully. Elsewhere we urge the writer to place an hourly dollar value on his or her time. Since each working hour is precious, scheduling one's time is vital to getting the best possible return per hour.

Out of every forty working hours, the writer probably expends at least eight hours on "overhead" chores that don't directly apply to material being produced.

For instance, 30 minutes a day are probably spent in getting, opening and reading mail. Another 30 minutes may go to retrieving carbons of prior letters, writing answers and filing. Posting records, buying supplies and handling "paperwork" (mailing manuscripts, paying bills, taxes, writing follow-ups, etc.) This chews up another three hours per week.

Thus only 32 hours a week are left for actual "production"— getting article material, rough-drafting, editing and final-drafting.

Appointments can rarely be scheduled tightly. It is frustrating to shut off a flow of good information because of need to meet another appointment! Appointment time must also be kept flexible because interviewees are often late or frequently interrupted.

This means being prepared to fill in the time-chinks between appointments or between interruptions—the "tag-ends of time," a friend calls them. The following are good chink fillers, depending on where you are and what's around you:

(1) Snapping up a pic-cap or a shorticle near or between the sites of successive appointments;

(2) A quick survey interview or two at firms near the appointment sites;

257

(3) A short bit of research, whether at a business firm, a laboratory, an institution or library;

(4) Scouting or "casing" leads for possible future stories;

(5) A necessary errand or bit of shopping;

(6) Study of a business magazine, possibly in the industry involved with your current appointment, or the industry connected with your next appointment;

(7) Reviewing notes from the interview just completed, possibly over coffee in a nearby diner. Fill in the details, rough out the opening two or three paragraphs, outline the sequence of points to be developed.

Reviewing Notes in the Field. Alternative Seven should always be the first choice, if you just had a rough interview and need to nail down the details in your mind while they're fresh.

Otherwise, leave this to do first thing on getting home. Your primary aim out in the field is to make the most of your time and cost of being there. Since you're in the field, try to use chink-fillers that depend on field-work, as a first choice.

It's a great temptation to reward yourself with a cup of coffee after a good solid interview. Reviewing notes can be a good excuse for taking such a break. We ourselves have done it often, and better stories resulted. I recommend it.

But we have to resist temptation to take breaks after *every* interview, or to prolong breaks between interviews. Those hours in the field are the most precious and most vulnerable of all.

Ronald Finney told how he and partner-wife, Selma, celebrated with a drink and a good dinner after an unusually good interview. They'd do it again when the story finally went into the mail. And again they'd celebrate when the check came. They did, that is, until they realized all the extra revenue from occasional outstanding stories was being chewed up with celebrating.

I rarely make more than one major appointment each for a morning and an afternoon. This gives complete flexibility in prolonging an interview at full steam, whenever it continues to well-up material.

Cold Turkey Calls Fill Gaps. If an interview proves brief or fruitless, I may go "probing" in the locality, or enroute home, to recapture the cost of travel and time. "Probing" is calling "cold turkey" without appointment on smaller firms, using survey questions to expose potential story material.

To some of us more timid freelancers, probing seems a presumptuous imposition on a busy business man! That a writer should take up his valuable time merely poking around in hopes of finding something newsworthy, seems almost like stealing!

In defense of probing, we find many business men enjoy the novelty of it, if they aren't under pressure—or if they have nothing to hide.

Secondly, many innovations first come to light in various industries due to such probing. Too often an innovator sees nothing remarkable in what he has done. Either his solution appears so obviously simple to him, or he has done it so long ago it is not longer novel to him.

This was impressed on me in my earlier writing for Commercial Car Journal in the trucking industry. For about five years I was their unofficial specialist in "shop-kinks." These are the special tools that mechanics in the truck maintenance shops devise to make their work easier.

One day I remarked to a shop foreman that I had uncovered seven shop-kinks in a competing truck garage across town. Promptly this foreman set out to prove *his* shop more innovative than the other. Before running dry he rounded up twelve shop-kinks.

By such competitive leverage, I ultimately uncovered one Shop with 17 good shop-kinks. Some were variants of ideas seen elsewhere, of course. But even the variants were newsworthy in their different applications.

The shop-kink market has long since dried up. Most such special jigs, stands, hoists, dollies, etc., are now made commercially. Moreover cost of shop labor is now too high to expend on making gadgets that can be brought more cheaply commercially.

Yet in the late Fifties, *Commercial Car Journal,* by publicizing the variants of so many shop-kinks, did much to speed up their commercial introduction.

Schedule to Fit Your Personality. Actually, scheduling, to be realistic, should be adapted to a writer's personality, as well as day-to-day circumstances.

Hazel was a "night owl" who just couldn't go to bed at night, or wake up in the morning. Yet her best creative work came in the morning, once she downed coffee black enough to open her eyes.

She bee-lined to her desk, ignoring breakfast and household chores, to get in four solid hours of creative work, if possible. The rest of the day she tapered off with overhead chores, correspondence, paperwork, housework. But any time Hazel got in that solid four morning hours, her day was "made!" She even refused to pick up the mail until noon, lest she get distracted by it.

I usually wake at dawn, no matter how late I retire. But I have to "crank up," I futz with paperwork, posting records, handling mail, filing. Finally I get productively rolling by 10 a.m. or thereabouts.

Once rolling, I'm usually good for all day, and sometimes half the night, if need be.

When I get my teeth into something I tend to stay with it to the bitter end and exclusion of all else. Preliminary futzing is excused as trying to eliminate all possible interruptions in advance.

Hazel preferred to rotate among several jobs. She thrived on variety. Like a fretful mare, she shied from what I call "hoeing corn," a nose-to-graindstone all-day push at one task until it's done.

Hazel would determinedly get in her creative four hours daily, but she'd always have several writing projects going. She would quickly switch whenever she bogged down.

No "Best" Way. Some writers prefer to tackle the typewriter in the morning, do their interviews in the afternoon, run errands on the way home. Others like best to interview in the morning "with clear minds," then do their writing after lunch.

Those who range widely from home base learn to interview intensively for several full days in a row. Then they settle at home to a week or two of solid writing.

Such scribes are more careful about filling out notes while they're fresh. They often spend evenings roughing stories in motels, sometimes even finishing one or two that involve deadlines.

A writer's hours are precious in terms of dollars earned by the hour. If an hour in the motel gives richer material, due to freshness of detail in the mind, than that hour's value is higher than two hours spent later trying to recall stale data.

Chapter 34

Help—Can You Multiply Yourself?

"Without a full-time unpaid worker around the house (my wife), I may not have made it freelancing!" frankly admitted John Stapp, a prolific business writer. "She's bookkeeper, typist, grammarian, re-writer and darkroom expert."

John might have added marketing, re-mailing, record-keeping, filing, purchasing, phone answering and more to that list.

During the Great Depression, the Stapps turned to freelance business writing for support of a new young family. In later years and better times, John and his wife put kids through college, acquired property and savings. Now semi-retired they live modestly but comfortably, even as productivity gradually lessens.

A freelance career is often born of financial desperation, whether due to unemployment or of need to supplement inadequate job income. It's a time when the wife or husband, the kids or grandma, are all likely to lend a hand for the common good.

There's no question then of adequate return, or fair treatment, or whether the work is pleasurable. If daddy or mommy can make a buck writing freelance, we'd better all help daddy or mommy write lots of freelance stories. It's a simple matter of groceries, rent and clothing!

But depression-born attitudes and practices often persist too long after crises are past. We continue to grind out as much copy as fast as we can, and indiscriminately take what we can get for it. If not enough money comes in, grind out more copy faster!

Choice Between Helping Or Working Out. Does a writer's family-help net more total net family income than if the helper(s) should work at outside jobs instead?

Suppose a writer, working alone, produces "X" income. With the help of his family they produce "X" plus "Y" income. The basic economic question then is whether the family helper(s) could earn significantly more than "Y" by working outside rather than helping the writer.

However, to make fair comparison, the *net* income earned outside should be used. That is, from outside wages you first deduct cost of commuting, lunches, clothes, beauty care, union dues, office collections, etc. *Then* compare to "Y" what remains of the outside wages.

On the other hand, if one family member does have an outside job, will it bring fringe benefits to the whole family, such as: reduced cost of car insurance, or of life, health and accident insurance; medical check-ups; pensions; merchandise or travel discounts; credit union availability; etc.?

The value of family support must be judged by balancing pluses and minuses of both writer support and of outside work. Set down the pluses and minuses on paper for careful study. Try to put dollar value on each plus or minus, even though some items must be estimated.

Not All Have Dollar Signs. Other factors affect this equation, to be sure. Is the wife already tied down at home, with kids or an invalid's care? Is the helper too handicapped for outside work? Or would a teenager, for instance, get experience useful to future outside employment.

Finally, *should* a family member stay home to help, even at proven financial advantage? Or might this confine the helper so closely to home, as to create psychological problems. The helper can get mildly "stir-crazy," if positive steps are not taken to prevent it.

For instance, a busy writer breaks up the days with interviews, surveys, plant visits, meetings, press conferences, grand openings. Admittedly these all can be drizzle-dull. But the writer does at least get out of the house, around town, and meeting people. Meanwhile the helpmate may drudge on without release day-after-day between the same four walls.

It isn't always so. But it can seem that way. In many little ways confined routine takes its toll of efficiency in the long run. Mistakes, procrastination and bickering chew into the productive time and dollars!

So, at least be prepared to grant the helper as many outside chores as possible to relieve the monotony! *Plan* to get the helpers out and away as often as can be managed.

Comes Back To Revenue-Per-Hour. The basic function of a writer is to ferret out, assimilate and organize certain facts, then convey them to a client, whether on paper, by phone, or by other media. This, presumably, is the writer's highest skill-level. It should be the most rewarding in revenue-per-hour.

Therefore the more total time a writer devotes to getting facts down on paper, the higher that writer's net income should be.

A freelance's billing rate is usually a compromise. It's a blend of varied tasks, weighted by skills and efficiency at each task. Moreover, it must be measured against the outside labor market where each task by itself commands a different pay scale.

A writer's net return at each task then varies with competence there-at. A journalist who touch-types 60 words-a-minute, yet falls into rigor mortis before a column of figures, obviously needs bookkeeping-help more than typing-aid.

Now, suppose a family helper can *net* only $3 per hour outside (1978 figures). But at home she or he can enable the writer to double production at an average *net* of $5 per hour. To this family the *net* gain would be $2 per hour for the helper to work at home.

If talents are *truly* journalistic, a writer generally needs help most with mechanical overhead functions—such as a good secretary provides.

On the other hand, only laymen regard writing as monolithic. Article production abounds with specialists—legmen, researchers, re-writers, editors, headline writers, abstractors, columnists, and even more.

Hence, suppose the people-contact of interviews inspires a journalist, while libraries and archives induce siesta. Then being provided with helpful research profits *that* scribe more than having another body out conducting interviews.

The Multiplier Effect. So independent professional people usually enjoy the best financial returns for their own efforts in direct ratio to their success in applying the "multiplier effect." This is a management engineering term for sharing as much of your work as possible with people who can do it more cheaply than you.

The theory is that if you are worth $10 per hour as a writer and communicator, you should "waste" as little time as possible on $3 per hour work such as re-typing, mailing, filing, clerical, bookkeeping and darkroom work. Every hour *you* spend on such chores, in theory, is "costing" you $7, rather than saving $3.

Of course, the assumption is that you have plenty of $10-per-hour jobs available. On the other hand, if you are buried up to here in $3-per-hour work, you are less likely to be alert to or to promote $10-per-hour opportunities!

There's another booby-trap to this multiplier effect, however. If it takes hour-for-hour of your time to supervise and/or service a $3-per-hour "multiplier" (i.e., employee), then what have you gained in the long run?

We ourselves have had a succession of one-day-per-week

domestics, plus several printing and darkroom services, only to conclude we don't profit very much from their use. By the time you instruct, supervise, transport, check, correct and keep records on everyone and everything—you're lucky if you make a nickel!

This appears to be part of the penalty of being small operators in a mass-oriented economy. As solitary individuals, we aren't important enough to anyone to command their full attention and dedicated service.

Social Security and Tax Load. In recent years another factor in the equation has become the cost of taxes and social security payments. If you hire an employee outright, the governmental burden is one-third to one half more on top of the take-home pay. The paperwork is horrendous!

If family members work out for someone else, the employer pays half the withholdings. When they work for you, as employees, *you* pay it all. Or if you don't pay it, your widow and dependent children get only minimal survivors' benefits, should you get hit by a truck.

In most states you can avoid some paperwork on unemployment insurance, etc., by forming a partnership with your spouse. A joint income tax return is filed, with separate reports on social security payments by you and your partner.

"Farming-Out" Is Next Alternative. It usually isn't too difficult to locate someone in your neighborhood to type manuscripts and transcribe recordings. Look in the newspaper classified ads first. Check the classified telephone directory. Inquire at the local business school or college.

But probably most cost-effective is to ask among your neighbors. For most typing businesses have offices and overhead to support and charge for. You are lucky if you find a gal with two or three young children to look after. She's homebound, but has secretarial experience and is eager to make the extra bucks. And hopefully she lives close enough so pick-up and delivery take only a few minutes.

To arrive at a fair rate of pay, see what is currently advertised in the writers' magazines for manuscript typing. Make allowance for whether you deliver and pick up, or she does. Pay a minimum for "clean" copy, that's easily and quickly read. Double the rate for "dirty" copy that chews up the gal's time in trying to understand it.

If you have to supply the typewriter, first check with a public accountant or the local tax office to determine whether in your state that makes the typist an employee, even if working in her own home.

In some states there's a very fine distinction between being an employee and an "independent contractor."

Yet a major benefit of farming-out your re-typing or transcription work is to avoid the government involvement and paperwork connected with having an employee.

How About Tape Recorders. They're wonderful! But they're expensive when used unnecessarily because of the extra cost of transcribing. They serve me best with technical material. But if they're to be transcribed for me, I still take notes on the obscure terms. The gal may not understand the words, and I may forget what they were, without the notes.

Greatest value for me has been dictating notes while driving on long trips, especially when returning from a heavily-programmed meeting. Your mind wanders while driving anyway, so it can be profitable to refocus it on the meeting program. Same is true if I've had a long difficult interview where I couldn't readily use the tape recorder, like wandering through a foundry or stone-crushing plant.

I often use the recorder only for back-up, without transcription. I depend on my notes for the story, but run through the recording for quotes or some detailed explanations. Never have been able to control the recorder so half what's on the tape isn't irrelevant stories, anecdotes, diversions, partial phone conversations, etc.!

There's rarely trouble using the recorder anymore. Virtually every business man or woman has kids playing with them around the house, or working with them in school. Many executives use recorders themselves in their own businesses.

And despite my referral to irrelevant material, the presence of a recorder exercises a bit of discipline. People are simply more careful when being recorded.

Which all gets back to my original caution. The big expense of tape recorders can be transcription, if you're hiring it done.

Teamwork That Pays. When two or more freelances team up, temporarily or permanently, each partner soon turns specialist, contributing the journalistic chores at which he or she is the more adept.

For instance, several husband-wife teams are or have been members of Associated Business Writers of America. And it is our observation they tend to be more successful than the average writer working alone. This is in terms of net return per hour of total work by both partners.

Utilization of best talents and experience appears to be the basic reason for the higher returns.

In our personal spells of teamwork it has proven so. On Hazel's stories I'd do the photography. I'd also dig out technical or mechanical details, write them up rough draft. Then she'd absorb my draft into her story, re-written in her own style.

On my stories Hazel would pull out the human interest, research the personnel relations and the training functions. Her drafted notes were then incorporated into my main draft.

Previously I described a group project whereon I became team photographer (by process of elimination). I was also specialist on all matters involving detailed paperwork. This latter was not so much due to my talent, as to the others' distaste for doggedly tracing controls of any kind.

But what most assures me of the value in utilizing separate skills is the variation among two-some situations (of any duration) in which I've been involved. I have always wound up with different chores, depending on the partner teamed with. In team situations I have been variously responsible for research, interviewing, rough drafting, polishing, photography, darkrooming, mechanical drawing and querying.

Typing and Typists. It is surprising how often a writer's deficiency involves poor typing skill. Many times the typing chore has fallen to me simply because I'm a faster typist than my partner (even though I'm not all that good a typist)!

Because Hazel and I were fast typists, she especially, we tended to revise copy even while typing a final draft. This is because the common mental block to doing a page over again was really no obstacle to us.

Either of us could re-type a page almost as quickly as we could mark up instructions for someone else to follow. Therefore typing help was less needed by us than some other skills.

This is highly important, in our opinion. Slow or poor typing creates so craggy a mental block for many writers, they let sloppy copy go out to clients, rather than force themselves, or a helper to retype a crisper, more legible draft.

Hunt-&-Peck Hamstrings. Anyone with normal dexterity *can* learn to touch-type fairly rapidly and automatically. The mind is then able to concentrate on composition, unhampered by keyboard concerns.

My own fingers are somewhat large, slightly stubby, and utterly clumsy at picking up small or delicate objects. As a bachelor, I couldn't darn socks without bleeding all over them.

Yet as a young man I did learn to type 60-words-a-minute

without error, even faster on rough-drafting. This is all without thought for what my fingers are doing. In fact, if I do think about my typing I start making mistakes.

The secret, of course, is touch-typing without looking at the keyboard.

Many successful writers hunt-and-peck at a fast pace on type-writers. Some can draft copy almost as fast as Hazel or I. But watch these folks re-type their final draft, or copy some printed material. They must study the copy to pick out a phrase or sentence, then glance down to watch their fingers work. Back-and-forth, back-and-forth.

This slows them to where editing and polishing become a sub-conscious mental block. Often they begin to take pride in whipping out unrevised first drafts that "can go as is" to clients—and are paid for accordingly. Or else final drafts are done by someone else, who usually *can* touch-type.

Learning To Touch-Type Is Easy. Actually, learning to touch-type is not all that arduous. Nor is formal schooling necessary. Major typewriter manufacturers all give away or sell good typing manuals. Stationery and office supply stores stock independent typing manuals, possibly school texts, for modest cost.

If you follow their exercises faithfully for a half-hour each working day, your typing speed will pick up noticeably in two weeks, and substantially before a month is out. Most rapid progress would come if you could space out four 15-minute practice sessions per day.

You may nearly go crazy the first week! Especially if you already are a rapid hunt-and-peck typist. For this reason, like giving up smoking, most would-be touch-typists do give up in their first week.

But persevere! In the long run you'll save yourself a lot of ex-pense for hired typing. This is because, in many, many instances, you can type something out yourself as fast as you can mark-up copy for some one else to type.

However, another secret of successful touch-typing is to never give up exercises entirely. Every now and then your fingers suddenly get fiendishly uncooperative. Certain letter combinations persistent-ly appear in the wrong places. You try to write "sink" or "sign," and it comes out "sing."

That's when you take yourself by the scruff of the neck and patiently type out "sink, sing, sign,; sink, sing, sign; sink, sing, sign" for five minutes each day for a week. Sooner, or later, your fingers will repent and behave again—on that particular letter combination.

In the weeks thereafter those little five-minute exercises will spare you from whole flocks of erasures.

Chapter 35

Yoga vs Fridge-Break

Refrigerator vs Tension

Health hazards of freelance business writers are less than for the average office or shop worker. But this is only provided the writer exercises self-discipline.

With fewer meals out, preferred or prescribed diets can be adhered to more closely. The problem is to halt refrigerator visits. For snacking is a reflex reaction for writers who actually only need an occasional break from the typewriter.

It might help, for instance, to paste a large sign on the "fridge" door reading "Three deep breaths!"

Creative typing is unlike clerical or transcription typing, where the mind usually coasts. As absorption in words and phrasing grows, one's breathing becomes short and shallow. Knees jam against typing table legs, shoulders lock and fingers pound. The words seem virtually thrust onto the paper physically. You come to each break in a state of semi-paralysis!

Hence, before you touch food, or cigarettes, try Stage One. Take a half-dozen real deep breaths. Slowly distend the abdomen first. Then fill the chest with *all* the air it'll hold. Now suck in the abdomen, followed by the chest, expelling the air as completely as possible.

This moves so much carbon dioxide out of the lungs, and fresh oxygen in, that you may even feel a trifle dizzy for a moment. But you'll also relax!

Then ask yourself, do you *really* need that sandwich or soft drink or piece of cake, or cigarette? Chances are, you're ready to go right back to the typewriter.

A Physical Break. If not, Stage Two is in order. This is either a short brisk walk, some vigorous calisthenics, or a bit of yoga. Actually you've probably finished a segment of your article, and need a few moments to think out or organize the next phase.

This you can do while exercising something besides the jaw and stomach muscles, then return to work refreshed.

Physical activity is preferrable to some sedentary hobby or

269

diversion. Tense muscles need to be stimulated and relaxed. Slumped in a chair reading a paper is not likely to do it.

If there are short physical chores around the house or office to do fairly vigorously, they are much better tension-breaks than are "fridge-trips."

"Business Writer's Syndrome." Professional freelance business writers are subject to a specific ailment we call the "business writer's syndrome!"

This is a constant or recurring stiff neck, a spot of pain just below and between the shoulder blades, and soreness in or to the right of the small of the back. It all comes from hours immobilized at the typewriter, alternated by hours with the right foot glued to the car's gas pedal.

There are a few minor helps for this syndrome. Arrange your typing set-up so that copy material can be moved into at least four positions.

That is, copy should be able to lie flat, or be stood up, on each side of the typewriter. Then be sure to shift it often, such as after every second or third page of typed copy.

In the car, when waiting for a stop light, tuck your accelerator foot under your left foot (which should be on the brake pedal). Roll the right foot repeatedly on its right ankle, until you feel a slight pull in the ankle. Wiggle your toes.

Change your seat adjustment occasionally, on long drives. If the back angle, doesn't adjust, insert a wedge pillow every once in a while. Move the seat back if necessary.

Turn the wedge upside down a time or two for short periods. This may make you slightly uncomfortable, but it shifts tensions to a different set of muscles. It relaxes those previously locked under tension.

Shift sidewise in your seat. You can move four to six inches toward the door under a seat belt without affecting your driving. (We have to shift this much to accommodate a third person in the front seat, for instance.) Then if you move that far from the door toward the middle, muscle tensions change again.

Over the years we found a good chiropractor or osteopath could temporarily break up this business writer's syndrome. If treated often enough, he could even ward it off. But the treatments get expensive and time-consuming!

Yoga Can Help. Our most effective solution has been yoga exercises. We don't buy the esoteric occult practices, but the physical stretching, and deep breathing of "hatha yoga" has greatly modified this syndrome for us.

This book is no place for elaboration on yoga. There are well-illustrated manuals by professionals on the subject. But I'd like to make a point or two about yoga vis-a-vis the business writer's syndrome.

We experimented with a couple dozen exercises. Now I concentrate on ten or twelve that seem most helpful. Almost all tend to stretch muscles of the neck, shoulders, back and hips. These are the ones tensed most over long periods at the typewriter or behind the wheel.

If you wish to check our choice of exercises in a yoga manual, they are: Handstand; Shoulder Stand; Plough; Fish; Forward Bend (seated); Head-Knee Post; Twist; Cobra; Ancestor worship; Shoulder Squeeze; Neck Rolls; Clock Circles (for the eyes).

The relaxing part is as valuable as the exercises! I lay flat on the floor for three minutes between each exercise and try to melt into the floor. That in itself relieves a lot of tension.

At my mature years (sixty-eight at time of writing), I haven't mastered the official headstand using the forearms. I do employ the old YMCA head-and-palms headstand. But for me it does the job!

Beneficial Side Effects. A writer sits so much of the time, his innards sag into the pelvic basin. Chronic constipation can result, with hemorrhoids as a side effect. Two or three headstands per day, for a minute or two each time, will markedly reverse this pelvic sag.

Low backache, caused by hours of typing can be replaced quickly in a headstand by the tingle of blood re-circulating at the small of the back. Rippling the abdomen muscles a time or two while upsidedown, aids this sag reversal.

Swollen ankles from sitting or standing long hours, especially in summer, will also be relieved by occasional headstands.

This yoga routine, after we employed it for a couple years, apparently solved chronic lifetime constipation attributed to business writer's syndrome.

The most effective yoga is done in a single session of forty minutes to an hour. The actual time depends on how long it takes to get relaxed between each set of exercises.

Non-Coffee Breaks. But to a writer, yoga is often more useful when done as "non-coffee breaks." In segments of two or three different exercises and relaxations, do it three or four times in the workday. Such yoga-breaks bring you back to the typewriter quite refreshed.

Yoga is a good relaxer after a long drive. As you lug the bags into the motel room, you usually still "feel the road going by." A quick headstand, against a wall if necessary, will cure that fuzziness almost instantly.

Or a full set of yoga exercises takes about the time needed to down a couple of highballs. Yet the yoga can refresh you so you wonder why you stopped driving so soon!

And again, yoga counteracts the constipation that comes from long hours behind the wheel.

We do drink coffee. But yoga keeps us from drinking so much we get the dark brown taste! We have just enough to truly enjoy coffee for itself, and not for the break. Too often coffee drinking is simply excuse to stop work for a spell!

Yoga also considerably reduced our resort to alcoholic beverages for relaxation. With the price of Scotch today, that's not an insignificant benefit!

Of course, another benefit of freelancing is that one does feel free to stretch out on the floor for yoga-breaks without upsetting office decorum.

Chapter 36

Good Ethics are Smart Business Writing

After a writer leaves an organization to freelance, one's total nakedness is the most difficult thing to accept.

As an employee, the writer is both protected and supported by the image of "the company." One is a *Time* man, a *Daily News* gal, the *Fur Breeder* reporter, a McGraw-Hill editor, or that *Women's Wear Daily* stringer.

Each publication has a unique image that's widely-if-subconsciously-accepted in its field. Its employees are cloaked (more or less) with that image. Their deeds and misdeeds are co-mingled with it. And responsibility for misdeeds are shared on a "don't do it again" basis with the editor or publisher.

But generally the freelance writer is strictly on his own. Any company mantle assumed in part-time or temporary assignment is porous and fragile at best. Editorial patience with freelance misdeeds is far shorter and more explosive than it is with "the company's" permanent hired hands.

Moreover, as a responsible independent contractor, a true freelance *must* build his or her own *personal image as a freelance.* The writer's availability in the communications marketplace will never be widely enough known or understood, if he or she is constantly disguised in the cloak of one magazine or another.

One's observed personal ethics, therefore, are a prime factor in building a writer's image and marketability. These ethics involve dealings in both directions: with editors and other clients; and with the persons interviewed or written about.

Ethical Standards Vary. Proper ethics for freelances is a perennial topic at writers' gathering, even when not on the official program.

Discussion is especially heated between freelances from different disciplines—editorial, advertising, public relations, education or government. Each discipline has a somewhat different ethical value-system, and they conflict at various points between disciplines.

Since the freelance often must work in more than one of these communications disciplines, in order to earn a living income in his locale, it is necessary to perform in a manner creditable all across the board.

Other factors becloud ethics considerations, too. For instance, freelancing combines an employer/employee relationship with that of buyer-vs-seller. There's an implied pledge of loyalty to the client that conflicts with the pragmatism of "independence."

Again, a freelance often works with separate clients who are themselves in direct competition with each other. Thus the freelance often is privy to information or insights that ought to be held in strictest confidence. A guarded tongue is a vital asset to an ethical freelance.

Subsidized Writing's Shadow. Much discussion of freelance writing ethics involves "subsidized" writing. This is material written for publication in magazines, but paid for by some source other than the magazine. The inference is that, if the magazine doesn't pay the writer, an article will not be "objective" or unbiased. It can't help, the contention is, but be unduly slanted to the sponsor's advantage.

Some subdized writing got a shady reputation, so far as I know, back during The Great Depression. There was a noxious racket involving subsidy all through the Thirties.

Some character would sweep through a town. He'd call on many small business men, and some not so small. To each he'd claim to be "reporter" or "field editor" of a leading trade journal in that man's field. His proposal was to publish stories about each firm, provided the owner thereof paid "expenses" or "publication fees."

In that era, most business people were unsophisticated about business magazine procedure. They often were gullible enough to pay off. I've even been shown "receipts" for such payments, complete with the magazines' names printed on them.

On payment, these characters would go through the motions of an interview. In the later years they even clicked an empty camera a few times. Then, after a fast sweep through a business district, they'd vanish. The stories, of course, never appeared in print.

It was a lucrative racket for some time, so much so the Chambers of Commerce and Better Business Bureaus inveighed against it for a decade or more.

At that time I was breaking into trade journals as an assistant editor. I quickly learned in those days that any businessman approached for a story would immediately ask, "What will it cost me?" Often it took real persuasion to assure him our magazine paid all costs, before we could finally get down to the business of an interview and pictures.

Occasionally I had to sign statements of assurance there would be no charge to the businessman, either after the interview or after publication. In some communities businessmen even had such statements already at hand, prepared by lawyers and circulated by the Better Business Bureau or other business organizations.

Ethics For A "Free" Lance. Before discussing subsidized writing of the more normal and commonly accepted kind, let's look briefly at the words "freelance" and "ethics."

A freelance is literally that—a "free" lance. He or she has *no* binding ties, is permanently beholden to no one.

Swiss soldiers guarding the Popes were freelances. Hessian troops fighting our Colonials were freelances. The famed French Foreign Legion was composed of freelances. They were professional fighting men hired out to anyone who paid a fair wage—often to the highest bidder.

Whomever they did serve received their complete loyalty and dedicated effort during the period of service. Swiss guards were especially noted for their integrity and faithfulness. They were much sought after. By contrast, of course, many freelance soldiers or sailors became full or part-time freebooters. When no one hired them, they turned to banditry and piracy. Too often, of course, their behavior was indistinguishable under either circumstance.

OK—as a freelance writer I serve any client who pays me a fair wage. While paid by him, or her, I will be loyal and dedicated. Even after such service is terminated, I will always maintain all confidences incurred.

But my basic ethic is that I will not serve for illegal ends a known criminal, subversive, fraud or pervert. I will not knowingly write anything false or misleading.

In other words, as a writer I'm simply a special tool, useful to the client who hires me. But as a human being, I strive to be principled and moral in the use to which I am put.

Writing The Subsidized Article. Swan Cleaners, a multi-million dollar group of textile service plants in Columbus, Ohio, retained me to write a lengthy story about them and place it in a leading drycleaning magazine.

At the editor's regular rates, I couldn't afford to spend more than a day in Columbus, let alone drive there. But Swan paid for a week in which to study the operation in depth.

As it appeared in the magazine, the story was completely factual. It was explicit about several unique Swan practices of real news value to other drycleaners. It deserved to be written. Feedback from the publication's readers on publication was uniformly good.

Swan's objective was strictly PR. They ordered thousands of reprints. They also re-cast the same story in tabloid format as an eight-page insert in the *Columbus Dispatch*. Extra copies of the insert were distributed from Swan's 30-odd stores for several years thereafter.

The magazine paid me nothing, though they regularly pay for everything else I contribute. This one exception was arranged for beforehand.

Did the editor abdicate his own objectivity? Was this project ethical? I believe it was.

The story *was* accurate and exciting. The magazine suffered in no way. Yet to have adequately paid my time and expense would have dislocated that editor's freelance budget for several months. They never could have ordered this story on their own. It would never have been told so comprehensively.

Suppose I had been Swan's regular PR man, whose task was to write and plant stories about Swan? Would that change the ethics?

Suppose the editor paid what he could normally afford, and Swan paid the rest? This arrangement is also occasionally made. Swan desired control of the story's flavor, not its accuracy. In fact, I had to completely re-write the first version. It had struck them as "too technical" to be understood by Swan's customers.

Some Editors Have No Freelance Budget. Without subsidy, some small magazines would never be markets for freelance writers. Yet they are significant publications in narrow fields of business and industry.

During the Fifties, *The National Rug Clearner* was a very skinny publication with zero funds for story purchase. To earn a full salary, its editor also served as assistant editor on two other publications. The magazine was so marginal that loss of one major advertiser could, and eventually did, throw it permanently into the red. Yet in the Fifties the magazine was the *only* voice of progress in the tiny rug cleaning field.

So one major manufacturer paid me a good fee and expenses to do six feature stories per year for placement in this magazine. I suspect two or three other advertisers did likewise with other writers, though this was never verified to me.

All the stories (mine and theirs) were good operational case histories, never unduly slanted to the subsidizing manufacturers. The sponsors' direct benefit was frequent appearance of their equipment in the pictures, (not always under ideal conditions either).

Again, was this unethical? My patron once said he'd thought of offering the publisher 24 more ad pages a year, if the publisher would just put most of the money into more good articles. How would that have differed from direct subsidy of a writer?

In actual practice an advertiser gets no more leverage with an editor through any subsidized writing he provides than with 12 or 24 extra ad pages. Of course the editor does have to insist more firmly on objectivity in articles than with ads, to sustain credibility with his readers.

Subsidized Writing Still Requires Principles. All I, the freelance, can do is write any story as honestly as I see it. If I do, it doesn't matter who pays, or what use is made of it, so long as the use is moral and legal.

I once flew to Chicago for an in-depth descriptive story on development of a truly new and significant process. To introduce it to the industry for the manufacturer, I was to place the story in a leading magazine.

My client didn't think the finished copy was laudatory enough. Yet *I* felt *he* would be stretching the truth to say more, and unnecessarily so! Actually the process *was* truly outstanding on its own merits. It didn't need inaccurate embellishment.

Ultimately I left the manuscript with him to use *without* my by line, and flew back to New York. I figured I'd really "blown this one."

After further thought, my client wound up adding a few slightly florid touches himself. But he showed much more restraint than he originally would accept from me. This version he ran as a six-page story-page *advertisement,* so labelled, under my by-line. And he sent my full check for fee and expenses.

I've described these experiences to show the elusiveness of ethics in any patron-writer-editor-reader relationship. What may be ethical often has to be a subjective decision by the writer. The beauty of freelancing is that the writer is never subject to organizational fiat to produce unethical copy.

Puff, Puff, Puff. "Puffery" is blowing your own horn frankly and openly. Advertising, the extreme, is paying outright for the privilege of puffing. External house organs are designed for puffing products or businesses. Direct mail is rifle-shooting puffs to specific individuals or families.

There are a hundred different ways of more subtle puffing, aside from case histories of a laudatory nature. Some thumbnail biographies, for instance, can be so quaintly or perceptively written as to rate very high readership. So advertisers and subscribers are eager to be mentioned in such columns.

Hence many publications have their special departments of

"Profiles," "Names in the News," "Who's Who," "Remember When," "Editor's Sportlight," "Know Your Industry Leaders," etc.

But Is It Honest? Thus we get down to the real moral issues: "Are the stories I'm telling essentially true? Do they describe advertisers, or others, honestly? Or are there obvious distortions and misrepresentations?" This is where the writer decides whether he can live with his own writing.

Also it may come down to a question of whether the story is unethical, or whether it's the image of the publisher or editor that's unethical or immoral. If the latter, your real concern should be seeming to ally yourself with, and therefore condoning, such publishing practices.

It's A Small World. The freelance lives in a small world—several small worlds, in fact. Each is a compact world, wired and tunnelled with many open channels of communication.

Firstly, a business writer deals mostly with a narrow slice of any given industry, the top five percent perhaps. For good stories rarely come from failures, except perhaps for a horrible example. The real news-makers are constant repeaters in a magazine's pages, because they are both innovative and aggressive.

These elite business people are in constant communication with each other. They frequently visit one another, phone each other, meet at conventions, serve as officers, attend seminars together, go on post-convention trips, etc.

Hence news of grossly inaccurate reporting wildfires through such upper business strata. The guilty writer's reputation is quickly reduced to cold ashes. Executive suites become inaccessible overnight.

A similar grapevine connects the leaders of any local business community. It is of vital importance to the freelance who mines a small territory, a city or town and environs, and who must work many industries to conduct a full-time freelance career.

For local business people are another small world that crosses industry lines. They meet regularly for fraternal luncheons, serve together in churches and charities, electioneer together, etc.

Therefore a shifty or unscrupulous writer will find local business doors closing so fast he or she will soon be forced to get a steady job, or else move on, move on and on.

Editors Move Around. In a different vein, editors are a fluid bunch, often transferring from publication to publication as they upgrade their careers. The generally small size of editorial staffs make promotion from within a snail-like process. To advance themselves, editors most often have to change publications.

Thus many a new account comes to a good freelance when his or her favorite editor moves to another magazine, usually in a stronger decision-making spot.

Conversely, many a writer finds an erstwhile market dries up suddenly, if the new editor proves to be one whom he or she badly fouled-up on another magazine.

Then there's always the editor who needles a competitor, "Boy your Larry Golightly was way off on that cactus juice story! Where the heck did he get his dope—er—facts?"

Defensively the editor's victim admits Golightly *was* a new correspondent, one he couldn't really recommend to anyone. That fixes Golightly with both editors. Also their associates, if they happen to work for multi-publication houses.

Readers Speak Up, Too. Misleading or false statements disillusion readers. They engender cynicism about the factualness of all one's business paper stories. Once business readers catch you off base a time or two, they tend thereafter to promptly flip the page at the sight of your byline.

Inaccurate writing involves your editors in arguments or awkward discussions with both their readers and their advertisers. It even can make you liable to subpeona as court witness to statements you can't support. For inaccurate reporting does expose both the magazine and you to court action.

Being too free with the facts *never* pays a freelance business writer. *All* his worlds are much too small!

ABWA Code Of Ethics. Thus "accuracy of fact and presentation is the first consideration, with nothing taken for granted." This statement is the first declaration in a Code of Ethics evolved over the 40-year experience of Associated Business Writers of America.

This Code's preamble reads: "Accepting their *responsibility* to editors and readers *as a public trust,* ABWA members and associates are bound by these standards of practice."

Impartial And Fair. The second point in the ABWA Code reads "impartial and fair treatment, without personal bias, shall be given both news and features."

Writers and reporters, as much as any human beings, are subject to strong opinions and to bias about many things. But we must not permit the *facts* of news or a story to get entangled with our personal opinions or bias.

A reporter's major function for editors and clients is communicating facts, as clearly and accurately as possible. If any coloring or shading of facts are to be done, that is the editor's privilege.

Careful distinction is necessary between slanting to a magazine's style and injecting one's personal bias. Distorting or withholding facts cheats the editor. It makes it more difficult for him or her to gain a complete, clear picture of circumstances. It can cause an editor to go off on a tangent, requiring a 180° turn later when full or true facts come to light.

Therefore, if certain newsgathering proves distasteful to a writer, it would be better to reject the assignment, than to pass in distorted, biased or incomplete facts.

Distortion quite often occurs in paraphrasing or condensing an interview. Choice of words can materially alter thoughts or concepts originally expressed to the writer.

"The full sense of a report can be changed," says veteran editor Fay Coupe, "according to whether you say the bucket is half-empty or half-full, both accurate statements in themselves, or whether you say a person spoke 'cautiously,' 'guardedly' or 'warily.' "

Omission of qualifying remarks often leaves unclear whether the interviewee is dubious, or positive or whether the facts are his actual witness, hearsay evidence or simple speculation. Omission of contradictory or substantiating evidence or testimony also affects the credibility of a story.

Hence the writer is under more compulsion to supply *all* essentials, than he or she is required to screen out trivia.

Grind No Private Axes. "Private interests of writers are not promoted; material offered in a public relations capacity is so labelled."

If you're crusading or promoting, level with your editor or clients. Remember, it's a small world!

A certain writer had a deal with Bushmeyer Beer (name altered). He got $50 for every picture published with a recognizable Bushmeyer bottle visible somewhere in it.

He kept this deal secret. Several pix appearing in different publications had Bushmeyer bottles clearly visible in the background, on window sills, cabinets, truck tailgates, boat seats, etc. Nothing in the stories themselves had to do with beer.

A couple editors got suspicious, and industry people commented to other editors about it. Word spread among editors in other industries. Suddnely Bushmeyer bottles were being cropped or painted out of this writer's illustrations.

His cries of anguish resulted in a few accommodations. But thereafter universal skepticism about every detail in that writer's photographs made editors more critical of *all* his photo content. Some editors even scaled down their pay on the assumption he was probably also being compensated from other sources.

Actually, few editors cared whether or how this writer made a few extra bucks. What they did question most critically was whether his pix made specific points about his stories, or whether the points actually were "piggy-backing" the beer bottles. That is, were his stories "manufactured" as vehicles for beer bottle displays.

Moreover, the best angles for a good illustration don't always accommodate a casually-placed beer bottle.

Confidences Not Violated. "Confidences imposed by news sources will not be violated under any circumstances."

A freelance once submitted a story from St. Louis to me, as editor. It included some revealing cost data about a certain business. After publication, we learned this data was given the writer in strict confidence, which he violated.

There *is* a black mark against *me*, for not phone-checking such sensitive copy. I can only say the industry was on a cost-comparison kick at the time. Such figures *were* being published every month. So I didn't think the check-back necessary.

But that writer was in the doghouse in St. Louis from then on, not only with that industry, but in the business community at large. Moreover, despite full apology and attempt at explanation, our own editorial staff wasn't able to get a solid story out of St. Louis for a full decade thereafter.

Yessir, it *is* a real small world!

A blabbermouth reporter also gets tagged quickly. It's one thing to pass along tips about solving business problems. But gossip is something else. It gets you a reputation you'll *never* live down.

When a writer details juicy tidbits about other firms, especially competitors, the listener usually wonders what the writer will say about him or her at the writer's *next* destination. So gossip can dry up an interview abruptly, even if the interviewee first appears to invite gossip.

Dependable Performance of Assignment. "Dependable performance of an assignment, once accepted, is to be made by every reasonable effort to get the story; hindrance to such performance will be reported to editors at once, whether the hindrance be economic or otherwise."

It is appalling how often a writer, supposedly expert in communications, fails to keep the editor or client informed about obstacles or delays in completing an assignment. This even includes dropping an assignment, or walking out in the middle of it, and never reporting the fact. Honest, some freelances actually do drop assignments without notifying clients, who in turn usually drop the writers. It's unbelievable!

Assignments are almost always tied to editorial schedules, however firmly or flexibly. As one editor moaned, "I *would* like a hint whether I can use that story *this* October or *next* October!"

Editors or clients should never have to call writers to learn of serious obstacles or delays. The writer owes it to a client to keep him or her fully posted.

As a practical matter, from the writer's viewpoint, prompt communication can often help solve the problem quickly. The financial arrangement can be adjusted, if that's the bottleneck. Or the editor can bring pressure or persuasion to bear on a subject who stalls off the writer. Or an alternative story might be arranged.

Frequently a writer is asked to report some new development, only to find it incomplete. Letting the editor know promptly does two things. It permits the editor to re-schedule the story for a later issue. It also may result in an interim progress-report by the writer. The result would then eventually be two stories from the same project and research.

Too often an assignment proves unwieldy because the writer accepted it too casually in the first place.

Did he estimate enough time to do the job, allowing for interruptions or delays? Does he have conflicting appointments around which he must work, that can stumble this job if it drags out? Has he estimated *all* costs?

Estimate your job from a check-list before accepting. Then try to carry it through past all obstacles. But, when really stymied, let the client know at once.

Prompt Acknowledgements. Another writer faux-pas is in ignoring assignments, or queries about whether the writer is available. No matter how ridiculous or impossible an assignment might seem, it must be promptly acknowledged and accepted or rejected.

First, any proffered assignment is a business proposition. It is usually offered in good faith, even if the terms are unrealistic.

Second, if the assignment cannot be handled, the editor should be enabled to re-assign as quickly as possible. This is not only common courtesy. It's an invitation to try you again sometime, as a truly business-like professional.

Third, *if* an assignment does seem "ridiculous," at least give the editor a chance to adjust. He may want a story badly enough to raise the fee. He may actually not understand the circumstances (i.e., Brown Town is a half-day's drive, and not a nearby suburb as the editor supposed). Or a new editor may even be unaccustomed to dealing with a freelance.

Fourth, even if the client historically offers impossible assignments (low rates, slow pay, etc.), still you should communicate, if only to say "no." Some day he may "get religion" and improve his methods or terms. Many do, often influenced by ABWA or its members. Some of the stingiest editors have become quite "good pay" over the years.

Of course, I may also have learned to write in the meantime! But how do they find out, if I don't communicate?)

And again, you may meet this editor on another better-heeled magazine some day!

Sources Are Credited. "Sources are credited in all instances where information is not obtained from original sources."

Nothing disconcerts an editor more than publishing the management views of John Doe in Oskaloosa, only to learn they're almost verbatim extracts from Prof. Smedley's research reported in *Harvard Business Review.*

The writer needs to be alert to all sources of information referred to by an interviewee, or uncovered in research. Cite them accurately and fully enough for clarity (partial quotes can even seem to contradict the basic message).

A frequent problem of this kind is statement by a primary source about an isolated instance, which the interviewee has in turn misconstrued as true of a whole class or group.

Syndication Clearly Identified. "Duplicate submission of a feature to more than one publication in non-competing fields shall be so marked, by words 'exclusive your field' or similar statement.

Syndication is the selling of an identical, or nearly identical article, column or story to more than one publication. It is generally done with a single publication in each field by verbal or written agreement or by contract.

This is a perfectly legitimate practice. But the editor or client has full right to be apprised of such multiple sales.

Syndicated material usually commands a lower price per submission than does fully-exclusive material. This is both because of the wider dispersion of syndicated information and because it is less directly tailored to a specific industry.

Assigned Material Is Exclusive. "Competitive publications will not be offered features already sold to or assigned by an editor, in original or re-written form, nor will ABWA members give, trade or sell notes or material from such features to other writers for their use, *except* at regularly-called press conferences."

A hardware merchant has perfect right to sell hammers to every contractor in town. The writer, however, sells exclusivity as an inherent part of his material, unless clearly agreed upon otherwise.

I had the embarrassing experience of submitting similar material to two magazines that I judged, without adequate study, to be non-competitive.

Fortunately I found out before publication that, while *Amercian Laundry Digest* did not consider *Executive Housekeeper* to be even indirect competition, the latter considered its hospital laundry department in hot competition with ALD. The material involved new laundry equipment.

Therefore I promptly returned his check to the EH editor (which happened to be in larger amount than the check from ALD).

The ALD editor was broadminded. The EH editor was jealously guarding his exclusivity. No writer can assume how editors regard their competition. It pays to check both editors when in doubt how close competition may be.

News Service Is For Everybody. "Duplicate sales of news is not restricted, even to competitive publications, except when sold under exclusive written agreement with an editor. Duplicated news should be so marked with 'syndicated news' or smiliar wording."

"The whole truth and nothing but the truth" sometimes suffers simply because one reporter can't cover all the elements of a fast-breaking event.

Therefore, in a tight or complex news situation, it is the mark of a mature reporter to check his findings against those of other reporters at the scene, each filling the gaps in his or her own material and assessing validity of what he or she has heard.

This is a legitimate mutual back-scratching function. If one reporter does ferret out unique data, however, it is also that individual's right to either keep this data confidential as a "scoop," or to share it for confirmation and fleshing out by the others.

The purpose of this clause in the ABWA Code is to assert the editor or client cannot condemn a writer for working cooperatively with competing reporters, if the situation is too big for one to handle expeditiously alone.

At the same time, the client has perfect right to be informed of non-exclusivity wherever and whenever it occurs.

Business-Like Submissions. "Plainly-marked rights and price should accompany all material submitted for publication, leaving no doubt as to rights offered, or terms on which they are offered."

This is not so much an ethics clause, as simple good business practice. It applies primarily to material submitted on speculation, or to cases where a query and subsequent assignment left the price-and-rights question open.

New writers are timid about declaring terms, lest they deter editors from using their material. Sometimes they're hopeful a higher fee will be paid if they don't set a price. But lack of such declaration infers the writer will just be, oh, *so* happy, simply to have his or her work published under any condition. Editors act accordingly, because they work for profit-making organizations.

That's alright if somebody else is supporting you! Otherwise you'd better start with the ABWA formula in setting prices from the beginning, and submit only to clients willing to pay what it's worth.

Good Stories Aren't Dashed-Off. Suppose you *are* trying to break in. It's better to work harder and longer on fewer articles. Then ask for fair prices based on what time you judge an experienced pro would have invested. That is, you take a day to produce a story a pro would whip out in an hour. Figure your price for an hour at the pro's rate.

In this way you more quickly establish your true worth in the field. You more quickly command a "living wage." And you more rapidly learn to produce marketable manuscripts in a reasonable length of time.

The novice is too often bemused, however, by the "dash-off" syndrome. In writers' magazines, experienced freelance journalists brag how they "dash-off" this story and that article, and how editor so-and-so sends fifty or a hundred bucks for it by return mail. These worthies keep mum about articles "dashed-off" and never heard from again!

One rarely dashes-off anything for good money. Not until you learn thoroughly the elements of the kind of story a given editor will buy. Then you do rapidly produce stories for this one editor according to his unique formula.

But in business writing, as in any other kind of journalism, one never leaps to full competence overnight. Price your article according to what you think it's worth, and say so on the "rights ear" of the manuscript.

Project A Good Image. For some editors a substantial mental block to using freelances is their concern about the magazine's image, as projected by a writer whom the editor never met.

While I was editor, I received an indignant long-distance phone call from one proprietor, because a freelance, on assignment by us, spent half his time making vigorous passes at a charming (but unresponsive) married model working in the proprietor's fur salon.

Another freelance became widely noted for pressuring interviewees to take her to lunch.

One long-time "pro," who actually is a highly competent writer, always looks as if he slept in his clothes in the barn, and stinks accordingly.

Don't Cadge Favors. It's also a mistake to cadge free materials and services from an interview host. ("Cadge" is a colloguialism meaning "beg for.") There is nothing wrong with accepting samples, voluntarily offered. These are usually samples of sales promotions or proof of quality or workmanship.

But "working" the interview host for free merchandise or services, free meals or lodging for instance, is definitely out. It smacks of the old subsidy racket of the Thirties! And word gets around about it in your small worlds.

True, there can be a thin line between accepting proffered hospitality and imposing on courtesies. Gracious interview hosts sometimes are most generous in extending courtesies. Yet the writer must be mature enough to distinguish between cordiality and imposition, and to say "no" when appropriate to do so.

Why? No writer is entirely his own man or woman during an interview. This is true even if the story is done on speculation, and the writer is unsure who will buy it.

For, once that story is sold to Blank Magazine, the performance and behaviour of the writer blends into the public image of Blank Magazine. This blending of image occurs at least in the subject's locality, but often it also spreads out in the small world of Blank Magazine's industry. Word gets around that one of Blank Magazine's reporters is "quite a moocher!"

The reader must not feel the characters described above prevail in the freelance writing field. Most *professional* freelance writers are sober, hardworking craftsmen, who take their responsibilities seriously and maturely.

The exceptions, however, though few in number, are legendary in the business publication field. They are cited so often by editors as bad examples of freelance writers, as to seem much more numerous than they actually are.

No Eccentrics Needed. Freelance business writers cannot afford the many eccentricities deemed normal to their poetic and dramatic brethren. For business writers are business men and women, who must deal empathically with other business men and women.

Stanley Marcus, of the famous Nieman-Marcus department store in Dallas, was described by *Business Week* as quick to weed out any merchandise that didn't fit that store's image. "Character editing," Marcus called it.

"A good store is comparable to a good magazine," he said. "What you edit out is just as important as what you put in."

The successful writer is always conscious of two images, his own and that of his client(s). He edits out those habits and procedures that reflect poorly on either his own character or that of his client.

One final warning that might seem to contradict much we've said before is directed mostly at the novice. The business writer cannot afford to idolize business people. The large majority of non-business writers find business, business people and profit-making offensive. On the other hand there are business journalists who think business people can do no wrong.

A business writer cannot ignore business peoples' evident humanity. Clay feet are to be recognized, though not condoned, in a spirit of humility, but not contempt.

Ethics are not an accounting term that measures buying and selling in the commercial world. Ethics involve only personal relationships. You'll note that an individual's "ethics" often change greatly depending on the person or persons affected by those ethics—customers, employees, suppliers, competitors, neighbors, relatives, social services, etc. But ultimately our ethics involve our ongoing relationship with just one Person—our Maker—by whatever name you wish to call Him.

"All are sinners and fall short of the Glory of God," declared St. John. Management and labor, consumers and politicians and bureaucrats, clergymen, and tax collectors, merchants, senior citizens and teenagers, are *all* very, very human. We're *all* subject to the Ten Commandments and the Sermon on the Mount, under the wrath of God and in hope of salvation.

Chapter 37

A Word About ABWA

Associated Business Writers of America has repeatedly been referred to in these pages as a source of basic information about freelance business writing. Therefore this association deserves some description and explanation.

ABWA was formed in 1946 by a half-dozen full-time freelance business writers. Its aims were to better the general image of the profession, to improve relations and communication with editors and other clients, and to strive for higher pay scales and more considerate handling of manuscripts.

In all these areas ABWA has been influential to an unusual extent for the relatively small size of the organization (never more than 200 members).

The founders were all writers who produced almost exclusively for business papers (trade journals). Eventually ABWA members were convinced that very few could ever make better-than-low-average incomes from writing single articles for business papers. Therefore many ABWA writers, aided by experiences shared through the Confidential Bulletin, have branched out into other phases of the whole wide spectrum of business writing (as described in this book).

This reduced dependence on the business papers has strengthened the bargaining position of members, especially as they were exposed to higher pay scales prevailing outside the business paper field.

ABWA aids members in "educating" or negotiating with editors, by supplying the facts and even the phraseology needed to relate pay scales to work input and quality. This contrasts with editor tendencies to simply base pay on what other trade journals have customarily paid in the past.

The sharing of experiences referred to above occurs in a monthly Confidential Bulletin. This features: News of concern to members; Announcements of new manuscript markets; Confidential experience reports on troublesome clients; Interchange of tips and observations between members; and Special features on different phases of freelance business writing.

A Directory carries profiles of members indicating their

backgrounds, as well as the business areas each writes in or is reasonably familiar with. It also carries 30 or 40 suggestions of ways to use freelance business writers, that editors or clients might not readily think of. There's a discussion of fair pay and an explanation of the ABWA Formula.

This Directory is market-oriented. That is, all its components were developed in response to repeated editor requests. Because it's frequently quoted back to us, we know the Directory is seriously studied by many editors and clients.

A strong feature of ABWA is that all members are "editor-approved." That is, to gain admission a writer must provide names and addresses of three users of his or her business writing, as references. These editors or clients must then vouch for well-written copy received from the applicant, as well as affirm his or her professional behaviour.

ABWA is *not* an agency. That is, we do not charge commissions for assignments traced to ABWA. We provide a "marketplace." Then clients or editors negotiate directly with writers.

However, members often voluntarily contribute 5% of net return on unusually good jobs obtained through ABWA connections. This revenue is fed into a "stamp kitty" for extra PR mailings. ABWA has been mailing geographically-arranged membership lists to potential users of freelance business writers. When contributions are good, we've mailed up to a total 15,000 possible users over a three-year period.

From 1946 until October 1, 1978, ABWA progressed by fits and starts through volunteer management. Writers serving the longer management terms were Ernest Fair, Evelyn Waugh and finally Hazel Palmer and the author. In October 1978, Association Headquarters, Inc., a new multi-management firm, took over management of ABWA.

AHI specializes in managing associations for freelances in writing, editing, photography and graphic arts. It offers greater stability and the economies of size and volume to smaller writer associations such as ABWA, that have struggled on with volunteer leaderships who must yet to make their own livings on the side.

Although completely independent, AHI stems from the National Writers Club. By 1978 the NWC reached a level of 6,000 membership, including a section of over 1,000 professionals. This was under management of what is now the AHI team. Therefore NWC was AHI's first client. ABWA became its second client. By the time you read this, there are likely to be more. Each client association retains its own identity. Each is functionally independent of all others served by AHI, even while sharing staff and facility costs.

Therefore the headquarters address of Associated Business Writers of America is now 1450 S. Havana St., Aurora, CO 80012; Tel. (303) 751-7844. Please write or phone there for further information.

Glossary

Most of the following are common usage in freelance business writing. A few terms may be of the author's coinage, and given limited use through the ABWA Confidential Bulletin.

ABWA—Associated Business Writers of America, 1450 S. Havana St., Aurora, CO; Tel.: (303) 751-7844. Non-profit association of freelance business writers started in 1946.

Ad/ed ratio—Comparative percentages of advertising and editorial matter in a publication. Advertising includes classifieds and "house ads" for publisher's own products. Editorial is all story material, news, columns, opinions, philosophy, statistics, etc.

Aperture—The adjustable opening in the shutter of a camera that regulates the amount of light admitted to a negative.

Assignment—Advance agreement between an editor or client and the writer for the latter to do a writing task or article (as opposed to a writer preparing an article unbeknownst to a client, then submitting it on speculation).

Author—Writer or creator of an article (as opposed to editor or publisher).

Axiom—A fundamental law or principle, established by observation and experience, that affects performance of an occupation or profession.

B&W—Black-and-white photographic prints (as opposed to color prints or slides).

Barnstorming—Travelling from city to city without leads or assignments, ferreting out story and article material as you go.

Bird-dog—Used as a verb for the process of ferreting out stories in unfamiliar territory.

Boiler Plate—Non-exclusive copy submitted to anyone that will buy it; commands lowest pay rates.

Client—Anyone using the services of a freelance writer; usually applied to non-editors for work not appearing in business magazines.

Cluster—Group of articles or creative writings based on one interview or piece of research; or, group of magazines and clients having general affinity with each other, or a writer's group of steady clients.

Columnist—Writer of special articles appearing regularly in a publication, either dealing with a specific subject, or presented from a particular perspective.

Contact prints—Photographic prints having the same dimensions as the negatives from which they're taken.

Contrast (photo)—Shading in a photographic print or negative; If shading ranges from pure white to jet black on prints, or clear to fully dense on negatives, they are said to have high contrast.

Correspondents—Term for freelances who regularly write for a publication; often used to distinguish from staff people on payroll.

Data utility—Computerized library containing substantial information on a specific subject, industry or discipline.

Deck—Introductory paragraph, set apart by different type, color, or graphics, that describes or "sells" the subject of an article or story.

Discipline—A well-defined function having its own laws of effective procedure, such as accounting, salesmanship, quality control, etc.

Editor—One who selects what is to be printed, and/or refines manuscripts to fit allotted space, style of presentation and publisher's policy.

Editorial—Narrowly the articles expressing an editor's personal opinion about events; more broadly any material in a publication not categorized as advertising.

Empathy—Intellectual understanding or identification with another person (as contrasted with sympathy, an emotional involvement).

Feasibility study—Preliminary research to determine if a certain proposed action or project appears promising enough to warrant further research and development.

Fillers—Timeless printed material used by an editor to fill out a page, or to fill one or more empty pages; usually has general application rather than industry import.

Film speed—A code number indicating the relative sensitivity to light of a given type of photographic film, used as basis for calculating exposures.

Finder's fee—Fee paid by editor or client to a writer who reveals or ferrets out the source of a good story which is then assigned to another writer or staff member.

Form—A block of magazine pages printed on one sheet of paper, always in multiples of four pages.

Freelance—A provider of services who is not on the buyer's regular payroll.

Function—Broad general term for the sphere of activity of a person or thing.

Ghost—Writer of an article or book published under name of another person.

Growing edge—That part of an industry, discipline or function subject to rapid change, innovation and development.

Guarantee—The promise that a product will perform as intended (contrasted with warranty, meaning that product is physically what it is supposed to be); You can guarantee a service but you can't warrant it.

House organ—Publication issued by a company or organization for employees (internal), or for customers (external), or both.

Kill fee—Compensation paid writer for article assigned but not used, for article cancelled before completion, or for assignment that proves unobtainable on investigation.

Layout—Noun derived from "lay out" meaning to position the elements on a page (text, illustrations, head and subheads); Arrangement of sequence of advertising and editorial pages in a magazine.

Lead—Suggestion where or from whom a story or article might be obtained.

Leaded lines—Lines of type spaced farther apart vertically; double-space typing is a form of "leading" (pronounce "lehding").

Legman—A reporter who's major function is obtaining facts and data, leaving writing to another.

Literature search—Research confined to library, data utility, guidebooks, etc. (as opposed to field and laboratory research).

Log—Or logbook, a daily record of significant details of work, for billing purposes, IRS defense, for follow-up or permanent record; a diary.

Masthead—List of personnel affiliated with a publication, often along with other basic information about it.

Multiple sales—More than one story or creative piece derived from the same interview or information source.

Nut, The—Amount of income needed to cover one's fixed or continuing expenses.

Overhead time—Time spent in work not directly attributable to a given manuscript or job, such as record keeping, correspondence, banking, tax reports, PR mailings, shopping, etc.

Parochial—Restricted to small locality, group, industry or discipline; self-centered.

Pic-cap—Short for picture-plus-caption.

Pix—Pictures, photographs (plural of pictures).

POA—Payment on acceptance, at some point prior to publication.

POP—Payment on publication, at some time after publication.

Proof-print—Roughly-finished photographic prints showing what's on each negative; proof-prints are marked by photographer to show processor portion of negative to be enlarged.

PR—Public relations, the deliberate creation, maintenance or modification of a personal or company image as seen by the public or by any concerned group.

Puffery—Exaggerated descriptions of products, places, people or services.

Random writing—Totally unscheduled or unassigned writing, taking up whatever comes to hand.

Reporter—Writer who gets facts and data, organizes them into reasonably well-structured articles or reports.

Retainer—Regular fee (usually monthly) paid a writer without reference to amount of actual work done; purpose is to "retain," or have writer always available when needed.

Round-up—Survey of a single question or topic, by one writer in several interviews or by several writers geographically dispersed.

SASE—Self-addressed stamped envelope.

Scribe—Writer, often in sense of correcting, editing, improving someone else's work, or of setting an oral consensus down on paper.

Shorticle—Short article, 50 to 150 words usually.

Sidebars—Separate information not belonging directly in a story or article, yet providing background, anecdotes, or explanations; often set apart in different type or treatment.

Sideline—Assuming article or news reporting for business publications is chief function, any other creative activity is a sideline.

Spec—Speculation; an article submitted without assignment is submitted "on spec."

Speculation—Submission of an article to an editor without assignment, in hope or anticipation he or she will find it suitable.

SRDS—Standard Rate & Data Service, a directory of all publications supported by advertising. Writers find Business Edition and Consumer/-Farm Edition useful for finding magazines serving specific fields or industries.

Spread—Two facing pages in a magazine or newspaper.

Stringer—Correspondent regularly serving a publication in an assigned geographic area, often on retainer.

"Stumble-overs—Stories or articles a writer happens onto while working on something else.

Sub-head—The sub-title of a story, usually amplifying the title, or announcing a secondary emphasis in the story.

Sustainer—Income earned regularly and dependably to cover "the nut."

SWGL—Single-weight glossy, instruction to photo finisher to make a photographic print on single weight paper with a glossy finish.

Syllabus—Summary or outline containing the main points, usually a detailed outline.

Washout—Assignment or lead that produces no marketable story.

Addendum

It was coincidence, we hope, for two editors to complain in the same week that freelance business writers never seemed to know how to submit a simple business expense account! (Of course, Hazel and I usually found that when freelances are being editorially lambasted, non-ABWAers are usually involved).

However, here are two reporting forms I evolved by trial-and-error. Together they have proven adequate for any type of client I have served. Obviously any item on the expense sheet may be altered, deleted or added to suit personal circumstances.

Mine are mimeoed, simply because we have the equipment. They can be printed or offset. Or a master drawing can be run through a multi-copier.

The forms could be combined on one sheet, if you prefer. Yet I have some clients pay a flat fee plus expenses, who require only the expense report. For others no chargeable expenses are involved, yet they prefer to be invoiced for my labor. One firm pays a retainer and expenses, plus labor over 10 days monthly quota, with some months involving no overtime at all.

Details are pretty much self-explanatory. Usually I rough the report in pencil on one form. Then I type an original, plus a carbon for my own records. Or sometimes an extra carbon is made to include with the original on request by the client. In fact, one client used to demand four copies of every expense report (they must have had four partners).

One could use the rough draft as the personal record. However an actual copy of the original as sent is better protection in case of dispute with either the client or IRS.

William R. Palmer
P. O. Box 135
Monmouth Junction
New Jersey 08852
Tel. 201 297-4891

EXPENSE REPORT

In behalf of: __Modern Acoustics__

From: __9/10/73__   To: __9/22/73__

Item	Sun.	Mon. 9/10	Tues. 9/11	Wed.	Thurs. 9/20	Fri. 9/21	Sat. 9/22	Total
Air Wash'n, DC Bus to RR Round Trip		52.30						52.30
Air Bus to RR								
Air Bus to RR								
Car pers./rent @ 12¢					** 24.60	5.30	27.90	57.80
Tolls, parking					4.00	1.25	2.80	8.05
Local Transport		5.20	5.60					10.80
Lodging		19.90			16.80	16.80		53.50
Meals		5.70	7.40		8.05	6.45	11.20	38.80
Entertainment		* 4.50						4.50
Regis. fees		15.00						15.00
Telephone			3.65		1.10	.85	1.75	7.35
Photography					1.50	5.50	.75	7.75
Tips; Misc.		1.00			1.00	1.00		3.00
Totals		103.60	16.65		57.05	37.15	44.40	258.85

Less advances by client 150.00

Balance expense refund due W. R. Palmer . . . . $ 108.85

REMARKS:

* Bar, John Whatsis, Acoustics Assn lobbyist
** To Harrisburg, Pa., re Cute Acoustics, Inc.

I retain hotel/motel bills, etc., for my own records,
and submit copies of them where requested. Again, one
stickler insisted on getting originals, in which case I
made and kept copies for myself. We have a small copier;
but it's still reasonable precaution to copy receipts at
the library, or wherever. You can often do three or four
to the page, lapping over material that is irrelevant
or blank spaces.

Some brief explanation may be helpful about the
expense report. It is designed to cover one Sunday-
to Saturday week. Sometimes, as here, partial weeks
can be combined on a single sheet, if dates don't
overlap.

You can enter the round-trip ticket on the day purchased, or split it for the particular days going and
coming. Though there's provision for only three entries,
it is practical to combine when the same mode of transportation is used. Normally this form can show, for

example: flight Newark, N.J., to Washington, D.C.; then via bus Washington to Harrisburg, Pa.; and finally railroad Harrisburg to New Brunswick, N.J.

Twelve cents a mile (or whatever inflation makes it by the time you read this) is indicated for use of your personal car; if a rental, you only enter the net bill.

Local transport includes taxis, airport limo, city buses, trolleys (remember them), or jitneys.

"Regis." means registration at meetings, conventions seminars. It's general practice for publications to pay registrations that include meals or other direct expenses Meeting sponsors usually do not charge the press when direct expenses are not involved. "Direct" means an expense you'd incur otherwise anyway, i.e., you'd probably eat lunch, whether with the group or alone.

Under "photography" is here charged cost of film used for a client that picks up all photo costs. A future statement will include cost of processing on this same line.

There always is reluctance among writers to get so detailed as these forms suggest. Yet filling out such forms can save a writer money.

"Look," you say, "I started out with $100, came back with $35. So expenses had to be $65 -- right?

Wrong -- maybe! Have you included: all costs incurred by credit card; payments by check; any other deferred charges; all appropriate mileage on your car (at the job, as well as going and coming); Federal tax on phone toll calls from home; cost of film or other supplies already purchased, including sales taxes thereon, etc. etc.

Accuracy on this expense sheet is almost insured by having to make your vertical and horizontal totals agree. If they don't you figured wrong somewhere.

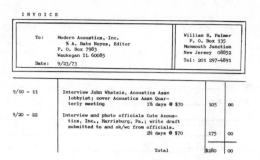

I N V O I C E

To:	Modern Acoustics, Inc. % A. Bate Noyes, Editor P. O. Box 7983 Waukegan IL 60085	William R. Palmer P. O. Box 135 Monmouth Junction New Jersey 08852 Tel: 201 297-4891
Date:	9/23/73	

9/10 - 11	Interview John Whatsis, Acoustics Assn lobbyist; cover Acoustics Assn Quarterly meeting 1½ days @ $70	105	00
9/20 - 22	Interview and photo officials Cute Acoustics, Inc., Harrisburg, Pa.; write draft submitted to and ok/wc from officials. 2½ days @ $70	175	00
	Total	$280	00

The invoices are on half-sheets, plus a few on full sheets (so far un-used). They aren't fancy, but seem to get the money as readily as handsome printed forms.

For memos, I replace the word "invoice" with "memo", and knock out the lines under the box. Color distinguishes them also. The invoices are on pearl gray paper, memos are on canary, both on mimeo stock.

Fold just below the date and the client's address appears at the window of a window envelope.

USE OF ASSIGNMENT SHEET

My own assignment sheet also evolved by trial-and-error. A supply of blank forms is kept by the phone, because their chief purpose is to secure all necessary information on phoned assignments or on queries phoned by me. However, these forms are used for all assigned work or speculative jobs. Only exceptions are stories obtained under contract or retainer, where compensation is not on a per story basis.

My name and address are on the form so I can make a carbon, should I wish to send it to the client as confirmation of our agreed-on terms. Frankly, I've rarely done this, except for a half-dozen clients who proved a bit slippery on prior experience, or who have that reputation among other freelance writers.

After trying a variety of record-keeping methods, I finally settled on "job numbers" as the simplest overall

```
                                            William R. Palmer
                                            P. O. Box 135
                                            Monmouth Junction
Assignment Sheet - Job #_____    New Jersey  08852


Date initiated_____        Date OK_____

Client (Firm) Name_____Phone No._____

Address_____

Contact:    Name_____Title_____

(if different) Address_____Phone No._____

Subject or Topic_____

Job description_____

                _____

                _____

                _____

Contact(s)   Name(s)_____Title(s)_____

                     _____    _____

                     _____    _____

Address_____Phone No._____

Who arranges?  Client_____I do_____

Am I expected_____When_____

No. words_____No. Pix_____No. Illus._____

Est. Time_____    Est. Expenses_____

     travel_____    Miles @ 15¢_____

     interview_____    Tolls, parking_____

     production_____    Meals @ $12_____

                                     Motel @ $20_____

Pay_____    Expenses_____

Deadline:_____

Job started_____Completed_____

     Submitted_____Accepted_____Paid_____
```

control device. When an assignment is received or a
query okayed, it is given the next consecutive number
available in my records. Or if I do an interview on
speculation (without assignment), that interview receives the next available number.

If more than one story derives from the same assignment or interview, the job number for each extra story
is followed by a decimal plus another number. For instance, suppose the story I went to get was #539. But
I also got a shorter story on maintenance, plus a human
interest shorticle, plus a pic-cap for a manufacturer.
These extra items are #539.1, 539.2 and 539.3 respectively.

If there are extra stories, they are indicated on
the job number line thus: #539 - 1 - 2 - 3. Then, as
each story is paid for, the proper number is circled in
red (i.e., "539" for the main story, or "2" for the
human interest item. The details on the extra items
are typed separately on the back of the form. But
they're always listed separately there because they may
go to different markets.

At first glance this form may seem cumbersome. But
it was the best means I could find for properly assessing
productivity per assignment, per interview or per day.
Keeping tabs on daily productivity also is one reason
for entering the numbers in my diary.

Forms are collected in a loose-leaf binder labelled "In Process". When the manuscript, bearing its
number, is mailed out, the related form is transferred
to an "Active" folder.

The carbon of the manuscript is filed in numerical
order. This has proven the easiest way to file manuscript carbons so they are readily retrievable.

This number is also entered in my diary in red
ink under the day assigned. Likewise numbered in the
diary are all stories done on retainer or contract,
so their carbons may be retrievable from the file.

"Date initiated" is the time the subject first
came up, whether phoned or written assignment, query
or unscheduled interview. Actually it is whatever
time you feel there's solid possibility of a sale.
The "OK" line then is the time a firm "go ahead" is received (except for speculative jobs).

The "contact" under client's data is the person
dealt with in connection with the story, whether editor,
PR executive, or whatever.

There is no separate line for the site of the
proposed story, since it could be any number of places
other than a business house. Hence the site is included in the "job description". "Contacts" listed
after job description are persons suggested to be interviewed, if known. These names are also handy for
future references on call backs or follow-ups.

```
Date Began Work: _____

Company_____Job#_____

Address _____(combined with Job#_____

Job Name_____

Assigned By_____Title_____Date_____

Original Estimate_____Date_____Ok'd By_____Date_____

Estimate Comment_____

          _____

          _____

Job Purpose _____

Job Mechanics

Photography:_____Layout:_____Artwork:_____Copy:_____

Mechanical:_____Type:_____Stats:_____Engravings:_____

Printing

Size_____Stock_____Color_____

Line/Ht_____Printing Method_____Folding_____

Delivery_____Other Data_____

Miscellaneous Costs

    Supplies        $_____Initial Selling _____Min. Gross $_____
    Telephone Calls       Interview        _____Min. Costs  _____
    Carfare               Creative         _____Min. Net $  _____
    Prod. Costs           Research         _____Min. Time    Hours_____
    Postage               Approval         _____Min.
    Photography           Revision         _____Min.
    Trips                 Prod. & Art      _____Min. Remuneration
    Other                 Copy Typing      _____Min.   Per Hour $_____
                          Office Work      _____Min.
                          Travel           _____Min.
           Total          Placement        _____Min.

Other Data

Amount Billed_____Date_____Invoice #_____

          _____     _____

Amount Paid_____Date_____Copy Received_____
                                           Meetings Attended _____
                                                             _____
                                                             _____

Date Submitted:_____
```

"Who arranges"? In discussion you may touch on
this point without deciding. This line is to pin the
matter down, as well as the following question of timing. If the client arranges, it often expedites your
interview or inspection.

It's good to pin down the acceptable number of
"words, pix and illustrations". If 1,200 words and
three pix or drawings are the client's absolute limit,
it's certainly not cost-effective to run off three
rolls of negatives.

By all means discuss the "time" and "expenses"
involved! Nothing delicate about that at all. This
is a business deal, not a social conversation. Make

sure the client realizes what he's getting you into
in the way of labor and costs. The 15¢, $12 and $20
were my going rates for 1976. Heaven knows what they
are by the time you read this!

*   *   *   *   *   *

The other form is used by a member of Associated
Business Writers of America who is heavily involved
in preparing and producing advertising brochures. Using this form he can actually produce a fairly complex
bid rather quickly. I have not personally used the form,
but present it here to suggest adaptations the reader
can design for his or her own unique needs.

*   *   *   *   *   *

AND IN CONCLUSION

Well, there it is, a distillation of 45 years
journalistic endeavor in business writing, much of
it freelancing.

I've deliberately tried to keep it low key. This
is in contrast to a number of writings over the years
that distort the opportunities in freelance business
writing. A major task in managing Associated Business
Writers of America has been counselling disillusioned
new writers beguiled by effervescent descriptions of
wide-open opportunity.

There is no glory in freelance business writing!
The occasional writer hits on a good thing and makes
a career of it. Yet he or she works just as hard at
it as those of us who plug away grabbing at all kinds
of feasible projects.

If I can leave any final thought, it's this.
There must be method in our madness. Freelancing is
not just doing what comes naturally. It's a business.
To survive we can't avoid being businesslike.

303